.cs of

THE HISTORY AND POLITICS OF VOTING TECHNOLOGY

THE HISTORY AND POLITICS OF VOTING TECHNOLOGY

IN QUEST OF INTEGRITY AND PUBLIC CONFIDENCE

Roy G. Saltman

THE HISTORY AND POLITICS OF VOTING TECHNOLOGY
© Roy G. Saltman, 2006.

First published in 2006 by
PALGRAVE MACMILLAN™
175 Fifth Avenue, New York, N.Y. 10010 and
Houndmills, Basingstoke, Hampshire, England RG21 6XS
Companies and representatives throughout the world.

PALGRAVE MACMILLAN is the global academic imprint of the Palgrave Macmillan division of St. Martin's Press, LLC and of Palgrave Macmillan Ltd. Macmillan® is a registered trademark in the United States, United Kingdom and other countries. Palgrave is a registered trademark in the European Union and other countries.

ISBN 1–4039–6392–4

Library of Congress Cataloging-in-Publication Data

Saltman, Roy G.
    The history and politics of voting technology : in quest of integrity and public confidence / by Roy G. Saltman.
      p. cm.
    Includes bibliographical references and index.
    ISBN 1–4039–6392–4
      1. Voting—United States—History. 2. Voting—Technological innovations—United States—History. I. Title.

JK1965.S25 2006
324.6′5′0973—dc22   2005048703

A catalogue record for this book is available from the British Library.

Design by Newgen Imaging Systems (P) Ltd., Chennai, India.

First edition: January 2006

10 9 8 7 6 5 4 3 2 1

Printed in the United States of America.

For my grandparents:
Nathan and Golda,
Salomon and Rosa,
who were born under imperialism
and came here just before and after 1900 to live in a
democratic nation;

and for my grandchildren:
Max, Daniel, and Sydney,
Joshua, Hannah, and Ellie;
may they be able to live beyond 2100 in this country,
assured that the voting process is fair and its integrity unquestioned.

CONTENTS

LIST OF TABLES

LIST OF FIGURES

Note: All figures, except for 5.1 and 7.1, are displayed with the permission of the Division of Politics and Reform, National Museum of American History. Figure 5.1 was taken by the author. Figure 7.1 is displayed with the permission of Diebold, Incorporated.

AUTHOR'S PREFACE

The idea for this book had its origin in the conflict surrounding the outcome of the 2000 presidential election. Soon after the resolution of the debacle in Florida, my son Steven, the Internet entrepreneur, called me and said, "Dad, you must write a book about the election." He knew that I had researched and published reports on the integrity of computerized elections and consulted internationally on the subject. I pondered the possibility for much of 2001. While I was considering the issue, many books covering that election suddenly appeared like wildflowers following spring rains in an arid region. All of them concerned that particular election: its statistics, the personalities involved, or the legal battles that immediately followed the close of polls. Additionally, there were a number of national reports produced in 2001 by distinguished citizens, universities, election administrators, and government officials that considered the specific administrative failings brought out in the Florida fiasco. These reports recommended many policy actions for correcting the problems.

None of these books and reports have taken a historical perspective in order to respond to the question, "Why did it happen?" An informed response requires serious reflection and research. The process of authorship on this subject, in order to be thorough, cannot produce a publishable product in a few months. The intention of this book is not only to answer the question of "why," but to answer it by providing the historical context out of which the process developed for conducting our federal elections. That context requires starting with the concepts that led to the statement in the Declaration of Independence that "Governments are instituted . . . deriving their just powers from the consent of the governed," with the understanding that implementing "consent of the governed" is what voting in America is all about.

It seemed to me that a multidisciplinary approach was necessary. As time progresses, new political ideas and technology are developed. In the case of the voting process, the application of technology partly depends on political conditions. The latter affects the demand for change in the way voting is conducted, particularly if an applicable technology already has been used in familiar products. An academic background in engineering and many years of work with information systems has made possible my understanding of the developments and implementation difficulties. Fundamental conditions of voting in the United States include its extreme administrative disaggregation and the intergovernmental conflicts that have served as a restraint to any uniform program of voting process improvements. My additional academic background in public administration and 27 years in government service have similarly assisted me in being able to elaborate the nature of this problem.

An important conclusion of this study is the following: Prior to the Florida crisis, it was not politically possible to translate federal/state cooperation, highly successful in issues of public health and safety, to resolving difficulties in the voting process. The problem first showed itself with opposition to the Election Clause (Article I, Section 4) in the framing of the Constitution in 1787 and has continued through 2005, as pointed out late in the final chapter.

In reviewing literature on American history, I found an unexpected situation. General works do not cover significant changes in voting technology. For example, discussions of political and social conditions in the middle and late nineteenth century do not often indicate that, as a consequence, the movement to adopt the secret (Australian) ballot had begun. While the participants in elections and the major issues of campaigns are described in detail in general histories, the chaotic process of voting before the adoption of the secret ballot is virtually ignored. The spread of the lever voting machine is not covered and misinformation is rampant concerning Edison's voting machine of 1869. One must go to publications devoted to more specific subjects, even to patents, to find appropriate information. I am indebted to historians who specialized in the voting process. Some of their works are cited in the references for chapters 2, 3, and 4.

In 2002, while completing a proposal, it was fortuitous that I discovered Alex Keyssar's impressive book, *The Right to Vote*. He was kind enough to take time to see me, and encouraged me to continue. When I began work in early 2003, after finding a publisher, I had to overcome the lack of a university connection. There were no graduate students eager to assist and no library at my disposal. Many books that I have cited as references, I bought secondhand off the Internet.

Early in my writing, I was most fortunate in establishing a working arrangement with Dr. W. Larry Bird, curator in the division of politics and reform at the Smithsonian National Museum of American History. Richard Smolka's *Election Administration Reports*, an authoritative source on current events in the election field, reported Larry's interest in acquiring *pro bono* expertise to aid in the mounting of an exhibit called *Vote: The Machinery of Democracy*. I applied and was helpful, it appears, serving as a "behind-the-scenes" volunteer. My position enabled me to use the museum's library, consult with Larry and his colleagues, and view some rare artifacts. Later, Larry agreed that I could publish some of the photos of materials from his exhibit and the museum's collection. His magnanimity has made this book considerably more interesting.

Others that I need to thank include the American people and their federal government for making available to ordinary citizens the Law Library Reading Room of the Library of Congress and the search facilities of the U.S. Patent and Trademark Office. Tony J. Sirvello III of IACREOT, an election officials' organization, smoothed the way for my attendance at the group's annual meetings and election equipment shows. Conny B. McCormack registrar-recorder of Los Angeles County, made herself available to answer questions on several occasions. Personnel formerly with the Office of Election Administration of the Federal Election Commission, Penelope Bonsall, Bill Kimberling, Brian Hancock, and Peggy Sims, have been very helpful over many years. Steven Hertzberg and Eva Waskell of the Election Science Institute provided information about the 2004 general election and its aftermath, which considerably expanded my knowledge. I have benefitted also from the writings of knowledgeable experts such as Douglas W. Jones and Michael I. Shamos. My wife, Joan, a professional in her own right, carefully monitored my compulsive work habits and ensured that I would rest for a sabbath each week. In addition, she acted capably in her appreciation that the way to a man's heart is through his stomach.

Roy G. Saltman
Columbia, MD
July 27, 2005

The 2000 Presidential Election in Florida: The Family Secret is Exposed

The presidential election of 2000 was the first one since 1876 in which the outcome remained uncertain for a significant period of time following the day of election. The delay was due to legal challenges to the reported results in Florida. The publicity attending the postelection legal contest in that state brought with it a fierce light of public scrutiny which uncovered election administration's family secret: the tottering and decrepit nature of U.S. voting technology. Exposed also was unabashed partisanship in supposedly evenhanded election administration. The flaws exposed during reporting of the election generated, in 2001, several studies. These included a review by *The New York Times* of decisions made about overseas absentee ballots, two meticulous examinations by media consortia of ballots unreadable by machine as well as several conscientious policy studies on the total voting process by respected groups. Congress responded in 2002 to the concerns raised with a law breaking new ground in public policy. It is appropriate, therefore, to review the 2000 presidential election in Florida to elucidate the problems of the voting process at that time. That election may have been an important turning point in a long-term effort to achieve a better quality of democratic choice for the country that invented the concept for national government.

Within a week or so after the presidential election on Tuesday, November 7, final results had been verified in all states but Florida. Vice President Albert Gore, Jr., the Democratic candidate, would receive at least 267 electoral votes, if all the electors pledged to him upheld their oaths. (One elector would not and would cast a blank ballot.) Republican candidate George W. Bush, governor of Texas, would receive at least 246 electoral votes. There were a total of 538 electoral votes at stake, and the winner would require at least 270 if all the votes were cast. Only the 25 electoral votes from Florida (winner take all) were not yet assured for either candidate, due to the legal challenge then proceeding in that state. If a political deadlock prevented the appointment of Florida's presidential Electors, then Gore would win according to the 12th Amendment of the Constitution: "The person having the greatest number of [electoral] votes for President shall be the President, if such number be a majority of the whole number of Electors appointed . . ."

Five Tuesdays after the election, on December 12, the U.S. Supreme Court, in *Bush v. Gore*, issued its decision that permanently ended recounts ordered by the Florida Supreme Court. The U.S. court's action allowed the previously attested Florida outcome to stand. That result of the state's popular vote, which showed Bush leading Gore by just 537 votes out of nearly 6 million cast, had been certified by Katherine Harris, the Florida secretary of state, and the redundant Florida Elections Canvassing Commission on Sunday, November 26. Thus, the 25 Electors for George W. Bush would be appointed. Bush's electoral votes would total 271 and he would be the next president. This result would obtain, notwithstanding the fact that Gore received 544,000 more popular votes than Bush out of more than 104 million cast nationwide.

The postelection legal battle that lasted until December 12 involved voting technology as an important factor. Whether or not some or all ballots should be recounted manually in order to determine if there were votes on those ballots that could not be read by machine became an essential question. If manual reviews were to be permitted, then human interpretation—likely to be subjective—was needed to decipher the nonstandard or ambiguous nature in which some voters had punched or marked their ballots. After the conflict was over, data analyses would show that voters' abilities to use different kinds of equipment varied, and that even among voters using the same type of equipment, socioeconomic factors played an important role. These facts had not been previously taken into account by political leaders, and were seldom investigated by social scientists.

During the legal contests, the voting equipment that voters used to record their choices (or failed to record their choices or mistakenly recorded their choices) became an issue. Votes were recorded by different methods in the several different types of ballot systems used in Florida. One particular type of voting equipment, based on prescored punch cards (PPCs) and used by a majority of Florida voters, presented ballot interpreters with an exceedingly difficult problem. The very nature of the system made the level of ambiguity of voters' choices exceedingly high. It was not surprising, therefore, that "intent of the voter," a concept recognized in Florida law, which began to be applied in this country long before there were computer-readable ballots, suddenly became a topic of interest at the U.S. Supreme Court. The court would characterize the different standards by which votes were determined in the different counties as a violation of that simply worded but consummately sublime clause of the 14th Amendment: "No state shall . . . deny to any person within its jurisdiction the equal protection of the laws." That would be part of its rationale for ending the Florida election imbroglio. There were several other instances of denial of "equal protection" in this contest, but they would not come before the court.

Another issue of the election was not contested in the legal disputes leading to the decision of the U.S. Supreme Court but, nevertheless, was vitally important. This issue was the quality of the information systems in Florida used for voter registration, an essential aspect of the voting process. There were persons who claimed the right to vote who, wrongly, were prevented from voting. There were also persons who were not entitled to vote but who were permitted to do so by election officials at polling places. Errors in voter registration did not affect the counting of the ballots actually cast and it was not a point of contention in the litigation. However, in the 107th Congress, elected at the same time as the president (except for senators continuing in office), the issue of voter registration loomed large in considerations of the federal response to the Florida fiasco. The Help America Vote Act, adopted in October 2002, almost at the termination of that two-year Congress, was the first federal legislation since 1899 mandating requirements for voting equipment. It was also the first adopted legislation ever to authorize federal funds for the conduct of federal elections. The law concerned both voting equipment and voter registration, but it was a controversy about the latter that generated the most animosity in debate and delayed its passage the longest.

1.1   THE SITUATION BEFOREHAND

Political bias by Florida election officials played an important role in the first part of the postelection legal struggle (the "protest" phase) in which the final results to be certified by the secretary of state were determined. This situation was not a new departure; there were strong antecedents. In the nineteenth century, in every state, political parties were more controlling of governmental processes than they are today. In the late nineteenth century, and into the twentieth century, reformers and "good government" advocates attempted to insulate aspects of governmental administration that could be nonpolitical from domination by political parties. The institution of the truly secret ballot and the establishment of a nonpolitical civil service at all levels of government were major steps. In some states and local governments, the positions of senior election administrators were made nonpartisan, but not generally in Florida.

The importance of nonpartisanship, or at least bipartisanship, in fostering integrity in elections cannot be overstated. If the power of the state can be brought to bear to favor one side over the other, then public confidence in the democratic process is reduced and many will see voting as a sham. The technology of voting is at the inner workings of democracy, nearly hidden from the political process except when, as in the situation at hand, it stumbles so badly it can't be ignored. Respect for the results that technology produces is dependent on the credibility of the government running the election. Credibility is maximized if the government does not favor one citizen over another in basic rights, as implied in the concept of equal protection.

The Florida secretary of state, the person responsible for assuring the administration of elections according to state regulations, was an elected partisan official in 2000. Soon after, the office was made appointive but still partisan. Katherine Harris was elected as a Republican and was cochair of the Bush campaign in Florida. During the postelection conflict, the closeness of the vote and the supreme importance of the outcome made it difficult for her to avoid slanted interpretations of law that favored her cause. Three of her important decisions were overturned by the Florida Supreme Court. These were her refusal to accept delayed submission of vote totals on two separate occasions and the narrowing of the requirements for manual recounting of ballots so as to make the concept of intent of the voter meaningless and irrelevant. A fourth ruling, advising the acceptance of absentee ballots with postmarks after election day, provided that they were "executed" on or before election day, was disregarded in some counties as inconsistent with Florida law. Her decisions were wholly consistent with Republican strategy: that is, no ballots cast at polling stations should be recounted (because Bush was ahead and nothing should be done that might change that fact) (Karlan, 2001, pp. 179, 180) and as many military ballots as possible cast absentee should be counted (because they were expected to favor Republicans). A legal scholar wrote later that she should have recused herself from postelection involvement, as her position in the Bush campaign "made it wildly inappropriate for her to remain in charge" (Kramer, 2001, pp. 115, 116).

The supervisors of elections (SOEs) in Florida were partisan, except in Miami-Dade County; that is, they were elected to office by running on the ticket of a particular political party. There was one SOE in each of the 67 counties. The function of the SOE in each county was to make all the necessary preparations and to administer the election. The partisan character of almost all SOE positions, the autonomy given those SOEs because they were elected officials, and the immoderate delegation of vote-counting responsibilities to local officials under Florida law provided opportunities for decisions by SOEs that affected the election outcome in this extremely tight contest.

In Seminole County, it was alleged that Republican SOE Sandra Goard invited Michael A. Leach, the Republican Party's regional director in north Florida, to sit in the county elections offices for 10 days to correct absentee ballot applications filed by prospective Republican voters who were missing their voter ID numbers. The absentee ballot applications would have been rejected if the numbers had not been added. When asked if the Democrats were extended the same opportunity to review their voters' applications for completeness, Bob Poe, the state Democratic Party chairman, emphatically declared that they were not (Correspondents of *The New York Times*, 2001, pp. 54, 55).

In Martin County, it was alleged that Republican SOE Peggy S. Robbins permitted Republican party workers to take away absentee ballot applications from the elections office on a daily basis, add missing voter ID numbers at the local Republican party headquarters, and resubmit them. At the same time, the elections office ignored other incomplete applications submitted by Democrats and independents (Correspondents of *The New York Times*, 2001, pp. 188, 189). (See section 1.15 for the resolution of the Seminole and Martin County situations.)

The three-person Canvassing Boards were partisan. There was one for each county, and the SOE was always a member unless he or she was running for reelection. The other two members were a local judge (supposedly nonpartisan) and another partisan elected official. The two partisan members (one in Miami-Dade) were very likely of the same party because their election would reflect the county's climate of opinion. One function of the Canvassing Board was to determine the total vote for each state-level and federal candidate in the county following the election and submit that total to the secretary of state. Additionally, the Canvassing Board was the group to decide, under Florida law, the validity of any particular markings or punchings shown on a ballot. In the establishment of the final vote total in the 2000 presidential election, the Canvassing Boards determined whether manual counting would occur or not (absent a court order), what rules about chads were to be used in analyzing PPC ballots, and what characteristics of absentee ballots would cause them to be accepted or rejected. For example, it was not surprising to find that the percent of absentee ballots rejected for counting was significantly different between some Republican-controlled and Democratic-controlled Canvassing Boards. As with Plunkitt of Tammany Hall, who saw his opportunities and took them (Riordan, 1963 (1905), p. 3) there were opportunities here for politically biased decisions, and they were taken.

In the design of ballot layouts, some implementations were disastrous. Each county SOE in Florida separately pondered the issue of how to arrange the statewide part of the ballot to accommodate the names of 10 pairs of candidates for the offices of president and vice president of the United States. Florida had not previously experienced a presidential election with so many candidates. The only guidance was a state statute that required the candidates to be listed in the order of their party's vote-gathering achievement in the most recent contest for governor. With each type of equipment, the question of how to display the names of all the candidates would need a different solution. Therefore, voters using dissimilar equipment would be differently impacted, although the Bush campaign would not protest these particular differences to the U.S. Supreme Court as an equal protection violation.

The poor choices in ballot design and instructions would not be recognized until election day. That was when voters actually had to solve the puzzle of filling out their ballots so that the voting equipment would sense exactly what they intended. Many voters would fail this challenge. Among counties using the same type of equipment, there was no evidence that the SOEs had consulted each other and agreed to achieve ballot uniformity. The assorted arrangements produced in the counties with the same type would demonstrate that fact.

In one county, Duval, voters had been instructed to "vote every page" on the booklet of the PPC ballot holder, but it turned out that the first two left-hand pages displayed different candidates of the contest for president. This arrangement had been approved by John Stafford, Duval's SOE. Over 22,000 voters, about 7.5 percent of the total number of voters in that county, attempted to cast votes on both pages. Each of them lost his or her vote in the contest because of "overvoting." Along with voter registration misfeasance, "the cumulative effect of these failures fell disproportionately upon our African-American population" (Duval County Election Reform Task Force, 2001, p. 6). In another county, Palm Beach, the PPC ballot layout, different from Duval's, would become notorious.

Five weeks later, the chief justice of the U.S. Supreme Court would declare "absurd" the need to count ballots that could not be counted by machine, despite a requirement of Florida law that "no vote shall be declared invalid or void if there is a clear indication of the intent of the voter as determined by the canvassing board."

Purging ineligible voters was another source of blundering. In 1998, the Florida state legislature enacted a statute that required the state Division of Elections to contract with a private company to purge all voter files of ineligible voters, that is, deceased persons, duplicate registrants, individuals declared mentally incompetent, and, most significantly, convicted felons whose rights had not been restored. An impetus for the legislature's action was a 1997 election for mayor of Miami whose results had been thrown out by court order due to registration fraud. The contract to develop the list of registrants to be purged cost the state about $4 million.

Registration files were maintained by each county. Two lists of supposedly ineligible voters containing almost 58,000 names were distributed to county SOEs in June 1999 and in January 2000. Matches to currently registered voters were graded as "possible" or "probable." However, the law was written by the legislature so that the list was to be accepted as correct unless proven incorrect by a prospective voter who found himself or herself cited. The county SOEs sent letters to all named individuals advising them of their right to challenge the list's correctness. Of course, a mix-up in names would not necessarily have yielded the right address for a letter's intended recipient. After distribution of the first list, the SOEs received notices from the state Division of Elections that some 8,000 citizens had been mistakenly included. Throughout the state, there were 7,837 appeals to the Florida Department of Law Enforcement about incorrectly listed convictions, and of these, nearly half were resolved in favor of the voter (Merzer et al., 2001, pp. 106–107).

Among the counties, Miami-Dade received a total of 7,150 names of supposedly convicted felons with unrestored rights, according to the statements of David Leahy, county SOE at the time. Of these, 469 successfully appealed and therefore remained on the voter rolls. In addition, the Division of Elections forwarded to Miami-Dade County a list of 485 additional names that should not have been on the list. Consequently, in that county, more than 13 percent of the names listed were incorrect (U.S. Commission on Civil Rights, 2001, pp. 22–24). Duval County SOE John Stafford is reported to have told an investigator from *The Miami Herald* that he never trusted the purge list because the husband of a worker in his office was mistakenly listed. Linda Howell, the Madison County SOE, was also wrongly listed. In some other counties, for example, Broward, Palm Beach, and Volusia, the lists were ignored. In Sarasota County, the only felons purged from the list were those who acknowledged letters and admitted that they were ineligible to vote (Merzer et al., 2001, p. 107). The mistakes on the list not reconciled before election day would frustrate the ordinary folks enmeshed in this bureaucratic blunder and would generate considerable indignation and legal actions from civil rights organizations.

1.2   VOTING SYSTEM SELECTION

In Florida, the selection of voting equipment was done at the county level, generally by consensus of the county's senior leadership. A Florida county looking for new equipment could select any model of voting equipment from among those already approved by the state. An approval program begun in 1990 involved testing the computer equipment against hardware and software standards after certification under the national testing system (see sections 6.10–6.12). There have never been any human factors standards—national or state—for the capability of voters to transfer their choices into computer-readable punches, marks, or direct electronic indications. Within each county, implementation of the selected equipment was countywide, except possibly for absentees. Six different types of voting systems were in use; five systems used hard-copy ballots; one was a non-ballot system. Among the five ballot-using systems, there were two different kinds of punch-card systems, and three types of systems in which the voter chose a candidate by filling in a small area on the ballot using a writing instrument. There were a total of thirteen different models of equipment, supplied by eight separate vendors.

Florida's use of several types of voting equipment, with selection occurring at the county level, was typical of conditions throughout the nation in 2000. There are about 3,140 county-level units in the United States, including some 44 cities that are independent of any county and that serve as county equivalents. About 2,870 of these units conducted elections for state and federal offices in the 40 states in which counties and equivalents performed this function. In the 6 New England states and in Michigan, Minnesota, and Wisconsin, subdivisions of counties, which may be called cities, towns, or townships, carried out these elections. There are several thousand of these units. In Alaska, elections are carried out as a state function. The District of Columbia conducts its own presidential election and names Electors as if it were a state (see section 5.3).

1.3   PRESCORED PUNCH CARDS

Prescored punch cards were used by 15 counties including the 5 largest in population. Listed in descending order of size, they were Miami-Dade, Broward and Palm Beach (all along the southeast coast), and Hillsborough and Pinellas (encompassing the Tampa–St. Petersburg area on the Gulf coast). The seventh largest, Duval, also used PPCs. The latter includes Jacksonville, northeast Florida's metropolitan center. About 61.5 percent of Florida's nearly 16 million population lived in these 15 counties. The name "Votomatic" was given to the system in the early 1960s by its inventor, Joseph P. Harris, at the time a professor of political science at the University of California at Berkeley. After the expiration of Harris' patents, other similar devices under different brand names were manufactured. These were based, also, on the use of PPCs. The mechanical device holding the card while the voter makes selections is very similarly designed in all brands (see figure 1.1).

The PPC system was, in 2000, the second-most common voting system used in the United States. It was used in Florida for many years. Broward County, for example, procured its PPC system in 1974 and Miami-Dade in 1978. In 2000, about 28 percent of voters used it, nationwide.

Chads, the small pieces of ballot card that are supposed to be fully punched out by the voters but may be retained on the card (due to voter error or equipment malfunction), are one of the PPC system's most distinctive and contentious features. If chads are rectangular, they are sometimes further distinguished by the condition in which they have been found. "Hanging" chads are those attached to the ballot card by only one corner. "Swinging" chads are those attached by two corners and a "tri-chad" is attached by three corners. A "dimpled" or "pregnant" chad is one that is indented or bulging, but is attached to the ballot by all four corners. A "pierced" chad is a dimpled or pregnant chad that is pierced with a hole (Correspondents of *The New York Times*, 2001, p. 90, Posner, 2001, p. xv). When ballots are manually reviewed, a rule must be in place to establish what condition of chad constitutes a vote. The system of chad classification was developed to provide people with a way of communicating about the rules. A society that is filled with amazing technological developments continued in 2000 to allow the use of a process not much more advanced than tea-leaf reading to determine its next president.

Chad is not a new word. As a data processing term, it appeared in 1961 in Webster's Third International Dictionary published by G. C. Merriam Co. Chad was specified in that publication as "one of the small disks produced in cutting code perforations on [paper] tape . . ." By 1970, it appeared in the American National Standard Vocabulary of Information Processing. It was defined there as "the piece of material removed when forming a hole or notch in a storage medium such as punched tape or punched cards" (Saltman, 1975, p. 103). Chad is an American term; the Oxford English Dictionary, in its 1933 edition or later editions through 1989, makes no mention of it, although it does report "chaff" as "refuse, worthless matter." In written reports of the 2000 election, for example, in *The New York Times*, "chads" is used as the plural of "chad." That is the usage adopted here, although earlier, "chad" was treated as the plural, as with "sheep" or "salmon." Since each chad starts out on a ballot card representing the choice of a citizen entitled to participate in one of the most important political

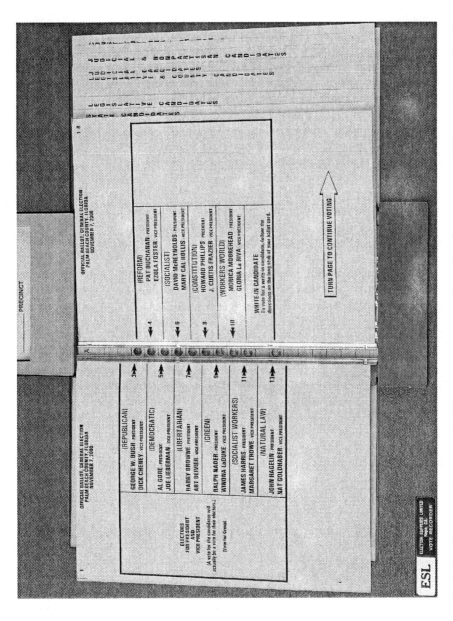

Figure 1.1 Ballot display of a pre-scored punch card (PPC) vote recorder, showing butterfly ballot arrangement, 2000 general election; Palm Beach County, FL.

processes of a democratic nation, it seems appropriate that each chad should be individualized and distinguished from the collective noun.

Each PPC ballot consists of a rectangular punch card the same thickness and size as an IBM punch card (7 ⅜ inches by 3 ¼ inches). That type of card was widely used for data processing in connection with IBM accounting machines in the twentieth century before electronic digital storage mechanisms fully replaced them. Data being processed was stored on the cards. The invention of punch cards for data processing use is discussed in section 4.9.

The IBM punch card was originally designed with places for holes at 960 "positions" on the card in a rectangular array, 80 along the long dimension and 12 across the short dimension. In a typical business application, each 12-position column was encoded with a hole pattern representing a single alphanumeric character. Thus, a card could store 80 characters and might be referred to as "an 80-column card." IBM cards were not normally prescored; the positions on the card (typically ⅛ inch by 1/16 inch) were punched out by machine when that action was needed. Even after the development of computers with electronic storage, IBM cards were still used for data input and sometimes output. Then, newer ways of entering data were developed, for example, keyboards, keypads, pushbuttons, document scanning, laser swiping of bar codes, cursor movement with mouse-clicks and touchscreens.

In a PPC, the positions are individually perforated so that they may be manually punched out. Harris based his concept on the "Port-a-punch," a special-purpose IBM product. This product consisted of a PPC, a backing for the card, and a punching tool called a stylus for directly entering data, that is, punching out chads, on the card. A typical application might be the manual recording, by a meter-reader, of the value of flow displayed on a pipeline meter in a remote location. The advantage of use of a PPC in this application was that writing of the value on a data sheet was avoided. Then, the later transcription of the value into a punch card was circumvented also, eliminating the possibility of a transcription error. In more recent times, such a value might be communicated electronically to a computer at a central station, dispelling the need for any person to visit the site just to manually record the data. The mass use of PPCs by untrained individuals was never contemplated for the Port-a-punch. Harris had obtained the help of William Rouverol, a professor of engineering at Berkeley, in converting the Port-a-punch into a voting device (Nathan, 1983, p. 132).

In 2000, elections were one of the few remaining applications of punch cards and possibly the only use of PPCs. When a PPC is used as a ballot, fewer than 960 positions are employed. In one arrangement, 312 positions in a rectangular array are used, 26 down the long dimension and 12 across the short dimension. (For a recent ballot implementation in Chicago, 456 positions were used.) The designated positions are prescored so that a voter, using a pointed metal stylus, may push out the chad from the card at the position that he or she believes corresponds to the candidate that he or she intends to select. Here, "believes" is used deliberately, because the names of the candidates are not on the card. Only numbers in small type, uniquely identifying each position, are printed there. Only one side of the card is used.

At a polling station, each voter receives a punch-card ballot with a stub attached to one of its short ends. The stub already has two holes punched into it; these holes are significantly larger than the holes that the voter is to punch out in the ballot. The voter is directed to one of several private booths containing a table on which is placed a ballot holder, also called a "vote recorder" or sometimes a "Votomatic device," and a stylus. The ballot holder is a thin hollow rectangle made of metal or hard plastic, and it is placed flat on the table. The voter inserts the PPC ballot into the hollow middle of the device from an opening near the top edge. When the ballot is properly inserted, the two holes in the stub must fit over pins.

Attached to the front of the ballot holder is a loose-leaf booklet. The pages of the booklet have the names of the candidates on them. In the center of the booklet, between the left-hand and right-hand pages, is a line of holes. The holes should line up with a single row (long dimension) of the punch card, which is located beneath. If the card is correctly located and the device has been correctly assembled, each punch-card position in that row lies directly beneath one of the holes.

The voter should start voting from the front of the booklet, that is, with the first page opened to the left and all additional pages under the next page on the right. The most important contest (the "top of the ticket") will be presented on the first pages. In most cases, the candidates will be presented only on the left-hand page. In the Florida presidential race, this could have been done by using small-sized type. Neither Duval County nor Palm Beach County would do it that way; voters in those counties would suffer the consequences.

Each candidate's name on the left-hand page of the booklet is listed to the left of a right-pointing arrowhead that points to the hole directly above the card position that is to be punched out to indicate a vote for that candidate. Each candidate's name on the right-hand page is listed to the right of a left-pointing arrowhead that has the same purpose. Additionally, each candidate's arrowhead has associated with it the number of the position on the ballot card that corresponds to that candidate.

To vote for a chosen candidate, the voter inserts the stylus into the selected hole and exerts pressure. This action is supposed to result in the complete punching out of the chad in the card position beneath and the creation of a hole in the ballot card. Each fully detached chad falls into the hollow space in the ballot holder beneath the ballot.

After the voter completes voting on the first pages seen, he or she turns over the first right-hand page of the booklet to allow a new set of pages to be viewed. A new line of holes should be seen also, and this line of holes is directly over the next row of the punch-card ballot. The voter votes on the new contests shown. Then, he or she continues to turn over additional pages and vote again until there are no more pages to be turned.

After completing the voting process, the voter removes the PPC from the holding device. He or she will have been instructed to remove all partially punched out chads from the back of the card, but many voters do not carry out that instruction. Additionally, the voter can check whether he or she pushed out each intended chad by comparing the number listed next to the candidate's name on the loose-leaf booklet with the small numbers next to the ballot positions.

To make this check for a candidate selection, the voter must find the position on the ballot card that has the same number given to the chosen candidate on the loose-leaf booklet. If the position on the ballot card with the candidate's number has been punched out, then the voter knows that he or she has voted as intended. It is unlikely that this check is made by a significant fraction of voters; if it were, in Florida in 2000, ballots cast with the mistaken punchings to be described would not have occurred with the observed frequency. The reality of the lack of voter friendliness of the PPC system is clearly shown in the analysis of the Florida ballots given later in section 1.19.

To tabulate the ballots in Florida in 2000, a "central-count" process was used. Voters deposited their ballots in a box at each precinct, and after the close of polls, ballot boxes were transported to a central computer installation. (Counting the votes at the precincts is possible, but it was not done in Florida.) At the central location, ballots were fed into card readers that sensed the holes in the cards and transferred that information to an attached computer. The computer should have been programmed to interpret a hole in a particular card position as a vote for the candidate that corresponded to that hole. Occasionally, a programming mistake is made by the election officials specializing the program for the particular election, and totals are reversed. This type of error is almost always caught by a reality check against expected outcomes, but the error typically creates concern among some voters that fraud was intended.

1.4   DATAVOTE PUNCH CARDS

In Nassau County, which occupies the area facing the Atlantic coast between the Georgia border at St. Mary's River and the Duval County line, SOE Shirley N. King was making her preparations. Nassau County was one of nine small counties that used the "Datavote" punch-card voting system at polling stations. It is significantly different from the PPC system. About 1.2 percent of Florida's population lived in the nine counties. Nationwide, about 5 percent of voters used it.

The Datavote system uses a ballot card the same size as the PPC card, but the card is not prescored when used at a polling station. The candidate names are on the card and both sides of the card are to be used. For an election with many contests, more than one ballot card may have to be issued to a voter. To vote the ballot card, the voter fixes the card in a holder. While in the holder, one entire side of the card is seen by the voter. A punching device is used to create a chad-sized hole in the designated space next to the name of the chosen candidate. The punching device includes a metal shaft to make the hole and a handle that provides the leverage to be used by the voter to force the bottom edge of the shaft through the card. The punching unit can be moved along the length of the card to bring a desired position under the punching shaft. The mechanism is supposed to prevent punchings except at positions that can be recognized by a card reader as votes for candidates. The voting spaces are close to the right-hand edge of the card, and when the card is turned over, the other long edge is available to be punched. The punch fully punches out the chad; partially punched out chads do not remain. The voter can clearly see whether the punches made correspond to the intended candidates.

After the voter completes the voting process, he or she drops the voted card or cards into a ballot box. As with the PPC process in Florida, a central-count process was used. Software must distinguish the types of ballot cards if more than one was issued to each voter as well as assure that the sensed holes are counted for the candidates for which they were intended.

1.5   MARKSENSE BALLOTS, PRECINCT-COUNT

The county seat of Leon County is the state capital, Tallahassee, 166 miles west of Jacksonville in the Florida panhandle. This county would use a mark-sense ballot system, where voters filled out their ballots with a pencil as they would a Scholastic Aptitude Test or a lottery form. These ballots were not limited in size to the standard IBM punch card, as were the PPC and Datavote ballot cards. Marksense ballots were typically larger, for example, 8½ inches wide by 14 inches long, and both sides of the ballot were used. Sometimes, the system is called "optical scan" because the marks on the ballot may be sensed by an optical scanner. However, some marksense readers operate with light in the infrared instead of the optical spectrum. The very first marksense ballots used fluorescent ink that was sensed in the ultraviolet spectrum (see section 6.4). Marksense seems to be a more preferable name.

Leon was one of 26 counties that used the marksense system with a small computer at each polling station. Voters individually fed their ballots into card readers that could sense the marks on the cards that filled the positions intended for voters' choices. The marks in the correct positions, assumed to be votes, were tallied in the attached computer. Therefore, the system was referred to as "precinct-count." One of the benefits of precinct-count systems is that the computer receiving the ballot data may be programmed to return the ballot to the voter if the voter has overvoted a contest. Then, the voter has the opportunity to request another ballot to cast it again without the error. All the marksense precinct-count systems in Florida were programmed that way on election day, except in Escambia and Manatee Counties. The SOEs in those counties ordered the return-if-overvoted capability to be disconnected, supposedly to speed up the voting process. About 32.3 percent of the Florida population lived in these 26 mostly moderate-size counties, and nationwide, about 30 percent of voters used a marksense system in 2000. (The latter percentage includes both precinct-count and central-count systems.)

Ion Sancho was the SOE of Leon County. Sancho would be drawn into the postelection legal contests by being requested by a Florida judge to supervise a recount (aborted before completion) of PPC ballots from Miami-Dade county. Sancho also would become recognized for his statement in 2001 that Florida spent $35 million teaching people how to use the statewide lottery and nothing to teach people how to vote.

1.6   MARKSENSE BALLOTS, CENTRAL-COUNT

Gadsden County is just northwest of Leon and it fronts the Georgia border, a surveyed line in this area. Denny Hutchinson was SOE during the 2000 general election, but he was defeated for reelection soon after. Gadsden County was one of 15 counties, containing 4.1 percent of Florida's population, that used a central-count, marksense voting system. Voters using a central-count system cannot benefit from the system's ability to return the ballot if an overvote is detected. The connection of the voter with his or her ballot is severed once the ballots are dropped into a ballot box and, in any event, the voter would not be in the vicinity of the computer to retrieve the ballot when the ballot data is sensed.

Rural Gadsden would be noticed in the aftermath of the election because of its unusual demographics as the only black-majority county in Florida and its unenviable distinction in the election results. It had the largest percentage of uncountable votes in the presidential contest of any Florida county. Marksense central-count systems showed themselves particularly vulnerable on this criterion.

1.7   MECHANICAL LEVER MACHINES—NO BALLOT

Martin County, located on the Atlantic coast just north of Palm Beach County, had 127,000 residents in 2000. Its poll-site voting units were mechanical lever voting machines; Martin was the only county in Florida continuing to employ them. In 1964, at the advent of computerized voting, nearly two-thirds of the voters in the nation, mostly in heavily populated areas, were using voting machines. (See sections 4.3–4.5, 4.7, and 6.1 for more on these machines.) By 2000, use had dropped to 18 percent of the national voting population. Since there are no ballots that can be transported, the system is basically precinct-count. Lever machines have not been manufactured since 1982; thus, there is no current vendor. Special maintenance experts are employed on contract to keep the machines in running order. Spare parts are obtained by the cannibalization of other machines.

The voter, upon approaching the lever machine, sees a rectangular array of small mechanical levers presented on its front. The machine is as tall as a person, and is intended to be used while the voter is standing in front of it. Each lever on the machine's front corresponds to the name of a candidate or a choice (yes or no) for a proposition. Identifications are presented next to the levers. The voter closes a privacy curtain before starting to use the machine, and then moves the free ends of selected levers to cover the names of the chosen candidates. Interlocks in the machine prevent the voter from voting for more candidates in a contest than are to be elected. Opening the privacy curtain completes the voting process; it returns the levers to their neutral positions and causes counters behind the levers within the machine to increase their stored numbers by one for each lever voted. There is no retention of the choices of individual voters, but the summaries of all votes for each choice are retained on the counters within the machine. Following the close of polls, administrators open the machines and record the values of each counter on official documents. Martin County used Datavote ballots for absentees.

1.8   HAND-MARKED, HAND-COUNTED BALLOTS

In little Union County, with just over 13,000 population, hand-marked ballots were hand counted. It was the only Florida county to still use this type of voting system. Babs Montpetit was SOE, and she was noted as distinctly hospitable by the journalists undertaking a recount of votes in her county. SOEs in certain other counties had the opposite reputation. Union's county seat, Lake Butler, is about 45 miles west-southwest of Jacksonville. It is estimated that 7 percent of voters nationally, in rural counties, townships, and towns, used this system in 2000. An estimate is required because usage data is only available on a countywide basis. Many of the deployments of hand-counted ballots are in the less-populated towns and townships responsible for their own election administration in counties designated as having "mixed" use.

1.9   ELECTION DAY IN PALM BEACH COUNTY

Problems with the ballot layout in Palm Beach County were noticed almost immediately. Other ballot design issues would become clear from later analyses of uncountable ballots.

SOE Theresa LePore had unwittingly approved (no partisanship was intended) a PPC ballot layout that might have contributed to a change in the outcome of the presidential election (figure 1.1 shows this arrangement). LePore had put the ten pairs of presidential candidate names on two facing pages of the loose-leaf booklet of the PPC ballot holder. This arrangement, with the line of holes in between the pages, suggested a butterfly to some observers. From top to bottom on the left-hand page were the candidate names for the Republican, Democratic, Libertarian, Green, Socialist Workers, and Natural Law parties. The arrowheads for these candidates pointed respectively (note that the photo shows misalignment) to hole numbers 3, 5, 7, 9, 11, and 13 of the ballot card's row positioned directly below the slot. From top to bottom on the right-hand page were the candidate names of the Reform, Socialist, Constitution, and Workers World parties, and their arrowheads pointed respectively to hole numbers 4, 6, 8, and 10. LePore had used this so-called butterfly arrangement, she said, to prevent having to use the smaller type that would be necessary to have all candidate pairs on the left-hand page. Many voters were elderly with poor eyesight, she explained.

As soon as the first voters in Palm Beach County left their polling stations, they reported being confused and upset. Many voters who intended to vote for the Democratic candidates, Al Gore and vice presidential nominee Senator Joe Lieberman of Connecticut, and who should have punched hole number 5, believed that they had erred by punching hole number 4 instead. (Of course, they hadn't checked the small position numbers on the ballot to be sure position 5 was punched before they cast it.) Position number 4 belonged to the Reform Party candidates, Patrick Buchanan and Ezola Foster, listed on the right-hand page. The mistake, if borne out, would be doubly dissatisfying to the blacks and Jews in Palm Beach County who intended to vote for the Democrats. To many of them, Buchanan was anathema.

The mistake of voting hole 4 instead of hole 5 was understandable. The Democrats were looking for the first usable hole directly below the Republican hole 3. If all candidates were listed top to bottom on the same page, the Democratic hole would be the first one below the Republican one, and there would be no intervening hole for the seventh-party candidates, Buchanan and Foster. It was this way in Broward and Miami-Dade Counties, where the need for smaller type was accepted and this type of error did not occur. With the allegation that the layout was incompatible with Florida law, the Palm Beach County arrangement was unsuccessfully disputed in a lawsuit against the county in the days following the election. A recent academic paper with extensive statistical documentation discusses votes for Buchanan that probably were intended for Gore:

> About 2,300 voters appear to have voted mistakenly for Buchanan . . . and at least 2,000 of the 2,300 would have been Gore votes . . . The evidence is very strong that . . . the butterfly ballot [was] pivotal in the 2000 presidential race. (Wand et al., 2001, p. 803)

Another study that analyzed overvotes (attempted votes for more than one candidate) made this observation about Palm Beach County:

> 8,170 voters . . . overvoted by punching Gore and one of the candidates who flanked him [on the ballot] . . . Another 1,668 voters punched Bush and Buchanan, the only name flanking Bush. The net effect of those errors cost Gore 6,502 votes. (Keating, 2001, p. 18)

Ballot arrangements in other counties (e.g., Duval stands out) also contributed to voters' mistakes, which might have overturned the election. The poorly designed layouts and lack of effective instructions created excessive numbers of undervotes as well as overvotes.

1.10 DISARRAY IN VOTER REGISTRATION

Florida, in 2000, had an administrative system to assist a voter who believed that he or she was registered to vote even though the voter's name wasn't on the appropriate precinct register and the voter did not possess a valid registration identification card. In such a case, the voter was permitted to sign an "affidavit," in which he or she affirmed that he or she was validly registered in that precinct. However, under Florida law, approval to vote must be given by the SOE and no one else. This, of course, required a phone call from the precinct to the SOE's headquarters, but there is considerable evidence that the phone lines to headquarters were terribly overloaded in many counties. Poll workers could not get through for hours. Consequently, many voters in this situation were not allowed to vote. However, some poll workers receiving affidavits from would-be voters, knowing that phone lines were constantly busy and that trying to connect would be a waste of time, permitted some citizens to vote anyhow. It would seem that equal protection was not uniformly applied in this situation, but this case would not reach the U.S. Supreme Court.

People who had applied to register to vote when they received or updated their driver's licenses also were having difficulties. A number of such instances have been documented. Poll worker Maria Desoto is recorded as stating:

> There were people who had registered to vote through motor-voter [the 1993 National Voter Registration Act] and somehow their registration was not transmitted to the supervisor of elections office. I saw that with married couples in my own precinct. One person would be registered to vote; the other person would not. The person who was not registered to vote couldn't vote unless they physically went to the supervisor of elections office and picked up a piece of paper, which they then brought back to me, because we couldn't reach them on the telephone. (U.S. Commission on Civil Rights, 2001, pp. 29–32)

Nonvoters were permitted to vote, according to a survey undertaken by *The Miami Herald*. The following was reported:

> Thousands of Floridians cast illegal votes on November 7; they swore they were eligible to vote, but they were not. The ballots, all of which were counted, came from unregistered voters, ineligible felons, and a handful of senior citizens who voted absentee first, then voted again at their local precincts after swearing that they hadn't voted before . . .
>
> A computerized review by the *Herald* of 2.3 million ballots from 22 counties found 1,241 votes cast by felons. If the pattern repeated itself statewide, more than 2,500 felons most likely cast illegal ballots . . .
>
> Several civil groups have charged . . . that black voters were harassed, intimidated and prevented from voting. There is considerable evidence of this . . . Some also claim that many legitimate voters—of all ethnic and racial groups, but particularly blacks—were swept from the rolls through the state's efforts to ban felons from voting. There is no widespread evidence of that. Instead, the

evidence points to just the opposite—that election officials were mostly permissive, not obstructionist, when unregistered voters presented themselves. (Merzer et al., 2001, pp. 97–110)

1.11   THE PROTEST PHASE OF THE POSTELECTION STRUGGLE

As it became clear that the result of the Florida election was in dispute, both national campaigns geared up for involvement by legal teams and political operatives from out-of-state. In 2004, the Federal Election Commission (FEC) stated that the Bush 2000 campaign agreed to pay a $90,000 civil fine for failing to properly disclose fund raising and spending for its postelection effort. The Bush campaign raised nearly $14 million compared with about $3.2 million in recount spending by the Gore campaign. Methods of spending (no accusations of bribery were made in Florida in 2000) should be compared with the 1876 presidential election dispute; see section 3.8.

1.12   VOTE TOTALS CHANGE AFTER PARTIAL MACHINE RECOUNT

After the first machine counting of ballots when polls closed on November 7, Bush led by 1,784 votes. State regulations mandate a recount if the totals for the leading candidates differ by less than one-half of 1 percent; the current difference was well within the requirement. In fact, Clay Roberts, the director of the Division of Elections issued a memo to all SOEs that "Florida law requires an automatic recount of all votes cast." After this machine recount, Bush led by only 327 votes. The change could have been caused by certain precincts failing to be included, or by errors based on double counting, or by changes in the conditions of PPC ballots. The latter could be due to chads falling out or to partially detached chads getting pushed back into the cards. When PPC ballots are handled, the status of the hanging or swinging chads may change. This statement was generally accepted as fact by both sides. After machine counts or recounts, loose chads are found in the readers and all over the counting room floors.

In Palm Beach County, Gore gained 643 votes due to ballots that hadn't been counted the first time. In Pinellas County, the machine recount yielded a net gain for Gore of 478 votes. In Nassau County, the recount yielded Gore an increase of 51 votes, but after a reconsideration, the Canvassing Board in that county decided that the first tally was correct. The board rescinded the second submission to the secretary of state. The unusual situation would cause the Gore team to include Nassau County in its contest of the election results approved as final by Katherine Harris.

According to two separate reports, however (Kaplan, 2001, p. 51; Toobin, 2001, p. 66), 18 counties had failed to run their ballots through the machines a second time.

> In Lake County, which did not run its ballots through the machines, the *Orlando Sentinel* found 376 uncounted ballots clearly intended as votes for Al Gore—and 246 uncounted ballots showing clear votes for George W. Bush. The swing in this one county—where Gore would have netted 130 votes—illustrates how important a true recount might have been. (Toobin, 2001, p. 66)

What this situation demonstrates also is the autonomy of the SOEs. Katherine Harris, as the state's chief elections officer, could have used the power of her office to assure uniformity in the application and operation of the election laws.

1.13   THE QUESTION OF MANUAL COUNTING

Following the second machine count, the Gore campaign requested a manual count of the ballots in four counties: Broward, Miami-Dade, Palm Beach, and Volusia. All four had produced majorities for Gore. Volusia, containing Daytona Beach, 91 miles south of Jacksonville on the Atlantic coast, was the tenth-largest county in population and had used marksense ballots with precinct-count. According to Florida law, manual recounts could be carried out if any of the candidates requests it within 72 hours of the election. Such recounts had been previously carried out in local contests. Gore's request was within the allotted time. It was up to the Canvassing Boards in each of these counties to order the recounts.

Very few Canvassing Boards voluntarily reviewed their ballots that contained no vote for president to determine if any of these undervoted or overvoted ballots contained a legal vote. Most Canvassing Boards apparently believed that running all the ballots through the machine, some only once, totally satisfied their responsibilities. By not manually reviewing the ballots that showed no-vote by machine, they were, by an interpretive reading of Florida law, voiding legal votes because the relevant statute provided that "no vote shall be declared invalid or void if there is a clear indication of the intent of the voter as determined by the canvassing board." On the other hand, if a Canvassing Board decided not to manually review the ballots showing no-vote by machine, the board members were clearly following the letter of the law that gave them the responsibility to make that decision. Thus, Canvassing Boards that wished to find no more votes because they were pleased with the outcome of the machine count did not need to manually review any ballots. "All politics is local," famously said the late Speaker of the House Tip O'Neill. The different actions of the Canvassing Boards could be classified also as denial of equal protection, but that particular set of wrongful acts was never considered at the U.S. Supreme Court.

Additional votes that might have been found to exist by a manual review might have been classified by a machine count as either "undervotes" or "overvotes," if the software of the machine could make that distinction. Some software could not cause the no-vote ballots to be distinguished by category.

With marksense ballots, a ballot that showed an undervote by machine might be shown in a manual review to contain a nonstandard mark, such as a circling of a candidate's name or an "X" next to the name of a candidate instead of the standard mark that could be machine-sensed. Under Florida's statute about intent of the voter, this ballot could be accepted as a vote if the Canvassing Board so chose. A marksense ballot that showed an overvote by machine might be shown to contain a machine-readable mark for an official candidate on the ballot and also a machine-readable mark and the name of the same candidate in the "write-in" location. This particular overvote situation, colloquially called a "double bubble," is specifically provided for by Florida law as a legal vote. Such legal votes would never be found if the Canvassing Board chose not to manually review the no-vote ballots.

With PPC ballots, a ballot that showed an undervote by machine might be shown (if a manual review were carried out) to contain a single partially detached or indented chad among the positions corresponding to choices for presidential candidates. That ballot would be classified as a vote if the type of partially detached or indented chad met the Canvassing Board's rule for a vote. There would be very few PPC ballots classified by machine as overvotes that could have been shown to be double-bubble legitimate votes. The process for writing in a candidate's name is complicated in the PPC system, and only two of the fifteen PPC counties provided a specific write-in punching location.

The Bush campaign officially responded to the Gore manual recount requests by filing a lawsuit in the appropriate U.S. District Court asking for an injunction to stop them. They would argue that Florida's manual recount laws subject the tally to capriciousness by allowing some, but not all, counties to recount by hand and by allowing counties to set their own rules for what constitutes a vote. They would say, on behalf of some Florida voters joining in the suit, that their 14th Amendment rights for equal protection would be violated under those circumstances. At a news conference in Tallahassee, James A. Baker III, who was U.S. secretary of state in the previous Republican administration and a leading Bush advisor, said that the manual count requested in the four Democratic counties would be far less accurate than the machine count. Baker stated that:

> It is precisely for these reasons that over the years our democracy has moved increasingly from hand counting of votes to machine counting . . . Machines are neither Republicans nor Democrats, and therefore can be neither consciously nor unconsciously biased.

However, federal judge Donald Middlebrooks denied the request for an injunction. He wrote in his order that the recount procedures "appear to be neutral" and that "the election scheme is reasonable and nondiscriminatory on its face" (Correspondents of *The New York Times*, 2001, pp. 40, 62).

The language of the Florida statute concerning recounts states that if the county Canvassing Boards found "an error in vote tabulation which could affect the outcome of the election," they could conduct a manual recount. Democrats understood this statement to concern an error in the entire process of vote tabulation. This view was supported by additional provisions of Florida law, which stated that a mismarked ballot should be discarded only "if it is impossible to determine the elector's choice" and as mentioned earlier "no vote shall be declared invalid or void if there is a clear indication of the intent of the voter as determined by the canvassing board."

Nevertheless, the Bush campaign would continue to press the courts for the end to manual recounts. They would be denied later at the Florida Supreme Court and at the U.S. Court of Appeals, but not where it really mattered: at the U.S. Supreme Court. In the meantime, Republicans prevailed on the office of the secretary of state, through Director of Elections Clay Roberts, to issue an advisory opinion on November 13, 2000, interpreting the statutes as follows:

> An "error in vote tabulation" means a counting error in which the vote tabulation system fails to count properly marked marksense or properly punched punchcard ballots. Such as error could result from incorrect election parameters, or an error in the vote tabulation and reporting software of the voting system. (Dionne and Kristol, 2001, pp. 12–14)

As one observer noted, Roberts offered no explanation for his conclusion—no statutory citation, no court cases that interpreted the recount statute and no analysis of the Florida election law generally (Kaplan, 2001, p. 81). According to a second observer, the opinion from the state government's election division was part of a Republican effort to prevent manual recounting by influencing the Canvassing Boards of the four counties that Gore had specified. The opinion responded to an arranged letter of inquiry from the state chairman of the Republican Party (Toobin, 2001, pp. 72–75). The advisory opinion was initially successful in that it caused the Palm Beach County Canvassing Board, at first, to vote not to undertake a manual recount.

The advisory opinion was contradicted the next day by a letter from Robert A. Butterworth, attorney general of Florida, who was, unlike Katherine Harris and Clay Roberts, a Democrat. Butterworth's letter extensively cited Florida statutes and case law (Dionne and Kristol, 2001, pp. 14–18). Eventually, supported by court decisions that rejected the advisory opinion, all four of the counties began the recount process. The Florida Supreme Court, besides dismissing the advisory opinion as incorrect, had extended the deadline for the submission of final counts.

Volusia's recount was completed on time and was included in the final count. (Volusia also had found an additional 320 ballots that it missed previously.) The Broward recount also was finished on time and was included, even though it took much longer because of the difficulty involved in evaluating each partially detached or indented chad. The recount from Palm Beach County was late. Their totals were determined over the extended deadline by two hours. The Palm Beach counters compromised their efforts by recessing for Thanksgiving Day on November 23. The secretary of state refused to accept the total recount, or the nearly complete recount finished by the deadline set by the Florida Supreme Court. The recount by Miami-Dade County was never completed; it was aborted. That occurred when the idea to abort surfaced at a Canvassing Board meeting while a noisy and intimidating demonstration by Republican operatives was going on just outside the doors. (It is likely that the $14 million spent by the Bush campaign included funds to pay for that operation.) The Board agreed that the recount would never be finished in time (Toobin, 2001, pp. 154–158).

1.14   THE CONDITION OF A CHAD THAT CONSTITUTED A VOTE

There was no state standard in Florida for what constituted a vote during a manual examination of a PPC ballot. (In Texas, such a state standard had been adopted in 1997 in a law signed by the governor, the very same George W. Bush, the Republican candidate for president.) It was generally understood that, in Florida, county Canvassing Boards were responsible for setting their own rules. When writing instruments were used, as with marksense ballots or even hand-read ballots, the human interpretation of ballot markings was reasonably clear to unbiased observers. For example, there was no controversy about accepting or rejecting marksense ballots in Volusia County while the manual recount was being done. With Datavote punch-card ballots, there was rarely a problem since the punches were typically clean and no chads remained. It was a different story with PPC ballots.

According to one report, when the Palm Beach County Canvassing Board started to manually recount ballots, they used the "sunshine rule" to determine if a ballot showed a vote. The substance of this rule was that if light could be seen through a chad that was partially punched out, then a vote was present; if no light could be seen, no vote could be counted. That rule was soon changed. The new rule went back to a standard established in 1990, which said that if a chad was detached by at least one corner, it would count as a vote, but if it was only indented (pregnant or dimpled) it would not count (Correspondents of *The New York Times*, 2001, p. 50). However, a legal scholar who has reviewed the record in *Bush v. Gore* reports that testimony in a lower court stated that Palm Beach began with the 1990 guideline before they switched to the sunshine rule. Then, following the second time that they adopted the 1990 guideline, according to the testimony, they "abandoned any pretense of a *per se* rule, only to have a court order that the county consider dimpled chads legal. This is not a process with sufficient guarantees of equal treatment" (Karlan, 2001, pp. 186, 187).

The Broward County Canvassing Board started its recount with a standard that required two corners of a chad to be separated to constitute a vote but later changed its rule to consider as a vote a chad that was detached by only one corner or just indented. Democrats had pressed for relaxing the standard in hopes that more votes for Gore could be found. Republicans objected to the changes, but a local judge agreed that the Canvassing Board had the right to set its own standards.

1.15   CONCLUSION OF THE SEMINOLE AND MARTIN COUNTY SITUATIONS

Very soon after the election, suits were filed by local Democrats asking that all the absentee ballots in Seminole and Martin counties be thrown out. Bush had a net gain of 4,700 votes in Seminole and 2,815 in Martin due to absentee ballots. While the suits failed and no absentee ballots were affected, the judges who heard the suits said that the actions of the SOEs violated Florida law. Judge Terry P. Lewis, who tried the Martin County case, wrote that the situation

> offered an opportunity for fraud and created the appearance of partisan favoritism on the part of the supervisor of elections.

However, the county court decisions stated that there was no evidence of any intentional wrongdoing. The Florida Supreme Court, which heard appeals of the two suits, upheld the results at the lower level but berated the election officials:

> Nothing can be more essential than for a supervisor of elections to maintain strict compliance with the statutes in order to ensure credibility in the outcome of the election. (Correspondents of *The New York Times*, 2001, pp. 271, 272, 309)

1.16   THE "CONTEST" PHASE

After the secretary of state certified the election outcome on November 26, opposition to the reported result by Gore would be called, under Florida law, a contest. There were several decisions by the Florida and U.S. Supreme Courts in this dispute. The decisions presented here are those considered most critical to the outcome. Note: case numbers are given for the decisions cited. These decisions have been reprinted and are available in a single volume (Dionne and Kristol, 2001, pp. 9–161).

1.16.1   The Florida Supreme Court—Decision of December 8

The first hearing after the certification, in the dispute called *Gore v. Harris*, was heard by Circuit Court judge Sanders Sauls in Tallahassee (in Leon County). Leon County was the venue established in state law to review all statewide election disputes. Gore's petition alleged that the certified results included "a number of illegal votes" and failed to include "a number of legal votes sufficient to change or place in doubt the result of the election" (the required basis under Florida law to achieve relief in this situation).

One of Gore's witnesses in this hearing was Kimball W. Brace, president of Election Data Services and highly knowledgeable about election equipment. Brace was seen to be carrying a copy of Roy G. Saltman's 1988 report on voting integrity (Saltman, 1988, pp. 1–132), which would be introduced as evidence. The report had called for the abandonment of PPC voting (see section 6.11). In 1996, Saltman had made a presentation to the group called Computer Professionals for Social Responsibility, stating that voting technology and administrative procedures would not be improved until there was "an absolute crisis." He was right about that. However, on November 6, 2000 (having first voted absentee), he had begun a trip of cultural education to Thailand and Cambodia believing that it was not the year in which a crisis would occur. He was wrong about that. Gore's plea was denied by Judge Sauls on December 4 (In the Circuit Court of the Second Judicial Circuit, in and for Leon County, Florida, Case No. CV-00-2808). Gore appealed and the case was taken up by the Florida Supreme Court after being forwarded on by the appropriate Court of Appeals.

The Florida Supreme Court was sympathetic to the Gore stand to require each vote to be counted. They succinctly stated:

> In the election contest at issue here, this Court can do no more that see that every citizen's vote be counted. But it can do no less.

In their four–three ruling (Supreme Court of Florida, No. SC00-243), they decided that the trial court had erred in rejecting three concerns raised by Gore. They ordered that 215 votes identified in a manual count in Palm Beach County should be added to Gore's total, as should 168 votes identified in the partial recount of the Miami-Dade ballots. They also ordered a manual count of approximately 9,000 Miami-Dade ballots that had been registered by the machines as non-votes and had never been manually counted, but they rejected Gore's contest of the Nassau County final totals.

In their most surprising ruling, the Court ordered that all undervotes previously rejected by the machines as non-votes should be manually counted throughout the entire state. The Court stated:

> We do agree . . . that a manual recount be conducted for all legal votes in this State, not only in Miami-Dade County, but in all Florida counties where there was an undervote, and, hence a concern that not every citizen's vote was counted . . . This essential principle, that the outcome of elections be determined by the will of the voters, forms the foundation of the election code enacted by the Florida Legislature . . .

With regard to the voting technology used, the Court majority produced the following footnote:

> This Presidential election has demonstrated the vulnerability of what we believe to be a bedrock principle of democracy: that every vote counts. While there are areas in this State which implement systems (such as the optical scanner) where the margins of error, and the ability to demonstrably verify those margins of error, are consistent with accountability in our democratic process, in these election contests based upon allegations that functioning punchcard voting machines have failed to record legal votes, the demonstrated margins of error may be so great to suggest that it is necessary to reevaluate utilization of the mechanisms employed as a viable system.

In his dissent, Chief Justice Wells, joined by two other justices, noted the differences in decisions that the several county Canvassing Boards were making about the acceptance or rejection of "dimpled chads." Additionally, the dissent raised the issue of overvotes, as distinct from undervotes. Presciently, the chief justice wrote that:

> Continuation of this system of county-by-county decisions regarding how a dimpled chad is counted is fraught with equal protection concerns which will eventually cause the election results in Florida to be stricken by the federal courts or Congress. . . . Also problematic with the majority's analysis is that the majority only requires that the "under-votes" are to be counted. How about the "over-votes?" . . . It seems patently erroneous to me to assume that the vote-counting machines can err when reading under-votes but not when reading over-votes. Can the majority say, without having the over-votes looked at, that there are no legal votes among the over-votes?

One significant decision that the Court majority had *not* made was to set the same standards in all counties for determining the condition of a partially dislodged chad that constituted a vote. The Court may have believed that setting statewide standards would extend their reach into territory properly belonging to the state legislature. *They would have been damned if they did and they would be damned that they didn't.*

1.16.2   The US Supreme Court—Decision of December 12

Immediately after the Florida Supreme Court ruling on December 8, lawyers for Bush applied to the U.S. Supreme Court for a stay of its implementation. A temporary stay was granted by a five–four decision on December 9 in the case to be known as *Bush v. Gore* [Supreme Court of the United States, No. 00-949(00A504)]. Oral argument was set for Monday, December 11. The U.S. Supreme Court issued its decision on December 12, with individual justices taking the same sides that they had taken on December 9 (Supreme Court of the United States, No. 00-949).

The unsigned (*per curiam*) judgment of the court, probably written by Justice Kennedy and/or Justice O'Connor, permanently enjoined the Florida Supreme Court from carrying out its ordered recount. The reason given was that the differing standards in the PPC counties undertaking manual recounting violated the Constitutional requirement of equal protection. Statements in the decision included the following:

> The recount mechanisms implemented in response to the decisions of the Florida Supreme Court do not satisfy the minimum requirements for non-arbitrary treatment of voters necessary to secure the fundamental right [of equal protection] . . . The problem inheres in the absence of specific standards to ensure . . . equal application [of intent of the voter]. The formulation of

uniform rules to determine intent based on these recurring circumstances is practicable and, we conclude, necessary . . .

The State has not shown that its procedures include the necessary safeguards. The problem, for instance of the estimated 110,000 overvotes has not been addressed . . .

On voting technology, the decision had this to say:

Much of the controversy seems to revolve around ballot cards designed to be perforated by a stylus but which, either through error or deliberate omission, have not been perforated with sufficient precision for a machine to count them. In some cases a piece of the card—a chad—is hanging, say by two corners. In other cases there is no separation at all, just an indentation . . .

This case has shown that punch card balloting machines can produce an unfortunate number of ballots which are not punched in a clean, complete way by the voter. After the current counting, it is likely legislative bodies nationwide will examine ways to improve the mechanisms and machinery for voting.

Of extreme importance for the future implementation of voting equipment throughout the nation was the following statement, which limited the applicability of the decision:

Our consideration is limited to the present circumstances, for the problem of equal protection in election processes generally presents many complexities.

There were four dissenting opinions, each written by a different justice, and each of the four opinions was joined, in part, by other members of the dissenting group. Justice Stevens, Justice Souter, and Justice Breyer each said that the proper decision would have been to remand the dispute to the Florida Supreme Court with an order that they institute a uniform standard for counting PPC ballots. Additionally, all three of these justices noted that different types of voting equipment are permitted in different counties of a state without having that situation rise to the level of an equal protection issue. Justice Stevens and Justice Breyer pointed out that "ballots of voters in counties that use punchcard systems are more likely to be disqualified than those in counties using optical scanning systems." "Thus," wrote Justice Breyer:

In a system that allows counties to use different types of voting systems, voters already arrive at the polls with an unequal chance that their votes will be counted. I do not see how the fact that this results from counties' selection of different voting machines rather than a court order makes the outcome any more fair. Nor do I understand why the Florida Supreme Court's recount order, which helps to redress this inequity, must be entirely prohibited based on a deficiency that could be easily remedied.

Additionally, Justice Stevens wrote that:

As the majority further acknowledges, Florida law holds that all ballots that reveal the intent of the voter constitute valid votes. Recognizing these principles, the majority nonetheless orders termination of the contest proceeding before all such votes have been tabulated. Under their own reasoning, the appropriate course of action would be to remand to allow more specific procedures for implementing the legislature's uniform general standard to be established.

Justice Stevens, Justice Souter, and Justice Ginsburg indicated dismay at federal judges substituting their views for those of the state judiciary on matters of state law. Justice Ginsburg's dissent was particularly detailed on this point. Justice Breyer wrote that disputes over presidential Electors, under the Constitution and the Electoral Count Act of 1887 (see section 3.9), are to be resolved by Congress and not by the U.S. Supreme Court.

Chief Justice Rehnquist, joined by Justices Scalia and Thomas, wrote a scathing concurrence to the majority ruling. With regard to the issue of counting the votes, the statement made the following points:

Florida's statutory law cannot reasonably be thought to require the counting of improperly marked ballots. Each Florida precinct before election day provides instructions on how properly to cast a vote . . . each polling place on election day contains a working model of the voting machine it uses . . . and each voting booth contains a sample ballot . . . In precincts using punchcard ballots, voters are instructed to punch out the ballots cleanly . . . No reasonable person would call it an error in vote tabulation when electronic or electromechanical equipment performs precisely in the manner designed, and fails to count those ballots that are not marked in the manner that these voting instructions explicitly and prominently specify. The scheme that the Florida Supreme Court's opinion attributes to the [Florida] legislature is one in which machines are *required* to be "capable of correctly counting votes," but which nonetheless regularly produces elections in which legal votes are predictably *not* tabulated, so that in closer elections manual recounts are regularly required. This is of course absurd.

The Secretary of State, who is authorized by law to issue binding interpretations of the election code . . . rejected this peculiar reading of the statutes. The Florida Supreme Court, although it must defer to the Secretary's interpretations, . . . rejected her reasonable interpretation and embraced the peculiar one.

Dissents to the Rehnquist concurrence were filed by Justice Stevens, Justice Souter, and Justice Breyer.

Justice Stevens pointed out that the Florida statutory standard on intent of the voter is consistent with the practice of 33 other states, which apply either a similar intent of the voter standard or an "impossible to determine the elector's choice" standard in ballot recounts. Justice Stevens named, besides Florida, 13 states that use an intent of the voter standard and 22 states (2 states appear in both groups) that employ a standard in which a vote is counted unless it is impossible to determine the elector's (or voter's) choice.

Justice Souter noted that the State Supreme Courts had to define the terms "legal vote" and "rejection," as definitions of these terms do not appear in the most relevant Florida election statute. The court looked to a related statute to define legal vote to mean a vote recorded on a ballot indicating what the voter intended. Similarly, the court defined rejection to mean simply a failure to count, and "that reading is certainly within the bounds of common sense." Justice Souter wrote:

> It is perfectly true that the majority [of the State Supreme Court] might have chosen a different reading [such as that chosen by the Secretary of State]. But even so, there is no constitutional violation in following the majority view . . .

Justice Breyer wrote:

> the parties have argued about the proper meaning of the statute's term "legal vote." The Secretary [of State] has claimed that a "legal vote" is a vote properly executed in accordance with the instructions provided to all registered voters . . . On that interpretation, punchcard ballots for which the machines cannot register a vote are not "legal" votes . . . The Florida Supreme Court did not accept her definition. But it had a reason. Its reason was that a different provision of Florida election laws (a provision that addresses damaged or defective ballots) says that no vote shall be disregarded "if there is a clear indication of the intent of the voter as determined by the canvassing board" (adding that ballots should not be counted "if it is impossible to determine the elector's choice") . . . This conclusion differs from the conclusion of the Secretary. But nothing in Florida law requires the Florida Supreme Court to accept as determinative the Secretary's view on such a matter. Nor can one say that the Court's ultimate determination is so unreasonable as to amount to a constitutional "impermissible distortion" of Florida law.

An important policy question is raised by Chief Justice Rehnquist about the effect of machine counting of ballots on the voter's ability to have his or her choices understood and accepted. According to the chief justice's concurrence, it is the voter's responsibility to learn how to use the voting system and to use it correctly, particularly as instructions are provided at the polling station. Whatever the machine's qualities, and regardless of a ballot arrangement produced with no understanding of human factors, if the voter fails to record choices the way the machine can sense them, then the voter has no right to have his or her votes counted. This viewpoint makes no allowance for poorly designed or poorly maintained machines, or for that matter, poorly designed ballots.

A different point-of-view is that the government has a responsibility to provide a ballot that is easily understood, that takes into account human factors of design, and maximizes the voter's ability to convert his or her choices into data that are correctly recorded by the machine. Unlike the requirements for becoming a lawyer, physician, or even a driver on the public roads, there is no certificate of competence required for becoming a voter. In fact, the Voting Rights Act of 1965 (see section 5.5) forbids any test requiring a voter to "demonstrate the ability to read, write, understand, or interpret any matter." If the work of recording one's choices on a ballot requires the execution of tasks beyond the ability of a percentage of citizens, then it is, in effect, a kind of test of problem-solving ability, even if not a literacy test.

Richard A. Posner (Posner, 2001, pp. 92–109), a judge of the U.S. Court of Appeals for the Seventh Circuit agrees with Chief Justice Rehnquist's interpretation of Florida law, but has somewhat more compassion for the less competent voter. He distinguishes between voter error and tabulator error and states that the Florida statute calls for manual counting only in the case of error in vote tabulation (meaning, to him, an error in the tabulating equipment). Furthermore, he states, the issue of "voter intent" arises only in the situation of a damaged or defective ballot. This "is different from its being spoiled by the voter." Nevertheless, Judge Posner says that:

> I do not suggest that the voters who failed to follow the voting instructions were seriously culpable, or even that voters who are utterly incapable, because of reading deficiencies, to follow simple and clear instructions should be disenfranchised; I argued [earlier] against literacy tests for eligibility to vote. The question rather is the amount of inconvenience that a voter who, however innocently, has failed to follow directions should be entitled to impose upon the election authorities, especially within the compressed timetable of a challenge to a Presidential election.

Thus, the issue, as Judge Posner sees it, is a question of priorities: inconvenience to election authorities versus the right of voters less capable in using vote-recording equipment to have their votes counted for president of the United States. The judge has clearly stated where he stands.

A protest against the use of the PPC vote-recording system that occurred in 1987 raised the issue of literacy tests. As reported by Ronnie Dugger (Dugger, 1988, pp. 40, 41), Michael V. Roberts, a black candidate for president of the Board of Alderman in St. Louis, contended in a lawsuit that "computerized voting is such a relatively complex process that it is tantamount to a literacy test, and literacy tests have been prohibited by federal law as an unconstitutional burden on the right to vote." Roberts had lost a very close election in which the percent of spoiled ballots was much higher in black sections of the city than in white ones (no person with national influence paid attention in 1987). The judge hearing the suit "ordered officials to count by hand all ballots that contained overvotes or undervotes and to intensify voter education in black wards." The Missouri secretary of state Roy Blunt said that a hand-count could "make punchcard voting unworkable" and successfully appealed the verdict. Blunt was, in 2005, the Majority (Republican) Whip in the U.S. House of Representatives (see section 7.8, *The State of Ohio*).

That Missouri defense and similar defenses of the indefensible PPC system paved the highway that led directly to the Florida conflict of 2000.

Judge Posner had made a point similar to that of Roberts, with regard to the 2000 election. He has written: "The problem was the use in 40 percent of Florida's counties of a voting technology that, despite the abolition of literary tests for voting, puts a premium on literacy . . ." (Posner, 2001, p. 88). The views of Larry Kramer, Samuel Tilden Professor of Law at New York

University (how ironic! see section 3.8), do not agree with those of the chief justice or Judge Posner. Professor Kramer has written:

> The statute is question refers to an error in "the vote tabulation" . . . Moreover, nothing in the language of the statute suggested . . . a narrower meaning was intended. On the contrary, when the Florida legislature wanted to refer specifically to the machines that did the counting, it used phrases like "the vote tabulation system" or the "automatic tabulating equipment" . . . (T)he provision governing how returns should be canvassed stated that a mismarked ballot should be discarded only "if it is impossible to determine the elector's choice" . . . This had been Florida policy for nearly a century . . .
>
>   (T)he Florida court had the better argument and more plausible interpretation . . . The deference ordinarily owed to . . . an executive official [Secretary of State Harris] charged with enforcing a statute . . . is reduced or eliminated when the interpretation in question is contrary both to long-established policy and to the apparent meaning of the statutory text, as was the case here. (Kramer, 2001, pp. 110, 111, 153)

Particular attention should be paid to Professor Kramer's statement that "This had been Florida's policy for nearly a century." What must be realized is that any policy on vote counting that has been in existence for almost 100 years must have been put into place before the commencement of computerized voting. The policy must have been devised for the hand counting of hand marked ballots, that is, certainly before 1964 when computerized voting first began to be used.

Then, a question that may be asked is as follows: to what extent did the introduction of the sensing by a computer reader of the choices punched into or marked on ballots change the philosophy of determining the results of an election? It is surprising that in a profession so concerned with precedent, lawyers for Gore did not argue strongly that the historical development of the vote-counting process demonstrates the intention of the Florida legislature in establishing the basic rules of interpreting ballots. The Florida statute cited by the secretary of state only provides instructions to a Canvassing Board if a machine fails to properly count. No evidence was presented that the introduction of machines changed the basic philosophy that the intent of the voter is what really mattered. Justice Breyer reported a Connecticut decision about a similar dispute:

> Whatever the process used to vote and to count votes, differences in technology should not furnish a basis for disregarding the bedrock principle that the purpose of the voting process is to ascertain the intent of the voters.

1.17   ANALYSIS OF OVERSEAS ABSENTEE BALLOTS BY THE MEDIA

In one of the first studies undertaken and reported about this election, *The New York Times* reviewed the postmarks and signatures of absentee ballots that were filed from overseas. These were both military and civilian. *The Times* reviewed the decisions made by the county Canvassing Boards as to whether or not the ballots should be counted or thrown out. There were different standards in different counties. The study showed that the decisions made were often partisan and contrary to Florida law. The July 15, 2001 article in *The New York Times* reporting the research states:

> Under intense pressure from the Republicans, Florida officials accepted hundreds of overseas ballots that failed to comply with state laws . . . *The Times* found 680 questionable votes . . . The flawed votes included ballots without postmarks, ballots postmarked after the election, ballots without witness signatures, ballots mailed . . . from within the United States and even ballots from voters who voted twice. All would have been disqualified had the state's election laws been strictly enforced. (Barstow and Van Natta, 2001, p. 1)

The "intense pressure" cited is that, after the November 17 deadline for receiving all overseas absentee ballots (10 days after the election), Republicans filed lawsuits against 14 counties. These suits intimidated some individual Canvassing Board members by naming them. The suits asked that rejected ballots be reconsidered. At the same time, Republicans undertook a public relations blitz that pressured Canvassing Board members with charges of a lack of patriotism for rejections of overseas military ballots. The Canvassing Boards of 12 counties won by Bush reconvened and accepted overseas absentee ballots that had been rejected previously. This reversal shows that the valid charge made against re-counters of hanging chads that they changed the rules in the middle of the game also applies to re-counters of overseas absentee ballots.

The difference in decisions by Canvassing Boards between counties won by Bush and those won by Gore is shown by statistics developed and reported by *The New York Times* in table 1.1 (Barstow and Van Natta, 2001, p. 18).

The *Times* could not relate the content of the ballots to their review of envelopes and signatures since the ballots had been separated. It is seen in table 1.1 that the aggregate set of decisions by Canvassing Boards in counties won by Bush was significantly different than the set of decisions in counties won by Gore. It is highly likely that counties won by Bush had Republican-majority Canvassing Boards while those won by Gore had

Table 1.1 Ballots with flaws that violated state election laws or administrative rules (adapted from Barstow and Van Natta, 2001, p. 18)

	Accepted	Rejected	Percent accepted
In counties won by Bush	530	523	50.3
In counties won by Gore	150	666	18.4
Total	680	1,189	36.4

Democratic-majority ones. The *Times* notes also the different strategies carried out by lawyers for Bush in different counties:

> The records reveal example after example of Bush lawyers' employing one set of arguments in counties where Mr. Gore was strong and another in counties carried by Mr. Bush . . . In Bush strongholds, they pleaded with election officials to ignore Florida's election rules, [while] urging strict enforcement of state election laws and rules in counties like Broward, which supported Al Gore.

As only the envelopes and voter documentation had been reviewed, it was not possible to precisely determine the effect on the election if all flawed ballots had been rejected. For an estimate, the *Times* approached Dr. Gary King of Harvard, an expert in statistical models. In the judgment of King and his associate Dr. Kosuke Imai of Princeton (Imai and King, 2004, pp. 537–549), Bush would have most likely suffered a net loss of 286 votes, resulting in a reduction in his margin of victory from 537 to 251 votes.

1.18   MEDIA REVIEWS OF POLLING-STATION BALLOTS

In 2001, two groups headed by media companies made intensive surveys of the ballots cast at polling stations that were not counted by machine. They were able to carry out this activity because Florida's expansive Sunshine Law permitted them access to all the individual ballots. A primary function of the studies was to determine the candidate who would have had the most votes in the Florida contest if all the undervotes and overvotes had been manually reviewed and votes had been assigned according to an intent of the voter standard. The studies also provided much information on the capabilities of the different types of voting equipment and the influence of ballot arrangements on voters' abilities to correctly record their choices.

One group (referred to as *The Miami Herald* Study) included *The Miami Herald* newspaper, its parent company, Knight Ridder, and USA Today. They hired the accounting firm BDO Seidman to undertake a detailed examination of the ballots. Their undervote results were published as part of a volume previously referenced (Merzer et al., 2001, pp. 221–301).

The second group was an alliance (identified as the Consortium Study) of The Associated Press, Cable News Network, *The Wall Street Journal, The New York Times, The Washington Post*, two Florida newspapers, and Tribune Publishing. The latter included *The Los Angeles Times, The Chicago Tribune*, and two other Florida newspapers. The Consortium Study hired the National Opinion Research Center (NORC) at the University of Chicago to perform its field research. A total of 174,500 undervoted and overvoted ballots were reviewed by the Consortium Study through NORC. The results presented here were made available by Dan Keating of *The Washington Post*, one of the two leaders who designed the methodology, obtained staffing, and managed the effort on the ground. Keating also presented a summary of the work to an annual meeting of the American Political Science Association (Keating, 2002, pp. 1–34).

1.19 PERFORMANCE OF THE DIFFERENT TYPES OF VOTING TECHNOLOGIES

Performance, calculated from data provided by Keating, is shown in table 1.2. The general figure of merit used is the ability of the voters to record their choices so as to allow them to be sensed by the machinery. The inability of voters to do so is shown by the percentage of undervotes and the percentage of overvotes not readable by machine in each technology. (These values do not consider votes recovered by manual review.) The two values—percentage of undervotes and percentage of overvotes—are not combined because the unusual problem of overvotes introduced by the presentation of the ten pairs of candidates on two columns, two pages, or two sides of a ballot leads to the conclusion that a combined value would have little meaning.

Results for each type of technology are shown in a separate row. Broward County is included with the PPC-using counties, even though its manually reviewed ballots were accepted by the secretary of state for inclusion in her certification. Special procedures were instituted to assure against double-counting or omission of votes. The 23 marksense counties that returned overvotes to the voters for re-balloting consist of the 26 counties with marksense precinct-count machines without Volusia, Escambia, and Manatee Counties. Volusia County's votes were hand-recounted under Gore's protest action and were accepted also by the secretary of state. None of Volusia County's ballots were examined by the Consortium Study and are not included anywhere in table 1.2. Escambia and Manatee Counties, which disabled their overvote-return capability, are included in the fourth row of table 1.2 with counties using marksense central-count machines. The special cases of Martin County, where only absentee ballots were recorded by ballot-counting machines, and Union County, where all ballots were analyzed manually, are shown in their own rows.

Table 1.2 Percentage of undervotes and overvotes calculated from the results of the Consortium Study

No. of counties	System type	No. of undervotes	Percent undervotes	No. of overvotes	Percent overvotes
15	PPC	53,215	1.46	84,822	2.33
9	Datavote	594	0.78	4,371	5.70
23	Marksense with overvote-return	4,937	0.30	4,604	0.28
17	Marksense, no overvote-return	1,903	0.37	19,563	3.81
1	Martin County, absentee ballots	177	0.56	56	0.11
1	Union County, hand-counted	25	0.61	233	5.71
Totals					
66		60,851		113,649	

The percentage of undervotes (1.46) when PPC systems were used is a significant item from table 1.2. While the percentage of undervotes for Datavote systems is only slightly more than one-half of the PPC value, the percentage of undervotes for marksense systems with overvote-return is just one-fifth of the value for PPC systems. The much higher value of the percentage of undervotes for PPC systems is consistent with data on this subject obtained for elections in other states and at other times. The higher value indicates that the PPC system is, in general, more difficult for voters to use than other systems.

System performance on overvotes was considerably poorer than on undervotes, as can be seen in table 1.2. There were nearly twice as many overvotes as undervotes, 113,649 of the former against 60,851 of the latter. It would appear that the Datavote system and Union County's hand-counted ballots had the worst records on percentage of overvotes. Some counties had much poorer results than others, due to ballot arrangements established without consideration of the human-factors impact. Datavote-using Desoto County (6.72 percent rate) listed eight of the presidential candidates on the front of the ballot card and the remaining two on the back. Among PPC counties, Palm Beach's overvote rate was 4.15 percent; Duval recorded 7.50 percent. In Duval, where the major parties' presidential candidates were presented on the first left-hand page and the remaining ones on the next left-hand page,

> examination of ballots by voters who chose just Bush or just Gore on the front page and one additional candidate from the second page indicates that Bush lost 4,465 votes from that error and Gore lost 7,050, a net loss for Gore of 2,585. (Keating, 2002, p. 18)

Among the marksense counties with overvote-return, all counties but one (Columbia) did very well with a 0.30 percent average, showing that the overvote-return feature was worth its cost. Columbia County's overvote rate was, at 3.20 percent, very puzzling. Staff of SOE Carolyn Kirby reported that "many voters . . . decided not to correct the error and submitted their overvoted ballots." If true, that would make Columbia County voters very different from voters in other counties. Among marksense counties without the overvote-return, Gadsden County's 11.59 percent overvote rate was the statewide record, although the Hamilton, Hendry, and Okeechobee County rates of 8.54, 8.50, and 7.23 percent, respectively, were not far behind.

Votes cast at blank positions is a characteristic of the PPC system, which occurs with no other system type. Data on the occurrence of these punches for the Florida election are available on a per-county basis from *The Miami Herald* Study. These uncountable punches are a special type of undervote. In each of the 15 PPC counties, an average of about 0.11 percent of all votes were cast in this matter, that is, slightly more than one vote in every one thousand cast (the percentage in Miami-Dade was somewhat higher). About 85 percent of these punches were fully punched through with no chad remaining. The existence of these votes at blank positions was recognized previously, that is, Florida in 2000 was not the first instance. They were noted, for example, in a special election in Wisconsin's First Congressional District in 1993 in which there was only one contest (also see section 6.14). (Their incidence in that election was considerably higher than here.) It was realized at that time that these were not deliberate protest punches, as it was highly unlikely that a voter would intentionally go to a polling station for just one contest and then punch for a blank position. The existence of these unintended punches for no candidate are not well known because they are not typically reported. They are another indication of the human-factors failure of the PPC system.

1.20   WHICH CANDIDATE REALLY HAD THE MOST VOTES?

According to the Consortium Study, Gore would have won if all ballots, including overvotes and undervotes, had been reviewed statewide. Gore's margin of victory would have varied up to a maximum of 171 votes, depending on the established condition of each chad that constituted a vote and the acceptance or rejection of certain marks on marksense ballots. On the other hand, for any subset of ballots excluding evaluation of overvotes, Bush would have won. For example, Bush would have won by 225 votes if the full recounts of all ballots in the four counties requested by Gore had been undertaken. Bush would have won by 430 votes if the Florida Supreme Court had had its way and all undervotes statewide had been manually examined (Keating, 2002, p. 8).

The particular results in table 1.3, derived from data provided by Dan Keating, show Gore picking up a net total of 585 votes (12,192 minus 11,607).

Table 1.3   Consortium data summary: votes retrieved for Bush and Gore (for a particular set of chad and mark standards)

No. of counties	System type	Bush votes retrieved		Gore votes retrieved	
		Undervotes	Overvotes	Undervotes	Overvotes
15	PPC	9,124	163	8,708	388
9	Datavote	72	38	61	34
23	Marksense with overvote-return	817	176	902	238
17	Marksense, no overvote-return	207	939	262	1,532
1	Martin County, absentee ballots	66	0	53	2
1	Union County, hand-counted	0	5	0	12
Totals					
66		10,286	1,321	9,986	2,206
Grand totals		11,607		12,192	

Given the official margin for Bush of 537 votes, the additional votes retrieved would have given Gore a victory margin of 48 votes. Note that review of all undervotes provides Bush 10,286 votes and Gore only 9,986 votes. In a review of the overvotes, Gore gains 2,206 while Bush gains just 1,321. The bonanza available from overvotes was never understood by Gore partisans nor, for that matter, by the Florida Supreme Court's majority. These valid but machine-uncountable votes do not occur often in use of PPC systems. As can be seen in table 1.3, the largest number of votes reaped from overvotes occurred with marksense ballots with no overvote-return capability.

The review of the ballots undertaken by NORC was very careful to assure objectivity. They required that three people review each ballot and determined that:

> The disagreement rate was much higher in punch card technologies. Consistency was much greater in viewing the paper optical ballots which, unlike punch cards, are designed to be read directly by voters and are clear to the naked eye.

1.21   SOME FINAL WORDS

The winner in this election was determined by a very small difference between two very large numbers. Determination of the final vote counts would be a question not of arithmetic, but of legal adjudication of how the final figures were to be obtained. The major error of the Gore campaign was their failure to ask for a recount of all undervotes and overvotes in all counties.

Voting technology played a pivotal role. The situation was significantly aggravated because of use of the PPC voting system by more than 60 percent of Florida voters. This system had been widely used in presidential elections throughout the nation for more than 30 years. It was destined to show its defects in public, if not in 2000, then at some future close election. The difficulty in using the system by a certain fraction of voters was known to election officials. Its difficulty in providing precise results because of the unstable condition of partially dislodged chads was also known. No operational difficulty that occurred in this election caused by use of the PPC system was new to administrators who had used it previously and to the few experts who had studied and denounced it. Some election officials, inured to the mistakes made by voters as an expected human condition, thought the system adequate. Others hesitated to speak out because they feared to propose significant expenditures to the local political leadership, and the remainder quietly prayed that the elections that they personally administered would not be close. There was no chorus of election officials demanding change.

The magnitude of the problem just wasn't previously appreciated by the public. At the highest levels, decision makers knew everything there was to be known about elections except how they were actually carried out. David Gergen, a senior policy advisor to Democratic and Republican presidents from Ronald Reagan to Bill Clinton, was heard to say on national television after the election, "We've all learned a new word—'chad.' "

The impact of the difficulties in determining the outcome of the 2000 Florida presidential election was large on the voters themselves. Many were disgusted with the inability of the world's greatest democracy to conduct an efficient national election in which all the collected relevant data makes the result clear within a short time to all with open minds. Chad became a subject for stand-up comedians. The widely disseminated photo of Broward County judge Robert Rosenberg peering at a PPC ballot through a magnifying glass became symbolic of the bumbling process. The United States promoted democracy to developing nations around the world, but it became clear to the U.S. public that its own elections were an embarrassment. How we arrived at this sorry condition is the subject of the subsequent chapters, except the last one. The final chapter concerns the aftermath.

From the Revolution to the Civil War: Consent of the Governed and the Election Clause

2.1 "Just Powers from the Consent of the Governed"

The Continental Congress, which began to meet for the second time in Philadelphia on May 10, 1775, adopted a resolution of independence on July 2, 1776. This resolution had been introduced several weeks earlier by Richard Henry Lee of Virginia. The resolution stated in part that

> these United Colonies are, and of right ought to be, free and independent states, that they are absolved from all allegiance to the British Crown . . .

The Congress, only a few days after Lee proposed his resolution and strongly anticipating that it would be approved, appointed a "Committee of Five" to "prepare a declaration to the effect of the said first resolution." The five—John Adams, Benjamin Franklin, Thomas Jefferson, Robert R. Livingston, and Roger Sherman (respectively from Massachusetts, Pennsylvania, Virginia, New York, and Connecticut)—agreed that Jefferson would write the draft of what would be called The Declaration of Independence. Jefferson was chosen because he was generally believed to have an unsurpassed "felicity of expression." The Declaration, which explained to the world why the Americans had so acted, was adopted by the Congress on July 4.

The second paragraph of the finalized Declaration provided the political philosophy that enunciated the ideals toward which the new country would strive:

> We hold these truths to be self-evident; that all men are created equal, that they are endowed by their creator with certain unalienable rights; that among these are life, liberty and the pursuit of happiness; that to secure these rights, governments are instituted among men, deriving their just powers from the consent of the governed . . .

The last part of that statement beginning "governments are instituted . . ." was adopted just as Jefferson had first put it down. Although there were changes made to Jefferson's draft by the Committee of Five and by the Congress itself, there were no changes whatsoever made to these particular words (Maier, 1998, p. 236).

Clearly, Jefferson's colleagues approved of the sentiments expressed. These political ideas were, in the late eighteenth century, "widely accepted as a commonplace," according to historian Carl Becker. The concepts were derived from the "natural rights" philosophy that was developed to replace the monarchial view that royal heads of government could not be opposed because they ruled by divine right (Becker, 1958 (1922), pp. 24–79). A major expositor of the concept of natural rights was English philosopher John Locke. His most famous works were the *Essay Concerning Human Understanding* and the *Second Treatise of Government*, and these works would have been brought to the attention of the sons of the prerevolutionary American gentry who expected their progeny to be well educated.

Locke had completed the *Second Treatise* in 1690 to justify the Glorious Revolution of 1688, and it provided an excellent rationale for American patriots in the years leading up to the revolution of 1776. In the initial paragraphs of Chapter VIII, "Of the Beginning of Political Societies," Locke often refers to "consent" and "consent of the majority." For example:

> For when any number of men have, by the consent of every individual, made a *community*, they have thereby made that *community* one body, with a power to act as one body, which is only by the will and determination of the *majority* . . . it is necessary the body should move that way wither the greater force carries it, which is the *consent of the majority* . . . (Macpherson, 1980, p. 52)

Historian Garry Wills presents for us the 1774 statement of James Wilson that contains similar sentiments, employing "consent." Wilson, of Pennsylvania, was a noted lawyer, influential delegate to the Continental Congress, and signer of the Declaration:

> All men are, by nature, equal and free: no one has a right to any authority over another without his consent: all lawful government is founded on the consent of those who are subject to it: such consent was given with a view to ensure and to increase the happiness of the governed . . . (Wills, 2002 (1978), p. 248)

The point of discussing "just powers from the consent of the governed" as an essential phrase of The Declaration of Independence is that implementing "consent of the governed" specifies the need for fair and honest elections and correctly operating voting technology that is at its core. Jefferson's words imply that a government not elected by the consent of the governed would not have "just powers." This interpretation has not been considered generally by historians of the Declaration. For example, Garry Wills' prize-winning book referenced earlier contains 27 chapters and each is titled by a different quotation from the Declaration. Not one of the chapters is headed by any part of phrasing that is contained in the title of this section. However, when the conduct of elections and the implementation of their results are considered, just powers derived from consent of the governed may be recognized to have the importance assigned to it here. Of course, in 1776, the concept of the "technology" of voting would have little meaning to the founders of this nation. Even so, the question of oral voting versus voting by ballot—which involves a selection of a voting technology—had been and would continue to be an issue. The question in 1776 was whether each individual granted the right to vote would be able to cast those votes without intimidation. Separation from Britain would assist that cause, in that it would foster some elimination of oral voting, but it would not fully assure secret voting for more than a century.

2.2   BEFORE ADOPTION OF THE CONSTITUTION

During the War of Independence, many thoughtful citizens recognized that the states would need a formal relationship regulating their political and economic interactions. The Continental Congress continued to meet to oversee the war, and the Articles of Confederation were devised. The Articles, completed in 1777, were eventually ratified by all the states; the last one ratifying was Maryland in 1781.

Recognition of independence by Britain came in 1783. The peace treaty provided for acceptance of U.S. claims to all territory east of the Mississippi River and south of Canada that were originally British possessions. At that time, the area west of the Appalachians was very sparsely settled by Europeans or their descendants. In addition to a few hardy settlers, there were some forts and trappers and traders. The indigenous residents were not considered in the accord. The mouth of the Mississippi at New Orleans, originally settled by the French, had been nominally under Spanish sovereignty since 1762. The French would regain it in 1800.

There had been elections in the colonies and they continued in the new states. Campaigning was subdued during the war. British troops were a presence in some areas, and members of the public were generally circumspect about revealing their views. Nevertheless, all the states but Connecticut and Rhode Island rewrote their constitutions in this period. These two states retained their seventeenth-century charters and only eliminated references to Great Britain. Gender restrictions were retained, except in New Jersey, where women could vote following adoption of its new constitution in 1776. That anomaly of the time was ended in 1807.

Regularization of elections occurred. Terms of office were set to be a specific whole number of years and, consequently, the dates of election were established at regular intervals. There was no uniformity among the states in setting these dates, except that they were typically in the spring or fall. Mondays through Thursdays were favored. More offices became elective by the people rather than appointive. This particularly applied to upper houses of state legislatures and governorships in New England and New York.

Other governors were named by the legislatures. Governors, except in Massachusetts, were refused the veto power, possibly a carryover from the hated vetoes of royal governors.

The duration of incumbency of many positions were set at one year. This was true for most governorships and all memberships in the lower houses of state legislatures except in South Carolina (Main, 1974 (1961), p. 18). Many people favoring close citizen supervision of the government believed that a short term—preferably one year—was essential for democracy. Upper house memberships had more variability in their terms: one year in New England, New Jersey and North Carolina, two years in South Carolina, three years in Delaware, four years in New York, and Virginia and five years in Maryland. Georgia and Pennsylvania initially had one-house legislatures that had a popular basis and therefore served more as lower houses than as upper houses.

The personal financial assets required for voting were generally reduced. There was considerable popular sentiment that those men who were fighting for independence should be given voting rights regardless of their financial status. In Maryland, in 1776, some soldiers denied suffrage rioted. In that situation, election judges enforcing the law as they understood it were removed under duress and replaced by those more sympathetic to voting by the active military. In some states, a two-tier system for the voting franchise was instituted. For example, in North Carolina, all freemen could vote for the lower house of the legislature, but only freeholders who owned 50 acres or more could vote for members of the upper house. A similar dual system was introduced in New York.

The financial assets required for membership in the lower houses were typically set lower than for the upper houses. The concept was that there should be consistency between the requirements for voting for a position and those for being elected to it.

Redistricting occurred in some legislatures to provide for more equal representation, but some retained a malapportionment that favored particular areas. If representation was initially on a per capita basis, then later increases in population in outlying areas would result in an inadequate number of seats for them. If representation initially had been based on an equal number of seats for each town or city, then more heavily populated cities would be underrepresented. States that failed to redistrict included Maryland, Virginia, the two Carolinas, Connecticut, and Rhode Island. South Carolina's malapportionment was sufficiently notorious to merit a mention in a speech by James Madison at the Virginia ratifying convention (see section 2.4). Redistricting of legislatures would continue to be an important political issue, but it would fester for a long time. Nearly two centuries after independence, a significant aspect of the general question with respect to redistricting would be resolved by the U.S. Supreme Court (see section 5.2).

The number of polling stations was increased in many places, allowing some voters to vote nearer their homes. Places favored for voting locations included churches, courthouses, taverns, mills, schoolhouses, and, in New

England, town meetinghouses. South Carolina continued its practice of using churches as venues for voting, defining precincts consistent with parish boundaries, and having churchwardens serve as judges of elections. Sheriffs and other election officials were more closely scrutinized to prevent personal bias from becoming fraud. Penalties for mischief by officials were increased.

Times varied during which polling stations were open. In New England, a one-day election was common because of the use of the town—a relatively small area—as the voting unit. In other states, the difficulty of travel to and from the polling location required the polls to be open for a longer time. In the Carolinas, polls were typically open for two days. New York permitted polls to be open for up to five days and New Jersey's polling times were measured in weeks, not days. The latter's Essex County is mentioned in several histories because its polling time was unique, at least five weeks. Even after ratification of the Constitution, polling times in some states remained longer than one day. In New York and several other states, a three-day election period was used well into the nineteenth century.

An increase in the use of ballots, as opposed to *viva voce* (oral) voting, began almost immediately following independence. The New England states and South Carolina, which had previously used ballots, continued to do so. Ballot voting began to be required in Pennsylvania, Delaware, North Carolina, and Georgia. Reformers had argued that "the *viva voce* method placed undue pressure on the elector, especially where tenant farmers were forced to vote in the presence of their landlord." Another view is that ballot voting advanced because it was "the quickest and easiest mode of taking the votes of a multitude." Tickets began to be published in newspapers for the edification of voters. In New Jersey, the voting method could be selected by county option under its new constitution. Of the thirteen counties then established, seven counties decided on voting by ballot and the other six selected oral voting. These county decisions changed from time-to-time. In that state, there was criticism of the use of the ballot with the claim that illiterates were being deceived by being given ballots not in accordance with their wishes. "Tickets were often palmed upon such as cannot write or read," it was said.

New York began an "experiment" to employ voting by ballot soon after independence was declared. The framers of its new constitution announced that the public appeared to have the opinion that voting by ballot "would tend more to preserve the liberty and freedom of the people." Ballot voting was officially adopted in 1787. In 1788, one faction handed out tickets supposedly for the other side, but folded over so that its own gubernatorial candidate could not be seen.

Maryland and Virginia generally retained *viva voce* voting statewide. On the day or days of election, each voter would make his way to the table where the judges of election and their clerks sat. A voter would be asked to verify his financial and residence status, and then requested to declare his choices. Votes would then be written down by the clerks, and any candidate present might publicly thank a voter who voted for him.

In some states using ballot voting, voters wrote in the names of their selections on paper ballots that they themselves provided. In Massachusetts, the voters prepared separate ballots for governor, lieutenant governor, and senator, as their selections had to be dropped into three separate boxes. In New Jersey, there were at least two ballot boxes for different sets of contests. In North Carolina, there were two boxes for legislative contests, one for senator and one for the lower house candidate. In other places, such as Rhode Island, the "tickets" printed by the factions were used, as was done before the revolution. Consequently, there was only one box for use by a voter for deposit of his ballot.

Ballot voting, in some places, provided opportunities for those of a felonious bent. In Boston, in 1782, there were more votes than voters. Collusion was a possibility then, and even now continues to be a concern. In Lancaster County, Pennsylvania, there were charges of ballot-box stuffing in 1778 and 1784. In New Bern, North Carolina, in 1782, a tin cannister without a top serving as a ballot box was left unguarded and received a number of fraudulent votes. In Hunterdon County, New Jersey, in 1788, in a case brought to the state legislature for resolution:

> it was admitted by the defendants that the inspectors had bet on the winning candidates; that the ballot box was placed in the custody of one of the candidates, even though it was not secured as the law directed; and that illegal votes had been received. Nevertheless, the election was held to be valid. (McCormick, 1953, p. 83)

Religious restrictions were lifted against voting by Christians of any denomination. "Only the Jews in certain states remained legally outside the fold," according to Dinkin (Dinkin, 1982, p. 40), although Keyssar has written that "the disfranchisement of Roman Catholics and Jews was brought to an end" (Keyssar, 2000, p. 20). Dinkin and Keyssar were referring only to the right to vote, but for Jews and Roman Catholics, the right to hold office was equally important. In 1786, Virginia eliminated all religious restrictions to office holding, adopting a measure proposed by Thomas Jefferson and spearheaded in the legislature by James Madison. It was the first state to do so. New York's constitution of 1777 allowed Jews to hold office, along with Protestants, but denied that right to Roman Catholics. In other states, there were religious restrictions for holding office well into the nineteenth century (see section 2.7).

The tendency to factionalism, that is, coalescence of voters into political groupings, continued to increase, as did electioneering. In each state, there were generally two significant factions. Main has characterized them as "Cosmopolitan" and "Localist" (Main, 1973, p. 32) and he used these terms to identify their worldviews. Cosmopolitans were more concerned with the progress of commerce and intellectual life. Localists were less worldly and more socially conservative; their constituents were mostly farmers of smaller acreage. Candidates continued to be nominated by caucuses, although some citizens claimed that these private meetings were inconsistent with democracy. In some places, to answer this criticism, open nomination meetings were called by county. It is not clear whether the public was there to ratify faction leaders' choices or to genuinely provide input.

Orderliness in the voting process was usual, although violence did occur in some places. There was considerable animosity between those who had supported the revolution and those who had not. The latter were called Tories. An oath of allegiance was required for voting for a while in some states, and many Tories refused to take it. Sussex County, the most rural of Delaware's three counties, was one of those places where violence occurred. The Tories actively defended their point of view and fighting ensued on election days. Burlington County, New Jersey, was another area of antagonism between patriots and Tories. In both regions, militias were called out to quell the disturbances. As time progressed, the oath requirements were repealed and the civil rights of Tories were returned. The citizenry moved on to more current issues.

2.3 THE CONSTITUTION: ESTABLISHING FEDERAL OFFICES

After the War of Independence was won, there would be a stronger focus on the defects of the Articles of Confederation. The Articles guaranteed the sovereignty and independence of each of the states. There was no national executive, only a president of the Congress. Amendments required agreement of all the states, and the Articles poorly covered a most important subject—the regulation of interstate commerce. Other difficulties, such as the lack of a requirement for states to obey acts of Congress, and Congress' inadequate taxing ability, encouraged all the states except Rhode Island to send delegates to a convention in Philadelphia in 1787.

The delegates to that convention had been charged with amending the Articles of Confederation but received, at the meeting's opening, a plan put forth by the Virginia delegation (that included James Madison) for a much stronger national government. The "Virginia Plan" received a surprisingly positive reception, although there were disagreements with some of its provisions. The convention received an alternative, the "New Jersey Plan," and finally the "Connecticut Compromise." With concessions from the various point of view, the convention proceeded to formulate, determine details, and approve the Constitution. There would be three independent branches of government with their checks and balances. The composition of the branches would include a single chief executive, that is, the president, plus two Houses of Congress with their different terms of office and separate means of selecting members, and a Supreme Court and "inferior" courts. There were also difficult negotiations, finally resolved, to establish the wording that would set a balance between the responsibilities of the national government and those of the states. One of the subjects of this compromise was the division of responsibilities between the states and the Congress for selecting the most senior executive and legislative officials of the new national government.

The president and vice president would hold office for a term of four years (Article II, Section 1). They would be elected in a process summing the votes of

a Number of Electors [in each state] equal to the whole Number of Senators and Representatives to which the State may be entitled in the Congress . . .

The Congress would take part in this process in that

The Congress may determine the Time of chusing the Electors and the Day on which they shall give their Votes . . .

However, the states would have some flexibility in the method of selection of the Electors, in that they would be appointed by each state

in such Manner as the Legislature thereof may direct . . .

The states would accept that challenge and would start out with a variety of different methods (see section 2.6). As of 2005, the method still is not wholly uniform throughout the nation. Congress did impose one uniformity. In both the original Article II and the 12th Amendment, which altered part of that article, it is stated that

The Electors shall meet in their respective States, and vote by Ballot . . .

At no time do the Electors from the separate states meet together. Thus, the "Electoral College" is only a way of collectively referring to the Electors, not an actual convocation.

Members of the House of Representatives would be elected by the people. The number of representatives from each state would be proportional to the population of the state, according to a census taken every 10 years. If, a priori, a total number of representatives is to be seated from all states, there must be a formula, approved by the Congress, that converts population figures into whole numbers of seats for each state. A sticky problem is the "fair" allocation of the fractions, and there are a variety of possible methods. (See later, in section 2.5, *The method of apportioning the House among the states*.) Representatives would be chosen every second year. As the delegates could not agree on a single national requirement for voting for representative, they decided that

the Electors in each State shall have the Qualifications requisite for Electors of the most numerous Branch of the State Legislature. (Article I, Section 2, Clause 1)

Thus, with different property, residence, and possibly religious requirements in the several states, men in similar economic and social circumstances might be treated differently in their right to vote by their states of residence.

The establishment of the Senate, consisting of two members from each state selected by their respective state legislatures, was a major subject of the Great Compromise. There was no need to specify requirements for voters as there would be no voting for senators by the public. A Senate term would be six years, and an arrangement was devised to have one-third of the Senate elected every second year.

2.4 THE ELECTION CLAUSE

The differing responsibilities of the states and the federal government in the election of members of Congress was set with the following statement:

> The Times, Places and Manner of holding Elections for Senators and Representatives shall be prescribed in each State by the Legislature thereof; but the Congress may at any time by Law make or alter such Regulations, except as to the Place of Chusing Senators. (Article I, Section 4, Clause 1)

The composition of this clause was controversial in the convention because of its provision for Congressional oversight. The first draft of the Constitution had a similar provision, but it included only "alter" rather than "make or alter," and it did not exempt the "Place of Chusing Senators" as the final product did.

Delegates from South Carolina objected to the draft, arguing that the states "could and must be relied on in such cases."

The clause was stoutly defended by Madison. He observed that:

> the times, places and manner of holding elections . . . were words of great latitude. It was impossible to foresee all the abuses that might be made of the discretionary power. Whether the electors should vote by ballot or *viva voce*; should assemble at this place or that place; should be divided into districts or all meet at one place; should all vote for all the representatives or all in a district vote for a number allotted to the district; these and many other points would depend on the Legislatures and might materially affect the appointments. Whenever the State Legislatures had a favorite measure to carry, they would take care so to mould their regulations to favor the candidates they wished to succeed. Besides, the inequality of the Representation in the Legislatures of particular States would produce a like inequality in their representation in the National Legislature . . . (Ferrand, 1911, v. 2, pp. 240, 241)

That Madison should have recognized, in 1787, the possibility that the national government might wish to determine the form of voting technology seems incredibly prescient in the light of the 2000 presidential election and the resulting Help America Vote Act of 2002. That act likely would have been unconstitutional if Congressional oversight had not been included in the Election Clause.

Rufus King, at the time a delegate from Massachusetts, joined in supporting Congressional oversight, saying that: "If this power not be given to the

National Legislature, their right of judging of the returns of their members may be frustrated." King was referring to that wording that would, without controversy, become part of Article I, Section 5:

> Each House shall be the Judge of the Elections, Returns and Qualifications of its own Members . . .

Significant antagonism to the Election Clause occurred during the process of ratification of the Constitution (required to be accomplished in convention by each state). Opponents of approval, called "Anti-Federalists," identified the Election Clause as one of their specific dislikes. These individuals were, to a large extent, those men who had been characterized by J. T. Main as "Localists." Main has described the Anti-Federalists as including "two major elements: those who emphasized the desirability of a weak central government, and those who encouraged democratic control" (Main, 1974 (1961), p. xi). In the Anti-Federalist view, the functions assigned to the president and the Executive Branch made for an excessively strong central government, and the existence of the Senate, with its membership by states and election not directly by the people, was significantly undemocratic.

It was the belief of some of the Anti-Federalists that, under the new Constitution, the states would wither away and that the Election Clause would be one of the instruments to assist that process. For example, in an article printed in Philadelphia newspapers under the pseudonym "Centinel," one Anti-Federalist wrote:

> The plain construction of [the Election Clause] is that when the state legislatures drop out of sight, from the necessary operation of this government, then Congress are [*sic*] to provide for the election and appointment of representatives and senators . . . (Ketchum, 1986, pp. 233, 234)

The speech by Patrick Henry on June 5 at the Virginia Ratifying Convention in 1788 provides another good exposition of Anti-Federalist thinking. He remarked about the Election Clause:

> What can be more defective that the clause concerning elections?—The control given to Congress over the time, place, and manner of holding elections, will totally destroy the end of suffrage. The elections may be held at one place, and the most inconvenient in the State; or they may be at remote distances from those who have a right of suffrage: Hence nine out of ten must either not vote at all, or vote for strangers: . . . The natural consequence will be that this democratic branch will possess none of the public confidence. The people will be prejudiced against Representatives chosen in such an injudicious manner . . . (Elliot, 1836, v. 3, p. 60)

Madison and Alexander Hamilton were active in supporting ratification in their respective states, Virginia and New York. At the Virginia Ratifying Convention, Madison responded as follows on June 14 to a prompting question from James Monroe asking how the Election Clause came to be formulated:

> it was thought the regulation of time, place and manner of electing the representatives should be uniform throughout the continent. Some states might regulate the elections on the principles of equality and others might regulate them otherwise. This diversity would be obviously unjust. Elections are regulated now unequally in some states, particularly South Carolina, with respect to Charleston, which is represented by thirty members. Should the people of any state by any means be deprived of the right of suffrage, it was judged proper that it should be remedied by the general government . . . And, considering the state governments and general government as distinct bodies, acting in different and independent capacities for the people, it was thought the particular regulations should be submitted to the former and the general regulations to the latter . . . (v. 3, p. 367)

Alexander Hamilton (who became the nation's first secretary of the treasury in 1789) discussed the Election Clause in Nos. 59, 60, and 61 of the celebrated Federalist Papers. These were distributed through newspapers in an effort to favorably influence ratification in New York. Included in Hamilton's writings are the following:

> The . . . propriety [of the Election Clause] rests on the evidence of this plain proposition, that every government ought to contain in itself the means of its own preservation . . . Nothing can be more evident than that an exclusive power of regulating elections for the national government, in the hands of the State legislatures, would leave the existence of the Union entirely at their mercy. They could at any moment annihilate it by neglecting to provide for the choice of persons to administer its affairs. It is to little purpose to say that a neglect or omission of this kind would not be likely to take place. The constitutional possibility of the thing, without an equivalent for the risk, is an unanswerable objection . . . (Kramnick, 1987, pp. 352, 353 (no. 59))
>
> there remains to be mentioned a positive advantage which will result from this [Election Clause] and which could not as well have been obtained from any other: I allude to the circumstance of uniformity in the time of elections for the federal House of Representatives. It is more than possible that this uniformity may be found by experience to be of great importance to the public welfare . . . the times of election in the several States, as they are now established for local purposes, very between extremes as wide as March and November. The consequence of this diversity would be that there could never happen a total dissolution or renovation of the body at one time . . . (pp. 362, 363 (no. 61))

Of course, ratification by each state eventually occurred. The ninth state ratifying was New Hampshire on June 21, 1788, and this action brought the Constitution, including its Election Clause, into effect among those ratifying it (see Article VII). Of the final four, Virginia and New York ratified, respectively, on June 25 and July 26 of 1788, leaving only North Carolina and Rhode Island not yet part of the United States.

Time has demonstrated that the fears of the Anti-Federalists were ill founded. The states have not "dropped out of sight," nor has the Congress attempted to force elections for itself to be held in inaccessible places so that only certain individuals would find it convenient to vote.

The state redistricting process was regulated through the Election Clause as desired by Madison, but not until more than 50 years after ratification.

On June 25, 1842, the Congress approved the following language:

> That in every case where a State is entitled to more than one Representative, the number to which each State shall be entitled . . . shall be elected by districts composed of contiguous territory equal in number to the number of Representatives to which said State may be entitled, no one district electing more than one Representative. (27th Congress. Sess. II, Chap. 47, Sec. 2)

The reason for this action was to end the practice of some states (e.g., New Jersey) in electing all of their representatives at large, winner take all. The Congress would never vote to require a similar single-member district arrangement for Electors for president, although attempts would be made.

A characteristic of single-member Congressional Districts is that it encourages a two-party system. Since only one person can win per district, coalitions are promoted. Smaller parties are forced into fusion arrangements with larger parties to create a combined majority that can win. Minor party candidates can win on their own only if their supporters are geographically concentrated. A "gerrymander," meaning a convoluted district design, can be used to promote or discourage minority representation. (The word was invented in 1812 in Massachusetts. It referred to a design approved by Governor Elbridge Gerry that looked to an opponent like the shape of a salamander.)

On other occasions, in the late nineteenth century (see section 3.7) and in the early twentieth century (see section 4.11), Congress would attempt to regulate the redistricting process. These later changes would not be permanent. Congress also gradually increased the number of members of the House of Representatives.

The Election Clause has been used for setting dates for federal elections and for the convening of Congress and Electors for president. It has never been used to establish dates for primary elections. In the late nineteenth century, the Election Clause might be identified as the basis for the Federal Election Law of 1871 (see section 3.6), the requirement for a printed ballot (see section 3.7), the Electoral Count Act of 1887 (see section 3.9), and for permission to use voting machines (see section 4.6). It was not applied in the nineteenth century in the adoption of a genuinely secret ballot. That action was taken by the states individually (see section 3.11). In the late twentieth century, the clause could be referenced as providing the basis for laws concerning voting by the elderly and handicapped, by overseas citizens, and for the National Voter Registration Act (see sections 5.9–5.11). It was not until the adoption of the Help America Vote Act of 2002 that the Election Clause would need to be cited again (see section 7.5).

2.5   Electing the President: 1789, 1792, and 1796

In the summer and fall of 1788, plans were put into effect to choose members of the first U.S. Congress and to name Electors for the first president and vice president. Members of the new House of Representatives were elected late that year (no uniform day had been established), and senators were named by their state legislatures. James Madison was a candidate for the House from Virginia. His enemies in the legislature had configured his district to his disadvantage but Madison, by strenuous campaigning, won anyway.

The First Congress was distinguished by its submission to the states of 12 proposed Constitutional amendments. In its submission, it wrote that these amendments to the Constitution,

> as extending the ground of public confidence in the government, will best insure the beneficent ends of its institution . . .

Ten amendments were quickly adopted and became known as the Bill of Rights. The issue of "public confidence" would be a question associated with the announced results of many public elections up through the present time, more than 200 years later. The concern would not diminish as machines began to be used; in fact, it would become particularly important as computer programs became part of vote counting, beginning in the early 1960s.

Electors for president were chosen on the first Wednesday in January 1789, and they would cast their ballots in their respective states on the first Wednesday in February (Cunliffe, 1971, p. 11). They were to:

> make a list of all the Persons voted for, and of the Number of Votes for each, which List they shall sign and certify and transmit sealed to the Seat of Government . . . The President of the Senate shall, in the Presence of the Senate and House of Representatives, open all the certificates, and the Votes shall then be counted. (Article II, Section 1)

The seat of government at the time was in New York City. The inauguration of the president had been set for March 4, but a quorum of senators and representatives did not arrive in time to determine the winner of the electoral count. The certificates could not be counted until April 6.

As the states had a choice in the process of choosing Electors, they made use of whatever method seemed appropriate to them. Some of the different methods for selecting Electors for president and vice president are, for example, (a) by a vote of the legislature, or (b) by a popular vote, in which the first two Electors are selected statewide and the others selected by districts, one from each district, or (c) by a popular vote in which all the Electors are selected statewide. Each of these methods has been used. While (c) is the method now used by 48 states and the District of Columbia (DC), and (b) the method now used in Maine and Nebraska, (a) was widely used through the 1820s. For DC, which is entitled to three Electors, and states similarly entitled, method (b) is the same as method (c). At times, some states used a combination of these methods, or other procedures.

In January 1789, the eleven states that had ratified the Constitution by that time could participate in the election of the president and vice president. According to Article II, Section 1, as initially ratified, Electors were to choose two favorites; the candidate obtaining the largest sum of votes from all states would be president ("if such Number be a Majority of the Whole Number of Electors appointed") and the person obtaining the next largest sum of votes would become vice president. Five states—Connecticut, Rhode Island, New Jersey, South Carolina, and Georgia—provided for selection of the Electors by their legislatures and successfully carried out that activity. In New York, which intended also to have its legislature name the Electors, the two branches could not agree nor could they agree to compromise. The result was that no Electors were chosen from that state.

In New Hampshire, the Electors were nominated by the voters, but the legislature actually chose them. In Massachusetts, where ten Electors were to be selected, two Electors at-large were chosen by the voters, and the remaining eight "were picked by the legislature from twenty-four names produced by the state's congressional districts" (Cunliffe, 1971, p. 17). There were popular elections for Electors in Pennsylvania, Maryland, and Virginia. In the first two of these three, two "slates" of Electors were made available for voters, but in Virginia, there were no slates.

The provision of the Constitution, in requiring Electors to select two persons without further identification as to which one they desired to be president, was becoming a serious concern. It was expected that George Washington would be chosen by almost all Electors. Alexander Hamilton, who had served closely with Washington during the Revolutionary War, importuned several Electors not to cast their second vote for John Adams, the next leading contender. Hamilton's purpose was not to prevent Adams from becoming vice president. It was to prevent confusion and a lengthened process should Adams equal Washington in the number of votes received, and also to prevent the remote possibility that Adams would obtain more votes than Washington. Either situation, had it occurred, might have been very embarrassing and could have created a crisis destructive of the new government. This Constitutional failure of specificity would create an ugly situation in the presidential election of 1800.

The outcome, when the votes were counted, was that every Elector had given one of his two votes to Washington. Adams received all the second votes from New Hampshire and Massachusetts, five of seven from Connecticut, eight of ten from Pennsylvania, five of ten from Virginia and one more from New Jersey. He would become vice president.

The method of apportioning the House among the states became a question to be resolved. As additional states entered the Union, and as total population increased, a formula would be needed that converted the respective state populations into whole numbers of members of the House of Representatives (and therefore the number of Electors) assigned to each state. In the first debate on this subject, in the 1790s, a method proposed by Thomas Jefferson was adopted. At the time, Jefferson's method, compared with a method proposed by Alexander Hamilton, gave one more seat to Virginia. Jefferson's method was used through the 1830s, when it came under severe attack as it favored the larger states. In 1840, a system proposed by Daniel Webster was adopted. Hamilton's method was considered also in the late 1800s, but it was found to produce "bizarre" results when the total number of seats in the House increased. In 1941, a method proposed by Census Bureau statistician Joseph Hill, and refined by Harvard mathematician Edward Huntington, was chosen to replace Webster's method. It was claimed to be unbiased between small and large states. However, it apparently favors small states, a reason for a proposal to return to Webster's procedure (Young, 2001, pp. 1–4).

Key dates for presidential elections needed to be set. On March 1, 1792, the Second Congress enacted legislation fixing dates for the "appointment" of Electors in each state, for the giving of their votes, for the transmission of those votes as certificates "to the President of the Senate, at the seat of government," and for the opening of the certificates and the counting of the votes so that "the persons who shall fill the offices of President and Vice President" could be "ascertained and declared, agreeably to the constitution" (Second Congress, Sess. I, Chap. VIII). The legislation provided also that the four-year terms of the president and vice president would begin and end on March 4 of the year following their election.

In 1792 and every fourth year thereafter, Electors were to be appointed within a period of time of 34 days preceding the first Wednesday in December, at which day they were to meet in their respective states and give their votes. Certificates were to be delivered to the president of the Senate by the first Wednesday in the next January, and the certificates opened and votes counted during a session of the Congress on the second Wednesday of the February immediately following.

The dates of appointment were different within each state, although limited by the 34-day window. Furthermore, by 1836, all states but South Carolina were determining their Electors by popular vote. To take advantage of the situation, "illegal voting by repeaters became common. In 1840 and 1844, both parties organized gangs of voters who went from state to state" (Argersinger, 1984, p. 496). To eliminate the opportunity for this type of fraud, Congress legislated on January 23, 1845, that "the electors of President and Vice-President shall be appointed, in each State, on the Tuesday next after the first Monday in November, in every fourth year . . ." (28th Congress, Sess. II, Chap. I). Thus began our national, single-day presidential election. The recent implementation of "early voting" has begun to change the single-day concept. All that is true now is that voting must end on the day established by Congress. With regard to absentee ballots, it generally means that those must be postmarked by that day.

For the presidential election of 1792, there were fifteen states in the Union, North Carolina and Rhode Island having finally come aboard and Vermont and Kentucky having been added. For selecting Electors, the continuing states used the same methods that they had employed in 1789. (This time, the New York legislature managed to agree on Electors.) North Carolina selected Electors by a popular vote by districts, but the legislatures of Rhode Island, Vermont, and Kentucky determined their respective Electors. As in 1789, all Electors gave one of their votes to Washington, who had reluctantly agreed to serve again. John Adams was reelected vice president with some competition from George Clinton, governor of New York. Clinton had been hurt by charges of vote fraud in the New York gubernatorial election earlier that year; it was said that he had "robbed" his opponent John Jay (Cunliffe, 1971, p. 22).

The election of 1796 was of extreme importance in that it would demonstrate that a transfer of power from the hero of the Revolution to a less monumental figure was possible in the new Republic. There were now two strongly dichotomous factions that were essentially political parties. They would be called Federalists, favoring a robust and "energetic" central government and the promotion of commerce and industry, and Republicans, favoring the small farmer and the supremacy of the states. John Adams and Thomas Pinckney (of South Carolina) would form a federalist ticket and would be opposed by Thomas Jefferson and Aaron Burr (of New York) on a Republican ticket. Both tickets were "balanced," implying a northerner and a southerner running together.

The election was not structured, as it is today, for a voter to make one selection for all Electors in his or her state pledged to a particular pair of presidential and vice presidential candidates. Electors ran as individuals, but they might state publically for who they would vote if chosen. "During the first hundred years after the adoption of the Constitution, Electors, wherever chosen by popular vote, were presented as individual candidates" (Albright, 1942, p. 101).

For the 1796 election, there were sixteen states, Tennessee having joined the Union. Its Electors were determined by its legislature. All the other states used the same methods of selecting Electors that they had previously, excepting New Hampshire, which experimented with a popular vote process. There were a total of 138 Electors who cast 2 votes each. John Adams won the presidency with 71 electoral votes, one more than he needed for a majority, and Thomas Jefferson was elected vice president with 68 votes. Thomas Pinckney had received 59, Aaron Burr 30, the next highest total was 15 and eight other names shared the remaining 33.

Following Adams's election in 1796, for the first time, "the nation experienced a party administration" (Cunningham, 1971, p. 103). The Federalists held all the Cabinet posts and they had a majority in Congress. Jefferson was the most significant non-Federalist office holder. Adams's signing of the Sedition Act in 1798 would be a stain on his reputation, as seen from a historical point of view. The act likely would have been declared unconstitutional as violating the First Amendment on freedom of speech if adopted at a later time.

2.6   ELECTING THE PRESIDENT: 1800
THROUGH 1832

Electors lost their individuality beginning with the election of 1800. Before that election, both the Federalists and the Republicans held Congressional caucuses to nominate candidates for president and vice president. A significant outcome was that Electors were now to be directed by the parties. That change was permanent. Electors would no longer be disinterested statesmen acting according to their personal understanding of which candidate would serve the nation best. Later changes in ballot designs would eliminate the names of the Electors; they would become totally faceless to the ordinary voter. (See section 4.11, *The presidential short ballot.*) Nevertheless, Electors could continue to make their presence known by violating their oath of support for the party that appointed them. These would be known as "faithless" Electors, and there have been a few of them. There was one in 2000, as noted in chapter 1.

The election of 1800 would pit the Federalists (the "ins") against the Republicans (the "outs"). In their preparations for the election, the parties considered the methods of choosing Electors. The choice of Electors with a popular vote by district maximized the chances that the Electors would be split between the two parties. Selection by the legislature, if controlled by one party, would assure a sweep of all Electors for that party. Selection by a popular vote for all Electors at-large would also assure a sweep for one party or the other; a party certain of carrying the state might desire the latter method rather than legislative appointment. Popular at-large selection would still permit the voters to have a direct voice, yet provide the dominant party with the maximum benefit.

In New Hampshire and Massachusetts, the Federalist-controlled legislatures decided to choose their Electors instead of letting the voters participate. That method would eliminate any possible Republican Electors. In Pennsylvania, also, the legislature took responsibility for appointing Electors, replacing its vote-by-district system. However, in the latter state, the two-chamber legislature (which replaced an earlier one-chamber body) was split between the parties. The result was a set of Electors similarly split. Kentucky, in a countertrend, adopted a popular vote-by-district system, replacing its legislative appointment. Similarly, Rhode Island moved from selection by the legislature to popular voting.

In Virginia, the Republican-controlled legislature agreed to change its system of popular vote by district to a popular vote at-large. They were certain that a statewide vote would favor their party. This action created an administrative difficulty, compounded by the continued use of oral voting in that state. With typical district voting, each voter indicates a preference for one Elector from his district and possibly two additional Electors running statewide. With at-large voting for 21 Electors, the number that Virginia was assigned in 1800, each voter was required to state his separate preferences for 21 individuals.

It is possible that lists of the names of Electors favorable to Jefferson and Burr (the same Republican candidates as in 1796), or Adams and C. C. Pinckney of South Carolina (the Federalist candidates) were made available to Virginia voters by political operatives and/or newspapers. The need to get out the message of which Electors favored which candidates required a viable statewide party organization. As a result, the necessary political machinery was constructed (in other states as well as in Virginia) and has been with us ever since. One can imagine a Virginia voter, given lists of Electors proposed by the parties, reading his selections aloud on the day of the election before the officers of election. A voter wishing to select some Electors from one list and others from the rival list could get confused as to how many of each he had specified.

The result of the election was that the winners, Jefferson and Burr, both received 73 electoral votes. Selection of Electors with an "unprecedented display of party regularity" (Cunningham, 1971, p. 131) had produced the tie. Final resolution of the contest would be up to the House of Representatives. The losers, Adams and C. C. Pinckney, received 65 and 64 votes, respectively. The latter's missing vote was cast for John Jay in Rhode Island, which otherwise voted the Federalist ticket. Two states that used a popular vote by district, Maryland and North Carolina, produced a set of Electors' split between the pairs. The former elected five favoring the Republicans and five endorsing the Federalists. The latter selected eight Republicans and four Federalists. All the other states but Pennsylvania voted solidly for one party pair or the other.

The electoral votes were counted on the second Wednesday in February before a joint session of Congress, and the balloting by the House of Representatives began very soon thereafter. Under Article II of the Constitution, the vote was by states, each state having one vote. A majority of states in favor of an individual, in this case nine, was necessary to name the president. In the first ballot, Jefferson received the votes of eight states: New York, New Jersey, Pennsylvania, Virginia, North Carolina, Georgia, Kentucky, and Tennessee. Burr received the votes of six states: New Hampshire, Massachusetts, Rhode Island, Connecticut, Delaware, and South Carolina. Two states, Vermont and Maryland, were internally divided and cast no vote.

After 35 ballots, there was no change in the lineup of states. Concern was mounting that the deadlock would be used to break apart the Union. Burr had made no clear, definitive statement that he did not wish to be president or would resign if he were named. Some thought that he really wanted the office. On the 36th ballot, some Federalist members of the House changed their choices. Jefferson received the additional votes of Vermont and Maryland, giving him the presidency. The votes of Delaware and South Carolina were cast as blank, leaving Burr with just four strongly Federalist New England states. The transfer of power from the Federalists to the new Republican administration would go forward quietly under the rule of law. The change of the party in control was the first in the history of this nation. That it occurred peacefully, given the situation, was a significant achievement.

Following the difficulty of the 1800 presidential election, there was wide agreement that the deficiency of Article II needed to be corrected. The 12th Amendment was ratified in June 1804, in time for the next presidential election. The amendment required that Electors file two separate ballots, one for president and one for vice president. Then, if no candidate for president had a majority of electoral votes, the House of Representatives would immediately choose the president "by ballot." In its choice, the House could consider one of the three candidates having the highest numbers of votes.

The procedure for choosing Electors in each state (presented in the order of its admission to the Union) through 1832 is shown in table 2.1. While the methods used varied considerably from 1789 through 1832, they became more uniform after that. In presidential elections from 1836 through 2004, all states except South Carolina, Maine, and Nebraska used the method of at-large popular voting, in almost all cases. (See, e.g., figure 2.1.)

South Carolina would continue to choose Electors by means of its legislature through 1860; it would adopt the at-large system in 1868 after returning to the Union. Maine has continued to use the particular district method identified above since it became a state in 1820; Nebraska used the at-large procedure before 1992, when it began to use the same method as Maine. Nebraska began employment of the district method in hopes of attracting

Table 2.1 Methods of electoral appointment by election year: 1789–1832

	1789	1792	1796	1800	1804	1808	1812	1816	1820	1824	1828	1832
DE	L	L	L	L	L	A	L	L	L	L	L	A
PA	D	D	D	L	A	A	A	A	A	A	A	A
NJ	L	L	L	L	A	A	L	A	A	A	A	A
GA	L	L	L	L	L	L	L	L	L	L	A	A
CT	L	L	L	L	L	A	L	L	A	A	A	A
MA	M	D	D	L	A	D	D	L	D	A	A	A
MD	D	D	D	D	D	D	D	D	D	D	D	D
SC	L	L	L	L	L	L	L	L	L	L	L	L
NH	L	L	A	L	A	A	A	A	A	A	A	A
VA	D	D	D	A	A	A	A	A	A	A	A	A
NY	L	L	L	L	L	L	L	L	L	L	D	A
NC		D	D	D	D	D	L	A	A	A	A	A
RI		L	L	A	A	A	A	A	A	A	A	A
VT		L	L	L	L	L	L	L	L	L	A	A
KY		L	L	D	D	D	D	D	D	D	A	A
TN			L	L	D	D	D	D	D	D	D	A
OH				A	A	A	A	A	A	A	A	A
LA						L	L	L	L	A	A
IN							L	L	A	A	A
IL								D	D	D	A
MS								A	A	A	A
AL								L	A	A	A
MO								L	A	A	A
ME								D	D	D	D

Note: L, Legislature; A, Popular vote At-large; D, Popular vote by District; M, Mixed.

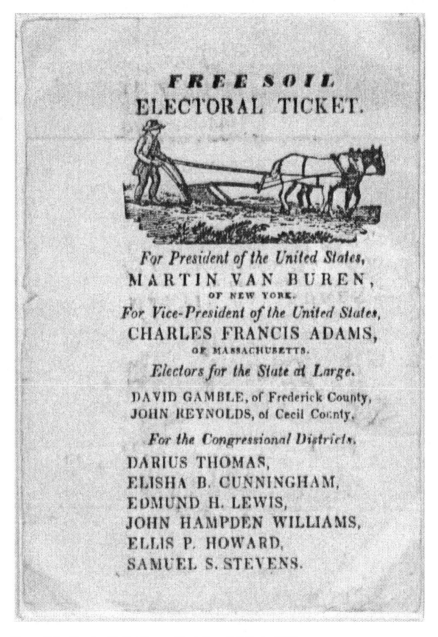

Figure 2.1   Maryland ballot for president, Free Soil Party, 1848.

more attention from the leading presidential candidates and with the hope that other states would follow suit.

There are a variety of other methods of voting by district. In 1804, for example, Maryland, in selecting eleven Electors, had nine districts: seven elected one Elector each; two elected two Electors each. In the same year,

Kentucky elected its eight Electors from two districts; presumably, each of the districts elected four Electors (Dauer, 1971, p. 164). Among other exceptions, legislative selection was used by Florida in 1868 and Colorado in 1876 (Dudley and Gitelson, 2002, p. 156). The method of presidential selection has been a long-standing concern to many thoughtful individuals. The outcome of the 2000 presidential election brought the issue forward again, temporarily.

The 12th Amendment was applied in the election of 1824. Andrew Jackson received a plurality of the popular vote and a plurality of the electoral vote over his three rivals, John Quincy Adams, William H. Crawford, and Henry Clay. Jackson was the military hero of the battle of New Orleans in 1815. Adams, the son of the second president, was secretary of state. Crawford, of Georgia, had been a senator and was secretary of the treasury. Clay, from Kentucky, was speaker of the House of Representatives.

As Jackson did not receive a majority of the electoral votes, the House of Representatives chose the president from the top three candidates. It was the second time for the House and the last time through 2004, except for an aborted role in 1876. Clay, who received the fourth highest number of electoral votes, was excluded from consideration. Thirteen states were needed to name the president and Adams received that number on the first ballot. Seven states voted for Jackson and four for Crawford. Jackson would try again in 1828; at that time, he would be successful.

It was an election without a competition of national parties, as the Federalists no longer were viable. All candidates claimed to be Republicans or Democratic–Republicans. Factions rallied around the aspirants instead. Soon after, a party realignment would occur, resulting in a National Republican party and a Democratic party. The former was soon replaced by the Whig party, which championed what might be called Federalist views. The Democrats were the heirs of Jacksonian ideals.

Additionally, it was the earliest presidential election in which the numbers of popular votes for each candidate were retained for posterity. Of course, there were no popular votes in the six states (out of twenty-four) in which the legislature appointed the Electors.

In 1828, conventions within the states began to replace the Congressional caucus. This new development was a necessity for state parties who had no representatives in Congress. At that time, the Jacksonian party was very weak in New England and supporters of John Quincy Adams had little strength elsewhere. Furthermore, the liberalization of suffrage requirements forced the decision-making process to be more inclusive. Improvements in transportation, including the development of railroads, made it possible for many delegates from various states to meet at a mutually agreeable location.

The first national nominating convention was held by the Anti-Masonic Party in 1831 in Baltimore. They wanted the visibility that they believed a national convention would provide. The National Republicans and the Jacksonian Democrats soon did the same. The national convention provided the venue where the views of different factions could be reconciled. The selection of a vice presidential candidate would often serve to conciliate factional losers for the presidential nomination or to balance the ticket.

2.7   ENDING RELIGIOUS RESTRICTIONS ON HOLDING OFFICE

Religious restrictions against holding office in the states ended slowly. The Constitution explicitly states that "no religious Test shall ever be required as a Qualification to any Office or public Trust under the United States" (Article VI, Clause 3). This clause did not apply to the states. The framers and ratifiers of the federal Constitution were extremely reluctant to make an equivalent ruling for their own states. That implied that it was useless for candidates for state elective office to appear on the ballot unless they were of the approved religious faith or faiths (but see later for North Carolina). It was not until 1925 in *Gitlow v. New York* that the U.S. Supreme Court was willing to rule that the Bill of Rights applied to the states as well as to the federal government. The First Amendment includes the statement that "Congress shall make no law respecting an establishment of religion . . ."

Between 1789 and 1792, Delaware, Pennsylvania, South Carolina, and Georgia joined Virginia in eliminating all religious restrictions, except that Pennsylvania retained its prohibition against atheists. New York removed its restriction on office holding by Roman Catholics in 1806. In Maryland, the bar to a non-Christian holding civil or military office or serving as an attorney was lifted for Jews in 1826 (after a three-decade struggle). In New England, New Jersey, and North Carolina, all non-Protestants were initially barred from holding office. In Connecticut, a religious restriction on office holding was eliminated in 1818, after the Toleration Party took control of the legislature. The revised Constitutions of Massachusetts, Rhode Island, and New Jersey eliminated their prohibitions in 1821, 1842, and 1844, respectively (Borden, 1984, pp. 24–52).

North Carolina required an oath of office that initially prevented non-Protestants from serving in any "civil department" of the state. Jacob Henry, a Jew, was elected to the lower house of the legislature in 1808. When his presence was challenged in his second one-year term in 1809 because he did not take the sectarian oath of office, the members of that body permitted him to retain his seat on the basis that the prohibition did not apply to the legislature. The prohibition against Roman Catholics serving in the executive branch apparently was not being observed, since the state's attorney general at the time was John Louis Taylor, a Roman Catholic. In 1835, North Carolina officially removed the barrier for any Christian, but retained it for Jews and others. After the Civil War, in 1868, the state government under Reconstruction removed the prohibition from all except atheists. New Hampshire was the last of the original 13 states to eliminate its religious requirement for office holding. It accomplished that act in 1876, although it retained other provisions of sectarianism. It does not appear that any of the states added to the Union after the original ones included a religious bar to office holding in its constitution, except possibly for atheists.

2.8   OTHER VOTING PROCESS CHANGES

In Pennsylvania, ballots were required initially to be handwritten. However, the formation of political parties had resulted in the wide availability of printed tickets usable as ballots. The original concern was likely that, if ballots were printed, it would be easy for them to be handed out to illiterate persons, or possibly, that many copies of printed ballots could be used to stuff ballot boxes. After 1796, the submission of printed ballots was allowed (Boorstin, 1965, p. 428). Tickets were published in newspapers and some voters cut out the tickets and handed them in.

In New Jersey, considerable change occurred in 1796 and 1797. A precipitating concern was the presence of only one polling place in each of several counties. A new law was enacted, which required one polling place for voting for legislators, sheriffs, and coroners to be made available in each township. Ballots, "which shall be a single written ticket," were to be used (McCormick, 1953, pp. 95, 96). Thus, the county option of using ballots or *vive voce* voting ceased. In addition, the practice of having a long period for open polls was stopped. Under the new law, the voting period was ended on the evening of the second day. Furthermore, a town meeting could designate two polling places within a township where polling might occur. The availability of many more polling places reduced the size of the electorate at each polling place and brought the voting location much closer to the residences of voters. A continuing defect was that the election officials were to be named at a town meeting. This process made it probable that the officials would favor the party of the majority in attendance at the meeting and could use their partisanship to their advantage in the voting process. Application of that advantage might include acceptance for voting of persons of dubious credentials.

In Connecticut, Federalists were totally in command prior to 1800. "Congregational ministers, in consultation with party leaders, determined policy and controlled nominations" (Williamson, 1960, p. 165). For the election contest of 1800, a Republican party organization committed to the selection of Jefferson was established. The new party called for the separation of church and state and the installation of a new constitution that would assure separation of powers of the three branches of state government. The Federalists strenuously fought these upstarts with the passage of the "Stand Up Law," which eliminated the use of the ballot in certain local elections. In these elections, voters were required to raise their hands or stand up when publicly polled. Reformers eventually got the upper hand with the formation of a fusion group called the Toleration Party or the Union Reform Ticket in 1817. One of their first orders of business was to repeal the Stand Up Law and require the use of the ballot in all elections. In addition, they eliminated property requirements for voting.

In Massachusetts and Rhode Island, during the eighteenth century and in the early nineteenth century, ballots were written by hand. In 1829 in

Massachusetts, a voter submitted a printed ballot for 55 candidates. The ballot was initially rejected, but the State Supreme Judicial Court ruled that it was acceptable. As a result, parties began to print ballots and each party selected its own ballot color. Secrecy was compromised. Then, in 1851, the legislature required that the ballots be put into standard envelopes, attempting to restore secrecy. In 1853, opponents of secrecy came into power and made the envelope optional; this allowed voters who were coerced or bribed to make public the ballot that they were voting. In Rhode Island, a similar situation occurred, with the same result.

In New York, voting by ballot for state-level elections had been adopted in 1789, but not for local elections. *Viva voce* voting was common. In New York City, landlords could vote in every ward in which they owned property. Several instances of landlords threatening tenants with retribution were reported in the 1790s if the rent payers did not vote as they were instructed. Election inspectors were still appointed in a partisan manner, and this fact made it likely that the lists of qualified voters were padded or pared according to voters' expected voting patterns. A new law in 1804 eliminated plural voting by property owners and established voting by ballot in city elections. Voting by ballot was extended to town elections in 1809.

In Maryland, efforts at election reform began in about 1797 with several proposals submitted to the legislature. Some of these measures were for universal manhood suffrage, elimination of restrictions against holding public office by Jews, and for increases in the number of polling places in each county. At that time, each county had only one polling place. Another suggestion was for the compiling of county voter registration lists "in order to curb abuses [by sheriffs] and the creation of fagot voters." The latter were persons temporarily assigned small plots of land to allow them to meet voting requirements (Williamson, 1960, pp. 141, 142, 149). In 1799, voting by ballot was adopted, replacing oral voting. Election districts were created that were almost equal in size and population. In 1802, universal white male suffrage was achieved, dropping landholding and taxpayer restrictions. In 1810, the state constitution was clarified to assure that all voters in state elections could also vote for members of the House of Representatives and for presidential Electors.

In South Carolina, complaints about fraud in the voting process had started to come forward in the last decade of the eighteenth century. It was stated that polls were opened and closed at the whim of sheriffs, that more ballots were found in ballot boxes than there were voters, and that some persons had voted more than once in an election. The concerns galvanized the opposition to the manner in which elections were being conducted, and resulted in a strong effort to equalize representation in the legislature. As noted by Madison in 1788, malapportionment of the legislature antedated ratification of the Constitution. Success was partially achieved in 1808 with equalization of representation in the lower house. The counties away from the coast would now have a fair proportion of seats, compared with Charleston and its surroundings. The upper house remained in the hands of the coastal planters and their allies.

In Virginia, there were significant property requirements for suffrage in the early years of the nineteenth century. As a result, "both east and west [sections of the state] witnessed a considerable degree of illegal voting and coercion of electors" (Williamson, 1960, p. 230). A state convention in 1829–1830, with its primary focus on reducing requirements for suffrage, did not increase the liberality of the voting process. The popular election of the highest state officials was not approved, nor was the elimination of *vive voce* voting in favor of the ballot. The state also denied reformers' desires to provide an increased number of polling places over the one per county then available. Virginia continued to use oral voting until 1867.

Kentucky, which had first been settled as part of Virginia, became a state in 1792. It continued to use oral voting until adoption of a new constitution in 1891. Kentucky was the last state to do so; it had permitted the city of Louisville to vote by secret ballot in its local elections in 1888 (see section 3.11).

The territory that became Ohio, Indiana, Illinois, Michigan, and Wisconsin was included in the United States under the 1783 treaty that ended the Revolutionary War. The Northwest Ordinance, adopted by the Continental Congress in 1787, included rules under which the new states could be formed. Support for education was contained in this legislation. There would be freedom of religion and no slavery in the new territory. Battles against the indigenous inhabitants were hard fought and bloody before resistance was crushed.

The *vive voce* method of voting was initially introduced into the Northwest Territory in the incorporating legislation of 1794. The first governor, Arthur St. Clair, was instrumental in obtaining approval of the territorial legislature in 1800 to adopt voting by ballot. St. Clair was concerned about excessive power of landlords under oral voting. He told the legislature that "creditors were using their power over debtors to make them vote for certain candidates on promises of extending the time for payment" (Evans, 1917, p. 6).

Ohio and Indiana provided for elections by ballot in their first constitutions, although Indiana, as a territory, had used oral voting before 1811. In Illinois, there was significant conflict over the issue of the voting method. Voting by ballot alternated with *vive voce* voting several times between 1813 and 1829. The state employed *vive voce* voting between 1829 and 1847. Advocates of open voting stated that "it enabled candidates to pledge a man before election" (Williamson, 1960, pp. 219, 220). The first constitutions of Michigan and Wisconsin required voting by ballot.

Soon after Maine became a state in 1820 by separating from Massachusetts, political parties began to distribute their own ballots. These ballots tended to be of different colors and sizes, and used different fonts and printing styles. The result was that secrecy of the ballot was lost, as anyone watching the deposit of ballots by voters could tell whose ballot the voter was casting.

Maine was the first state to try to assure secrecy by enacting legislation in 1831 that required specific ballot color and design. Other states did the same, at varying times. Some states tried to implement this process after the Civil War. The law stated, typically, that each ballot shall be upon plain white printing paper, without any "peculiarity" to distinguish its appearance, and shall be printed with plain black ink. These laws generally failed their purpose because of the different shades of white that were used. Poll watchers could still distinguish party ballots from each other (Evans, 1917, pp. 7, 8).

Missouri became a state in 1821 and used oral voting until 1863.

Arkansas achieved statehood in 1836 with oral voting, but abandoned it in 1846.

Oregon's first constitution of 1857 in preparation for statehood required oral voting but allowed legislative discretion: "In all elections by the people, votes shall be given openly or viva voce until the legislative assembly shall otherwise direct" (Ludington, 1911, p. 168). During the Civil War, Oregon used *vive voce* voting to assure loyalty to the Union. In 1872, the Oregon legislature directed voting by ballot, in response to the federal law of 1871, which required voting by ballot for U.S. representatives. The quoted sentence from the 1857 Oregon constitution has not been replaced, according to the Reference Desk of the State Legislative Library.

West Virginia, which broke away from Virginia in 1863 during the Civil War, required voting by ballot in its first constitution.

The act of voting in the 1850s has been reviewed in a recent study. The analysis, based on testimony in 48 Congressional hearings, provides detailed information on how elections were conducted, from the point-of-view of the voters themselves, in the time period considered (Bensel, 2004, pp. 1–85). Many of the examples elucidate conditions in rural areas.

During that period, the polling location might have been at a private home, a store, a post office, or any other convenient building. In some states, this situation still pertains. An essential feature of the situation, as described by Richard F. Bensel, was that the election officials were inside the building and, typically, the voters were outside. Inside, there were ballot boxes and records kept by the officials, often called "judges of elections." The atmosphere inside was calm. An open window in the side of the building fronted on a porch or platform, reachable by a few steps up from the ground. The porch providing the location where the voters handed in their tickets. On the ground, around the steps, there was much "chaotic" milling about by a throng of prospective voters, ticket peddlers, onlookers, and, in some places, toughs whose job it was to keep members of opposing factions away from the polls. (This situation would continue until the adoption of the Australian ballot; see section 3.11.) The arrangement is presented in the painting "*The County Election*," by George Caleb Bingham (1811–1879), in the possession of the St. Louis Art Museum. In Bingham's depiction, a voter is being sworn as to eligibility by an election judge on the porch while a candidate or his representative tips his hat and offers a ballot to a prospective voter. Spectators hang around, enjoying the excitement.

Eligibility was an important issue in those times, as it continues to be now, but then there were few records. There was no prior voter registration, and if property and asset requirements had been abolished, the question of eligibility was determined right there at the polls. In smaller localities, persons were known by sight and those not recognized might be challenged as to how long they had lived in the vicinity and whether they were citizens. Many men were not literate. If there were records available stating their age and length of residency, unlikely at best, they could not read them. If they were native-born, they had no certificate of naturalization; their natural accent, if different from the local one, may have created suspicion.

Some of the onlookers at the polls might have been involved tangentially in the voting. Illiterate individuals were assisted in selecting their tickets by supporters of one party or another. Wily voters would try to obtain the largest possible bribe from the different parties, playing off one against the other. The throngs at the polls might be viewing the negotiations, watching the dance between a prospective voter and various ticket peddlers, or determining which ticket a bribed or intimidated voter really cast.

2.9   NATIONAL EXPANSION BEGINS TO FILL THE LAND AND THE CONGRESS

Between 1803 and 1848, an enormous expansion of territory occurred, followed by a minor increase in 1856. This significant augmentation extended the borders of the United States to the Pacific Ocean and established our currently existing borders of the contiguous 48 states with Mexico and Canada. In 1803, on the initiative of President Jefferson, U.S. representatives approached French officials to find a diplomatic solution to the problem of U.S. access to the Gulf of Mexico at New Orleans. The French responded with an offer to sell the entire Louisiana territory for $15 million. The purchase would include the entire watershed of the Missouri and other rivers flowing into the Mississippi from the west, plus the land bordering the Gulf coast from New Orleans west to the Sabine River. The latter was the eastern border of Texas, then part of Mexico, at the time a colony of Spain. The United States accepted the offer, doubling the area of the country.

In 1810 and 1813, the United States annexed the areas along the Gulf coast between the Mississippi River east to the current western boundary of Florida. This territory was not included in the 1783 peace treaty with Great Britain or the Louisiana Purchase. The area annexed in 1810 became part of the state of Louisiana. The other area, claimed by Spain, was captured in the War of 1812 when the port of Mobile was being used by the British. The territory was divided between Alabama and Mississippi. U.S. sovereignty over both areas was confirmed in the treaty that ended the latter war. In 1819, the United States purchased from Spain what is now the state of Florida, obtaining the only territory east of the Mississippi and south of the Great Lakes not yet part of the nation. In 1842, the Webster–Ashburton treaty with Great Britain fixed the border between Maine and Canada.

Texas, which had received many settlers from the United States, declared its independence from Mexico in 1836. (Mexico had become a republic in 1823.) Texas allowed slavery. It had been illegal in Mexico, although immigrants were permitted to bring their slaves with them. In 1845, Texans requested annexation by the United States, and the Congress adopted the necessary legislation. The Mexican War began in 1846; the pretext was the clashes that had occurred in the area between the Mexican-claimed border at the Neuces River and the US-claimed border at the Rio Grande. By 1848, the Mexicans were defeated. They accepted the Rio Grande boundary and ceded California and other territories that became the southwestern region of the United States. An additional strip of land, called the Gadsden Purchase, was obtained from Mexico in 1856. It would finalize the Mexican–U.S. border between Texas and California.

The settlement of California and Oregon by Americans had already begun before the Mexican War. Some prospective settlers took ships around Cape Horn to San Francisco or to the narrower part of Central America. In the latter case, following a trip across the isthmus, emigrants took another ship on the Pacific side north to California. In a land route, wagon trains began the trek west from Missouri. The Great Plains were crossed, generally following the Platte, North Platte, and Sweetwater Rivers. The highest peaks of the Rocky Mountains were circumvented by crossing the Continental Divide by the easiest route, at South Pass in what would become Wyoming. Then the trail split: through the Great Basin and over the Sierras to the Great Valley of California or along the Snake and Columbia Rivers into Oregon. The Oregon country was claimed by both the United States and Britain, but with large-scale immigration from the United States, the British would have difficulty enforcing their control. The result was a treaty in 1846 that extended the border along the 49th parallel from Minnesota to an arm of the Pacific Ocean.

The population of the nation increased significantly along with the territorial expansion. The first national census in 1790 had shown a population of not quite 4 million. A decennial census was required under the Constitution, Article I, Section 2, for purposes of apportionment of the House of Representatives. Through 1860, it showed an average increase of about 34 percent every 10 years, resulting in a population in the latter year of over 31 million. By that year, there were 33 states in the Union, including all the states east of the Mississippi (except West Virginia, still part of Virginia), all the states bordering the Mississippi on the west, that is, Louisiana, Arkansas, Missouri, Iowa, and Minnesota, as well as Texas, California, and Oregon. In the 1860 presidential election, all the Electors that could be named were appointed, and all of them voted. There were 303 electoral votes cast, consistent with 66 members of the U.S. Senate and 237 members of the U.S. House of Representatives. The reconstituted Republican party, specifically antislavery, would win with Abraham Lincoln. That assured the start of the Civil War.

2.10   THE FEDERAL GOVERNMENT CONTRIBUTES TO NATIONAL DEVELOPMENT

The needs of commerce were understood by the framers of the Constitution. Among other powers, they specified (Article I, Section 8) that Congress would have the authority:

- To regulate Commerce with foreign Nations, and among the several States, and with the Indian tribes;
- To establish . . . uniform laws on the subject of Bankruptcies throughout the United States;
- To . . . fix the Standard of Weights and Measures;
- To establish Post Offices and post Roads; and
- To promote the Progress of Science and useful Arts, by securing for limited Times to Authors and Inventors the exclusive Right to their respective Writings and Discoveries.

In addition, there is more language in this section that Congress could utilize to justify relevant legislation. Congress would have the power to "provide for the general Welfare of the United States" and to enact "all laws which shall be necessary and proper for carrying into Execution [the powers enumerated in section 8]."

In the developing industrialization, patents would be found to be particularly valuable. The regulation of interstate commerce would become significant as rivers were cleared of obstacles, while roads and canals provided the infrastructure by which people and goods moved from place to place without regard to state lines. The federal bankruptcy responsibility fostered interstate commerce in that it prevented individual state sovereignties from interfering with the ability of creditors to achieve their due. It also prevented bankrupts from avoiding responsibility by crossing state lines. The establishment of "post Roads" would be very important for the knitting together of the vast territory that the nation was destined to have. The federal government helped fund the National Road, now U.S. 40. The road started in Cumberland, Maryland, in 1811 and was extended by 1838 to Vandalia, Illinois, not far from St. Louis. "When its 834 miles had been completed it had cost $6,821,200 and had required thirty Acts of Congress" (Johnson, 1999, p. 366).

2.11   FEDERAL REGULATION FOR PUBLIC SAFETY COMMENCES

The development of the relatively high-pressure non-condensing steam engine occurred around 1800 in the United States and England. The American inventor was the ingenious Delawarean Oliver Evans. The utilization of steam engines to power boats is associated with the name of Robert Fulton, who demonstrated it by a trip up the Hudson River from New York City to Albany in 1807. Soon, many steamboats were operating on major American rivers. Unfortunately, boiler explosions were common. In 1824, the Franklin Institute was founded in Philadelphia, dedicated to "the study and promotion of the mechanical arts and applied sciences." In 1830, the institute began to investigate and undertake research on the subject of these detonations. In that year, a particularly deadly blast occurred on a steamboat near Memphis, and Congress asked Secretary of the Treasury Samuel Ingham to investigate. Ingham funded the Franklin Institute to cover costs of experiments. "This was the first research grant of a technological nature made by the federal government" (Burke, 1997, p. 114).

Congress passed regulatory legislation in 1838, but it was ineffective. Boiler explosions continued to occur. In 1850, Congress asked the commissioner of patents to collect data and estimate the losses. He reported that in the period 1816–1848, 233 steamboat explosions had occurred in which 2,563 persons had been killed and 2,097 injured. Property losses were in excess of $3 million. Finally, in 1852, Congress passed a second law. The new law established safe technical operating conditions for boilers and set a schedule for repetitive testing. Nine supervisory boiler inspectors were to be appointed by the president. Under them, there were boards of inspectors "empowered to investigate infractions and accidents, with the right to summon witnesses, compel their attendance and examine them under oath" (Burke, 1997, p. 124). Following passage of the law, steamboat explosions significantly decreased, and one knowledgeable observer commented that explosions on the Atlantic had become almost unknown.

2.12   THE RELEVANCE OF FEDERAL INVESTMENT TO THE VOTING PROCESS

The solution to the problem of marine boiler explosions involved a set of actions that would be applied to similar public concerns about health and safety in the future.

1. The problem was seen to be important enough such that a sufficiently strong interest group or the public-at-large demanded Congressional action.
2. The Congress responded with a grant to a capable and disinterested organization (i.e., the Franklin Institute) to undertake research and propose a solution.
3. The Congress asked another disinterested party (i.e., the commissioner of patents) to collect data on the national losses as a result of the problem.
4. The Congress formulated legislation that set technical standards and established an administrative structure to supervise adherence to the standards. The legislation was considered in Congressional committee, amended, and ultimately adopted. Civil and criminal penalties were included in the Act for violations by the regulated industry.

While no one has been reported to have been scalded to death by a hanging chad and no person's physical health has been put at risk immediately because the candidates for a single contest were presented on two separate pages, the protection of the voting process is as important for the well-being of the body politic as is protection of public health and safety for the bodies of our individual citizens. The extent of involvement or the lack of involvement of the federal government in the assurance of free and fair elections will be elucidated in the forthcoming chapters.

3

THE LATE NINETEENTH CENTURY: STRUGGLING WITH CORRUPTION AND FRAUD

Slavery was abolished by the 13th Amendment to the Constitution, ratified in late 1865 after the carnage and chaos of the war had ended. Lee had surrendered in April of that year, and Abraham Lincoln was shot less than a week later. Republicans, in command of Congress since the inauguration of Lincoln in 1861, were not deterred by his assassination. They imposed military rule on the defeated region after becoming dissatisfied with the results of conciliatory moves by the new president, Andrew Johnson. Occupation would remain in some states until the adoption of an 1877 understanding that helped end the stalemate over the national election of 1876 (see section 3.8).

3.1 POPULATION, IMMIGRATION, AND THE CITIES

National population during this era expanded from about 35 million in 1865 to about 76 million in 1900, an increase of 117 percent. In the same period, the number of immigrants was over 15 million persons; that is, of the total increase of 41 million, over one-third was due to immigration. The highest immigration level in a decade of the late nineteenth century was over 5 million between 1881 and 1890.

Concurrent with high levels of immigration, there was a general movement of population to the cities. While a tendency to urbanization was a fact before the Civil War and would continue afterward, it was a major factor in the last third of the nineteenth century. In 1860, with the national population at 31.4 million, the urban population was a little over 6 million, or just about 20 percent of the total. In 1900, there were 30 million dwellers in places of more than 2,500 population (which defines urbanization), about 40 percent of the whole. New immigrants tended to settle in the larger cities. "The percentage of native-born residents in cities smaller than 25,000 exceeded that of larger ones throughout the late nineteenth century" (Barrows, 1996, p. 94).

There was a strong association between urbanization and industrialization. Many of the newer factories needed a large labor force, but the majority of workers could not be expected to travel far to jobs. Thus, many factories that were not specifically site-dependent on a rural location were placed in cities. In the decades following the Civil War, "cities and their factories transformed the United States from an agricultural debtor nation into a manufacturing and financial power" (Chudacoff and Smith, 1994, p. 107).

The situation just described had an impact on the voting process. The largest cities provided the greatest variety of opportunities for careers, including jobs for new immigrants. The political group in control of a large city, that is, the "machine" headed by the "boss," could take advantage of any situation. Considerable amounts could be reaped as money flowed in from taxes, permits, and usage fees and money flowed out for salaries and payments to contractors. In New York City in the 1880s, there were 12,000 municipal jobs and a payroll of $12 million. The dynamic quality of a large city is enjoyed by many who live there.

The winning of elections was fundamental to the success of the machine. If a party was not "in," it could not carry out any of the nefarious activities that brought its leaders large and unsavory monetary rewards. As a result, men with the right to vote were under great pressure to vote "right." Additionally, the circumvention of rules on entitlement to vote was not difficult to accomplish, with selection of "cooperative" individuals to serve as election inspectors. The continuous increases in population and movement in immigrant neighborhoods would make difficult the assurance of correct records of residents. It would improve the chances that false names and addresses would be accepted by unknowing, uncaring, or bribed election officials. Votes were easily augmented with the use of "repeaters" and "floaters" who voted early and often, and with the suborning of those supposedly opposition officials among those who counted the votes. (Floaters were men who made themselves available to vote a particular ticket in exchange for money. The machine arranged for them to vote in a variety of precincts. "Colonization" described the process of bringing men in from other cities for fraudulent voting and putting them up in flophouses.)

3.2   THE TWEED RING

Several "rings," that is, groups of corrupt and colluding officials who were in power in large cities, were active. Philadelphia had its Gas Ring, for example. A notorious example of the worst of municipal politics was the Tweed Ring, which was in power in New York City from 1866 to 1871. In 1878, that city's Board of Aldermen issued a report of its investigation of the "Ring" frauds, along with a transcript of testimony. The following often-cited interaction between the Board's questioner and William Marcy Tweed, the disgraced former boss of the eponymous Ring, sums up one essential requirement of the Ring's procedures for retention of power (Board of Aldermen of New York City, 1878, pp. 133–137):

> *Questioner:* What were they [election inspectors in the pay of the Ring] to do, in case you wanted a particular man elected over another?
>
> *Tweed:* Count the ballots in bulk, or without counting them announce the result in bulk, or change from one to the other, as the case may have been.
>
> *Questioner:* Then these elections really were no elections at all? The ballots were made to bring about any result that you determined beforehand?
>
> *Tweed:* The ballots made no result; the counters made the result.

To achieve this systematic nullification of the public will, a considerable effort went into assuring control of many positions in the city government. In addition, there was an unspoken and, for the most part, accepted understanding among city employees and contractors that doing business with the city or accepting its paycheck involved fraud, graft, and kickbacks. The Ring exacted its percentage of many transactions of which it was a part. It is instructive to review this situation that has "received the singular distinction of being labeled the model of civic corruption in American municipal history" (Callow, 1966, p. vii).

Tweed won election as an alderman in 1851. The Board of Aldermen was the city legislature, but it was not the only group with power to pass laws. Due to the State of New York's desire to retain control, there was also a Board of Supervisors for New York County; it had overlapping jurisdiction. An alderman had powers in his district over some patronage and city improvements. He appointed the police of his ward, from patrolman to precinct commander; he granted licenses to saloons, and franchises to streetcar lines and ferries.

In 1858, Tweed became the Democratic leader of the 7th ward, one of about 22 or so into which the city was divided. (At the time, the city consisted only of the island of Manhattan.) In those times, there was no concept of "conflict of interest," which would keep a person holding a government office from also holding a partisan political position. In that year, George Barnard was city recorder, Peter Barr Sweeny was district attorney and Democratic leader of the 20th ward, Richard Connolly was county clerk and one of the leaders of the 21st ward. These gentlemen would have major roles in the Ring as it would be organized in the next decade.

Tweed also had a "Supervisor's Ring" while he was a member of that board, and arranged with some colleagues to accept or reject certain contracts according to the kickbacks that they could receive. In 1859, Tweed attempted to fix the mayoralty election of that year by conspiring with other supervisors to appoint a large majority of election inspectors favorable to Tammany Hall, Tweed's Democratic political club. Although the Board of Supervisors was split half-and-half between Democrats and Republicans (by its charter from the state), a Republican supervisor was bribed $2,500 to stay away from the meeting at which the inspectors were named. Nevertheless, Tweed's man lost the election.

The year 1863 was especially fruitful for Tweed, although it was the year of the Draft Riots in New York (see Asbury, 1928, pp. 108–157). He was named chairman of the General Committee of Tammany Hall and later that year grand sachem (supreme leader). Also, in that year, he was named deputy street commissioner of the city and held that position until 1870. He was chief operating officer for that function, which employed thousands of men. Without the constraints of civil service, it was an enormous opportunity to be used for political purposes. It could be used to help influential people who needed jobs for their poorer relatives or for partisans in their wards. It provided the manpower to help secure desired election results by providing a reservoir of repeaters and "shoulder-hitters." The latter term (also "shoulder-strikers") was commonly used for toughs "accomplished in the arts of scuffling and ballot-stuffing" (Fredman, 1968, p. 26), who created disturbances at polling locations and intimidated opposition voters into either staying away entirely or accepting the machine's proffered ballot. Employees could be used for any purpose for which Tweed needed them. Satisfaction of political obligations was first priority. If there were a "job description" that limited a worker's function, no one paid any attention. Each man knew that he could be discharged and someone else hired to replace him.

In 1864, Tweed bought a major interest in the New York Printing Company, which henceforth was the city's printer of all documents. All companies with city franchises understood that they had better obtain their printing requirements from it. Additionally, Tweed was part of a group purchasing a marble quarry; the stone for the new County Courthouse was procured from it at exorbitant costs.

Another senior member of the Ring was A. Oakey Hall, who became mayor of New York during Tweed's ascendency and continued in that position until his term ended in 1872. As mayor, Hall had to countersign all vouchers for payment to contractors. Many bills were inflated; that was a major way in which the Ring made its money. Of course, Hall signed without protest and would later claim that he had only "ministerial" responsibility; that is, he paid no attention to their content.

In 1868, the Ring was in the midst of its best days. Tweed became a state senator, but was not required to relinquish any of his other positions. Peter Sweeny now was city chamberlain, the equivalent of a county treasurer. Richard Connolly was city comptroller; his annual salary was $3,600, but he was also cashier and general manager of a private bank. (In 1871, he would be worth $6 million.) James Watson had become city auditor in 1866. The fact that Watson had been previously convicted of financial manipulation did not seem to matter to Tweed; indeed, it may have made him seem more valuable.

Cooperating judges were on the bench. For example, George Barnard, formerly city recorder, was on the Supreme Court (not the highest court in the state). The control of the legal machinery assured that an operation essential to the Ring, that is, the capability of assuring certain election outcomes, was not in danger of being compromised. The judges would find excuses to release repeaters who were caught voting more than once. Additionally, they ran a naturalization mill that allowed aliens who did not meet the minimum requirements for citizenship to easily achieve that important goal. October, the month just before the general elections, provided the largest number of aliens naturalized. Certain individuals vouched falsely for hundreds of persons to be naturalized and Tammany judges ignored the obvious contradictions clearly in front of them. Of course, Tweed and Company were generally rewarded with the votes of the new citizens.

The national election of 1868 was one in which significant dishonesties were perpetrated by the Tweed Ring. Gangs of repeaters were organized at particular Tammany locations during days of registration and election day. Each gang member would receive a paper specifying a name and a residential address to use for registration and later for voting. After the first falsification was used, each repeater would return to the headquarters location where an additional false name and address would be given to him to be used. This process would be continued throughout the day (Davenport, 1894, pp. 168–171).

Ballot stuffing was widely employed on election day. At voting locations where the Republican poll workers would not cooperate or could not be bribed, ways would be found to distract or remove them. Shoulder-hitters might be used to create confusion to divert their attention. Incorrect information might be given to them that their services were needed elsewhere. False arrest was not unknown.

After the close of polls on election day, a method using telegrams was employed by Tammany Hall (the telephone had not yet been invented) to determine how the contending parties were faring in the vote upstate. Reports of local vote totals were held back by Tammany until it was determined how many extra votes might be needed to overcome the out-of-city deficit. The Board of Aldermen's 1878 report on the Tweed Ring scandals estimated that the vote cast in New York City in 1868 was 8 percent in excess of its entire population and that there had been more than 50,000 illegal votes cast.

The fall of the Tweed Ring began when County Auditor James Watson died in a sleighing accident in January 1871. Thoughtlessly, the Ring appointed supposed supporter Matthew O'Rourke in his place. Unbeknownst to the Ring, O'Rourke was embittered over his inability to collect a claim. Another anti-Ring Democrat, former sheriff James O'Brien, had hid his disgruntlement over a similar failed claim and had persuaded Comptroller Richard Connolly to hire a friend, one William Copeland. Both O'Rourke and Copeland diligently and independently reported their discoveries of the records of financial frauds to *The New York Times*, a strongly anti-Tammany newspaper (Callow, 1966, pp. 259, 260).

The disclosures by the *Times* began in the summer of 1871, and continued for several months. The public paid attention and reform rallies were held. Many New Yorkers who had become apathetic were suddenly excited that possibly the Ring could be beaten in the state and local elections of

November that year. On election day, reformers guarded the polls to prevent disorder and repeating. The reformers were successful; it was a quiet election. Almost all elected members of the Ring was beaten, although Tweed himself retained his State Senate seat.

A special state attorney general was named to prosecute the miscreants, and a special investigator was named to gather evidence. Tweed himself was convicted, but almost no others were. Several Ring members fled the state or country. Judge Barnard was impeached and removed from office. Estimates by different reviewers of the total amount stolen by the Ring ran from $40 million to $100 million (Mandelbaum, 1965, p. 86). Others have suggested that as much as $200 million might have been pilfered. The widely differing values of the estimated thievery is perhaps indicative of the primitive state of record-keeping, the extensiveness of the false documentation, and the lack of outside oversight.

3.3   CONFLICTS OVER VOTING RIGHTS FOR FREEDMEN AND INDIANS

Andrew Johnson of Tennessee had been selected as Lincoln's running mate in 1864 because of his Southern origin. As president, his intent was to return political power in the South to the same class of men who had withdrawn their states from the Union. Under his plan of 1865–1866, the former Confederate states were allowed to form new governments. The intent of some legislators in the Southern states was to return blacks to a condition close to slavery.

In the West, wars against the Indians continued as white settlement proceeded. Custer's "last stand" would occur in 1876. While these campaigns to appropriate lands of the indigenous inhabitants proceeded, any movement to ameliorate their political condition would have no chance of success. In the late 1880s, an effort to grant citizenship to assimilated Indians bore some fruit.

In the adoption of the Reconstruction Act of 1867, Congress retook the reins of the federal government on the issue of Southern reconstruction. It adopted, on March 2, *An Act to provide for the more efficient Government of the Rebel States,* overriding Johnson's veto (39th Congress, Sess. II, Chap. 153). Of the 11 former Confederate states 10 were put under Union military rule; provisional legislatures were dissolved, and former members of the Confederate military were denied suffrage. The states could apply for readmission if they ratified the 14th Amendment and enacted enforcing legislation. (Tennessee had done so and was exempted from military control.) The occupied states were required to grant suffrage to all eligible male voters, black and white. Of course, with many former Confederates denied the right to vote, the votes of blacks were more significant. In the South, there were about 627,000 white voters and more than 700,000 blacks with suffrage [Robinson, 2001 (1968), p. 23]. Congress assumed that blacks would vote Republican, the party of Lincoln.

Under Congressional Reconstruction, by the autumn of 1868, all of the former Confederate states excepting Mississippi, Texas, and Virginia had been readmitted to the Union. Those three cast no electoral votes in the 1868 election. Republicans were temporarily in control of most of the readmitted states. Ulysses S. Grant was elected president with 41 electoral votes of those states, including 3 from Florida that were determined by its legislature. Horatio Seymour, the Democratic candidate and governor of New York, won in Georgia and Louisiana. During Reconstruction, "two Negroes from Mississippi served in the U.S. Senate and fourteen Negroes were elected to the House of Representatives" [Robinson, 2001 (1968), p. 24].

However, violent groups had been formed by white southerners who continued to favor subjugation of blacks. These organizations had the goal of harassing, intimidating, beating, and sometimes murdering blacks and their white supporters. Their intent, besides obtaining the barbaric satisfaction of hurting the beneficiaries of the Civil War outcome, was to demonstrate that the Reconstruction governments were unable to protect their citizens. They succeeded in achieving that result.

Ratification of the 14th and 15th Amendments would require implementing legislation directed at conditions in the former Confederacy. The 14th opens with a statement about citizenship:

> All persons born or naturalized in the United States, and subject to the jurisdiction thereof, are citizens of the United States and of the State wherein they reside.

This statement applied to African Americans, but would be understood by the government not to apply to American Indians at that time. In 1870, the Judiciary Committee of the U.S. Senate issued a report affirming this interpretation. According to the report, Indians maintaining tribal allegiance were not "subject to the jurisdiction" of the United States and therefore were not citizens.

Section 1 of the 14th Amendment continued with a clause that would join the Bill of Rights as one of the most important statements of civil rights in many other areas besides racial conflict, for example, by the U.S. Supreme Court in December 2000, as reported in chapter 1:

> No State shall . . . deprive any person of life, liberty, or property, without due process of law; nor deny to any person within its jurisdiction the equal protection of the laws.

The 15th Amendment in its Section 1 specifically addressed the right to vote:

> The right of citizens of the United States to vote shall not be denied or abridged by the United States or by any State on account of race, color, or previous condition of servitude.

The Enforcement Act of 1870 was adopted by Congress to try to end racial discrimination in voting. Administration of the act was enhanced with the establishment of the Department of Justice as a Cabinet-level department in

1870. There had been an attorney general previously but, before 1870, he had no significant cadre of officials to assist him.

The act (41st Congress, Sess. II, Chap. 114) defined as federal crimes any action to prevent or attempt to prevent persons from voting or from registering to vote. It identified, as criminal, actions of election officials who, in the wrongful performance of their duties, prevented or hindered the registration, voting, or counting of votes of any persons lawfully so entitled. Administration of the act was put in the hands of local officials of the Department of Justice. These officials included district attorneys, federal marshals and their deputies, and special commissioners of elections. The act gave federal courts jurisdiction over voting rights cases, gave the president authority to use troops or state militia to help enforce federal guarantees, and most importantly, gave the Department of Justice the power and responsibility to enforce all of the provisions relating to the "elective franchise" (Goldman, 2001, p. 17).

At about that time, the U.S. Supreme Court would rule that the 15th Amendment did not require that blacks were to be given the right to vote without qualification; only that blacks and whites would have to meet the same qualifications in order to vote. Thus, literacy tests and poll taxes, if they were administered without racial bias, were Constitutional at that time. As the nineteenth century wound down, the public would have had its fill of racial concerns and the effort needed to assure racial justice. They would want to move on. Thus, the problem of black rights in the South began to be ignored by the great majority of whites nationwide.

3.4   THE APPORTIONMENT CLAUSE

Although much of the effort to assure the voting rights of African Americans was humanitarian, a part of it was self-serving. The Constitution, in Article I, Section 1, had stated the following:

> Representatives and direct taxes shall be apportioned among the several States which may be included in this Union, according to their respective Numbers, which shall be determined by adding to the whole Number of free Persons . . . and, excluding Indians not taxed, three-fifths of all other persons.

This wording was superseded by the 14th Amendment, Section 2, which redefined apportionment according to the "whole number of persons in each State, excluding Indians not taxed." The revised clause omits the word "free," which was no longer needed, and the phrase "three-fifths of all other persons."

A concern of Republicans was that, with the former slaves now being counted as full persons (instead of three-fifths of each), the population of the Southern states would relatively increase for purposes of Congressional apportionment. If the freedmen were not permitted to vote, then the (white) voters in the South would overwhelmingly vote for the Democrats. Republicans would have no chance to gain any of the extra seats. With that concern in mind, the following clause had been inserted into Section 2 of the 14th Amendment:

> But when the right to vote at any election . . . is denied to any of the male inhab-
> itants of such State being twenty-one years of age and citizens of the United
> States or in any way abridged . . . the basis of representation therein shall be
> reduced in the proportion which the number of such male citizens shall bear to
> the whole number of male citizens twenty-one years of age in such State.

No application of this clause was ever implemented, but the situation was not dire for the Republican Party. The great majority of immigration and population expansion after the Civil War and up to World War I was in the North, Midwest, and far West, counterbalancing the temporary increase in the South's apportionment. Additionally, voters outside of the South were often importuned by Republican politicians "waving the bloody shirt." The message was to vote against the Democrats, the party of disloyalty, rebellion, and postwar racial violence. Immigration to the South was relatively low, because of the lack of job opportunities in a mainly agricultural region and the general xenophobia in that part of the country. The South would remain nearly solid for the Democrats until the Civil Rights movement of the 1960s. This renewal of concern in the late twentieth century, strongly supported by northern Democrats, drove many white southerners out of that party.

3.5   PROGRESS TOWARD INDIAN CITIZENSHIP

"Indians not taxed" were those aboriginal inhabitants who continued to live on lands not yet settled by whites or on lands specifically exempted from taxation by treaty. A few Indian tribes had been granted citizenship as a result of treaties. In 1884, the U.S. Supreme Court had ruled in *Elk v. Wilkins* that the 14th Amendment did not apply to American Indians in general. John Elk, born in a tribal area, could not under this ruling become a citizen by assimilating and living in Omaha, Nebraska. In 1887, Congress made the court's decision moot by adopting the General Allotment (or Dawes) Act (49th Congress, Sess. II, Chap. 119, Sec. 6). It stated that Indians "who adopted the habits of civilized life" and those who accepted private allotments of what had been tribal lands, were eligible to become citizens (Keyssar, 2000, p. 165). The number of American Indians who were citizens was too small to significantly affect apportionment and, assuming states would permit them to register and vote, it was not clear that they would vote overwhelmingly for one party, as in the case of African Americans.

3.6   COUNTERING ELECTION FRAUD IN THE
CITIES, 1868–1894

The situation in cities needed to be addressed differently than denial of voting rights in the South. The anonymity of city living, together with the failure to enact into law effective administrative procedures for elections, had made possible enormous frauds. The Tweed Ring had been a prime exemplar. The primary issue, differently than the South, was frauds related to voter registration and ballot counting.

> Most states did not have meaningful (or even any) registration laws, making it exceedingly difficult to determine voter eligibility . . . election officials were generally partisan, rather than nonpartisan or even bipartisan and mobs of excited party workers surrounded the polls. (Argersinger, 1986, p. 672)

The fraudulent 1868 general election in New York City, which included a presidential contest, had been brought to the attention of the Congress soon after it occurred. Of importance to the Republicans in New York was that the bogus inflation of votes perpetrated by Tammany Hall had cost them the governorship of the state as well as the electoral votes of New York State for U. S. Grant, their presidential nominee. Congress appointed a special committee (U.S. House of Representatives, Select Committee on Alleged New York Election Frauds, 1869) to investigate the New York situation, and it did so. Congress' apprehension was not limited to New York. Distress over similar situations in other large cities would be demonstrated by its forthcoming legislation.

U.S. Senator Roscoe Conkling, Republican of New York, was successful in having a section of legislation adopted in July 1870 to obtain federal supervision of voting for members of the House of Representatives. This enactment gave the U.S. Circuit Courts and its marshals authority to appoint deputy marshals and bipartisan supervisors of election in Congressional elections if a request were made for them. The legislation was used by Republicans to petition the local U.S. Circuit Court to appoint supervisors to observe the 1870 general election in New York City. According to historian Albie Burke, President Grant granted 10-day leaves of absence to all federal employees in the city to allow them to serve as the Republican members of the bipartisan supervisors of election. Military weapons were placed at the disposal of the deputy marshals. Tammany Hall, at that time under the control of Boss Tweed, supplied the Democratic members of the supervisors, and responded with press notices asking voters to come to the polls armed to assure their right to vote. Violence was narrowly averted by a last-minute agreement to let each side perform its official duties without interference. The effort at close observation of the election was successful. Despite an increase in the population since 1868, "the 1870 return counted was considerably less than that of 1868. In addition, two Tammany lieutenants, as a result of the surveillance, had been arrested and convicted for violating the state registration laws and given the maximum sentence" (Burke, 1970, pp. 24, 25).

The Federal Election Law of February 28, 1871 (41st Congress, Sess. III, Chap. 99) was an improved version of Conkling's legislation of 1870. The subject of the Law, except for its last two sections, 18 and 19, was voter registration for the election of representatives or delegates to the Congress. Section 1 was applicable to all places, not just to cities. It defined as a federal crime a large variety of actions that resulted in or attempted to perpetrate frauds in voter registration. It also made clear that any voter registration made for purposes of a state or other election and that might be used also as a registration for voting for Congressional representation was also covered.

Sections 2 through 17 of the Federal Election Law were only applicable to cities of more than 20,000 population. In these sections, an administrative structure was established under control of local federal judges to have voter registrations and elections for representatives or delegates to the Congress "guarded and scrutinized." ("Delegates" represented U.S. territories that were not states.) In any city meeting the population requirement, this activity could be put into place by a letter written by two citizens to the local judge of the U.S. Circuit Court. The judge would then be required to appoint, for every election district and voting precinct, a pair of citizens of "different political parties and able to read and write the English language" who would be designated as "supervisors of election." The judge would be required, also, to appoint a "chief supervisor of election" to assure performance of all the other supervisors. The chief supervisor could be partisan.

The application of the Federal Election Law was concentrated in the largest cities. The U.S. marshal was required to obtain special deputies, but their political affiliations were not required to be balanced. In many cases, they were not, "a weakness in the law which proved to be a great source of conflict as deputies were used over the years" (Burke, 1970, p. 19). The use of supervisors and deputy marshals slowly increased, reaching their highest level in 1892.

"In the early 1890s," states Burke, "the principle of national regulation of elections as a permanent program began to be looked on with disfavor." The work of John I. Davenport, a highly partisan Republican and the chief supervisor of election in New York City under the 1871 law, was pointed out by opponents. Davenport, whose book on election frauds in that city has been cited earlier, had compiled a highly accurate voter registration list. Nevertheless, he had been severely criticized for his overzealous actions, including extralegal attempts to invalidate and retrieve falsely issued certificates of naturalization. Also, the selection of deputy marshals had been shown to be deliberately partial:

> As the deputies were federal appointees, they were invariably Republican. Indeed, deputies were usually chosen from lists supplied by local Republican party officials . . . Some marshals even aided Republican repeaters in illegal voting and impersonation. (Argersinger, 1986, p. 686)

The 1871 law was repealed in 1894, during the second (Democratic) Cleveland administration. The Democrats had a majority in both Houses of Congress during 1893–1895 (53rd Congress).

3.7   FEDERAL LEGISLATION TO ALTER THE VOTING PROCESS, 1871–1872

Section 19 of the Federal Election Law was the first-ever Congressional legislation on voting technology. It states, in its totality:

> SEC. 19. *And be it further enacted*, That all votes for representatives in Congress shall hereafter be by written or printed ballot, any law of any State to the contrary notwithstanding; and all votes received or recorded contrary to the provisions of this section shall be of none effect.

In 1871, when the law was enacted, only Oregon and Kentucky were still using *vive voce* voting on a statewide basis. Oregon would adopt the ballot the very next year. The use of *vive voce* voting, should it be readopted or adopted by new states, would thwart the work of the supervisors of election and deputy marshals in identifying falsely computed vote totals. There would be no voter-approved hard-copy record of individual votes cast. With bribery and intimidation rampant, the use of *vive voce* voting would be a step backward. Additionally, the Federal Election Law gave specific instructions to the supervisors of election to position themselves close to the ballot boxes during voting and during ballot counting. If there were no ballots, these directions would be meaningless.

Section 19 was not repealed in 1894 with the other sections of the Federal Election Law. Note that it does not specify a "secret" ballot. The use of the term "ballot" only means that the voter's choices are conveyed by writing or printing on a piece of paper or other hard copy. It has been noted already that differences in the ballots supplied by political parties often made their identification nonsecret by poll watchers.

A reapportionment of the House of Representatives was established under the act of February 2, 1872 (42nd Congress, Sess. II, Chap. XI, Section 1) according to the ninth census of 1870. Section 2 of that act tightened the specifications for design of the single-member districts under which members of the House were to be elected. In 1842, Congress had required that the districts be composed of "contiguous territory." In the new legislation, it was required that representatives were to be

> elected by districts composed of contiguous territory, and containing as nearly as possible an equal number of inhabitants . . .

This law would not be considered in force beyond the reapportionment of the next census.

Dates for election of representatives and the start of each new Congress were set under Section 3 of that same act of February 2, 1872. The act established that elections for members of the U.S. House of Representatives were to occur on a uniform day every second year and, in every fourth year, that day would be same as previously established for appointment of presidential

Electors. Additionally, Section 3 reiterated that Congress would commence its new sessions on the fourth day of March next. Thus, if ballots of presidential Electors were to be opened in front of Congress on the second Wednesday in February, that action would occur with the old Congress, not the new one. Specifically, the Act stated:

> That the Tuesday next after the first Monday in November in the year eighteen hundred and seventy-six and . . . in every second year thereafter is hereby fixed and established as the day for the election . . . of Representatives and Delegates to the Congress commencing on the fourth day of March next thereafter.

The day for the convening of the new Congress and the day for the inauguration of the new president and vice president would be changed under the 20th Amendment in 1933.

3.8   RESOLVING THE HAYES–TILDEN ELECTION, 1876–1877

The presidential election of 1876 pitted Republican Rutherford B. Hayes, governor of Ohio, against Democrat Samuel J. Tilden, governor of New York. After the resolution of the 2000 presidential election between George W. Bush and Albert Gore, Jr., similarities would be seen between the two contests. In both races, the loser had a plurality of the popular vote and the winner was not finally established until a significant time after the election. After the nineteenth-century match-up, some were noting that Hayes prevailed over Tilden by just one vote, eight–seven, in the special Electoral Commission established by Congress to consider contradictory certificates of election from four states. In 2000, some would claim that Bush won over Gore by just one vote, five–four, in the U.S. Supreme Court. In both cases, the vote count from Florida was controversial but, in 1876, the situation in Louisiana was even more contentious.

Conditions during the previous administration headed by U. S. Grant helped set the stage for the close balance of the political parties in 1876. While Grant was personally honest, many of his close associates were not. In the Congress and in the Executive Branch, graft and bribery were rampant. Special privileges were for sale. Soon after Grant was reelected, the Panic of 1873 caused serious financial harm to the country, putting millions out of work and causing the bankruptcy of many businesses. A result of that disaster was that the Democrats gained control of the House of Representatives in the Congressional election of 1874. The Republicans retained the Senate. This divided outcome would be most significant in creating the stalemate that prevented a quick conclusion to the 1876 election.

As the date of the election approached, the common wisdom was that Tilden would win. That appeared likely despite the fact that the Republicans were very well funded. The latter had been in office since Lincoln's first election, which meant that they could count on the support of nearly all federal employees. As noted by Roy Morris, Jr.:

> thousands of federal employees owed their very livelihoods to patronage. Government workers earning over $1000 a year were expected, in return, to contribute a strict 2 percent of their salaries to the Republican party campaign fund; those who refused would find their names on a list of uncooperative individuals forwarded to their immediate superiors. (Morris, 2003, p. 120)

By the autumn of 1876, Union troops had been withdrawn from eight of the eleven former Confederate states and the Democrats were now in control of them. (They had been "redeemed" in the vernacular of the time.) That was possible because, in 1872, the mood of the Congress had begun to be less punitive toward the South. A law had been adopted in that year restoring office-holding rights to many of those southerners who were previously disqualified under the 14th Amendment, Section 3, for having "engaged in insurrection or rebellion."

In the days immediately following the election, it appeared that the electoral votes of the states won by the Democrats added to 184, but 185 were needed to win the election. Hayes' uncontested electoral votes added to 165, so far; but there were 19 votes in the three doubtful Southern states with federal troops and Republican governors: South Carolina, Florida, and Louisiana. Additionally, one electoral vote from Oregon would be contested. If Hayes could win the three unredeemed Southern states and hold the vote from Oregon, then he, not Tilden, would obtain the necessary 185 electoral votes. The keys to the election in the Southern states were in the hands of the state-level election boards. These panels had complete power to produce the final returns in their states. In Louisiana and South Carolina, they were totally in the hands of Republicans. In Florida, the board consisted of two Republicans and one Democrat.

Soon, politicians from the North came to all three contested southern states. Supposedly, they were there to assure that deliberations and results announced by the election boards were consistent with the votes cast. W. E. Chandler, a member of the Republican National Committee, brought a valise to Florida filled with $10,000 in cash.

In South Carolina, turmoil was such that two legislatures were sworn in, one dominated by Democrats, the other led by Republicans. On December 6, the day of meeting of the presidential Electors, two sets of Electors voted. A certificate for Hayes was signed by the incumbent Republican governor; a certificate for Tilden was submitted by the Democratic legislature and signed by the Democratic gubernatorial candidate. The latter claimed victory. Both certificates were separately forwarded to Congress, directed to the president of the U.S. Senate, per the 12th Amendment to the Constitution.

In Florida, there were serious attempts at bribery of the state election board. Zach Chandler, chairman of the Republican National Committee, had written a letter to one board member containing the following language:

> W. E. Chandler has gone to Florida to see you with full powers to act and make terms. You can put a man in the Cabinet or elsewhere if you choose to demand it. . . . Agree to carry the state . . . and you can have your own terms in your hands. [Robinson, 2001 (1968), p. 124]

Other communications between Zach Chandler and the head of the Florida Republican Party suggest that at least $2,000 was paid through that channel to further Hayes' chances. In a similar vein, Democrats thought that they had made a deal to carry Florida and its governorship for $200,000. This deal fell through; it is likely that Tilden vetoed the plan.

Initially, the returns showed that Tilden had won by a margin of less than 100 votes. The state election board voided many Tilden votes under its absolute power to eliminate returns "so irregular, false or fraudulent that the board shall be unable to determine the true vote." Based on the election board's decision, the Republican Electors met and voted for Hayes. They submitted a certificate to Congress on December 6 signed by Republican governor Marcellus Stearns who, supposedly, had been reelected. The Democratic Electors also met and voted for Tilden, submitting a certificate signed by the attorney general.

A recount was ordered by the State Supreme Court in the contest for governor, and it showed that Democrat George Drew had really won over incumbent Governor Stearns. Drew was inaugurated in early January; the Democratic Electors met again and voted for Tilden again. They submitted a second certificate for Tilden signed by Drew on January 19, 1877. The last certificate was produced "on the basis of a careful re-canvassing of returns" (Morris, 2003, p. 220).

In Louisiana, the state election board consisted of four Republicans. A fifth member, a Democrat, had resigned in disgust over some of the board's unsavory activities in the past. The other members of the board had the power to replace him with another Democrat, but had failed to exercise it. (Both parties had to be represented on the board, by Louisiana law.) Thus, when the board went into a closed session, there would be no way the Democrats would find out the details of the discussion.

The election board had the absolute power to throw out any vote that they considered fraudulent. They threw out 13,211 votes for Tilden and 2,412 votes for Hayes. It was important for them to throw out enough ballots to prevent any of Tilden's Electors from winning. (Electors were still running separately). If only one of his Electors won, he would have the necessary 185 electoral votes to become president. On December 6, the Republican presidential Electors voted for Hayes; two of the Electors were federal office holders (see later, *In Oregon*). In Louisiana, there was a Democrat-dominated rump legislature and a Democrat shadow governor who filed a certificate for Tilden. They had existed since a disputed election of 1872 but federal troops assured the dominance of the Republican legislature.

There was evidence that the Republicans in general and U.S. senator John Sherman in particular had provided funds to smooth the way for Hayes' election.

In Oregon, the state's voters had elected the three presidential Electors to which Oregon was entitled. They were Republicans but one of them was a U.S. postmaster. This employment made him ineligible, under the Constitution, Article II: "no . . . Person holding Office of Trust or Profit under the United States, shall be appointed an Elector." John Watts, the postmaster, had been told that he could resign after the election and then be rehired after he cast his vote. He resigned one week after the election. Others read the law differently. The contrary opinion was that votes cast for a presidential Elector who was a federal office holder were void; the person who received the next highest number of votes should be appointed.

The governor of Oregon, a Democrat, decided that Watts had not been eligible to appear on the ballot, and appointed the next-highest vote getter among the candidates for presidential Elector. That person was a Democrat, and would vote for Tilden. A certificate signed by the governor was submitted to Congress showing two votes for Hayes and one for Tilden.

The two clearly elected Republican Electors decided that there was a vacancy for the third Elector, and they followed Oregon law for such vacancies by meeting together and appointing a third person. That person was Watts. Their certificate for Hayes was signed by the Oregon secretary of state.

In Congress, it was not clear who was to make the final decision to accept or reject a specific certificate. The Constitution, Amendment 12, stated: "The President of the Senate shall, in the presence of the Senate and the House of Representatives, open all the certificates and the votes shall then be counted . . ."

The Republicans controlled the Senate. They insisted that the wording of the 12th Amendment meant that it was the president of the Senate who would decide which certificates to accept or reject. They assumed that the certificates favorable to Hayes would be accepted and all others would be rejected. In the Democrats' view, all competing certificates should be put aside and results announced based on the uncontested certificates. Then, neither Hayes nor Tilden would have the majority of the electoral votes cast, and the election would be thrown into the House of Representatives. Tilden would be the beneficiary of this process, as the Democrats controlled the House. Negotiations finally produced a compromise.

A bipartisan Electoral Commission would be empowered to review all the competing certificates and choose the ones to be accepted by Congress. The fifteen-member commission would be composed of ten members of Congress including five Democrats and five Republicans, four Supreme Court justices, including two Democrats and two Republicans, and a fifth justice selected by the other four. It was planned that the fifth Supreme Court justice would be David Davis of Illinois, an independent. No one had taken the trouble to ask

Davis if he would serve. Almost immediately after the Electoral Commission had been established, it was discovered that Davis would decline the honor. The justices selected Republican justice Joseph P. Bradley of New Jersey. That decision would prove to be the death knell of Tilden's chances.

The deliberations of the commission occurred while Congress was counting the electoral votes, beginning on February 1, 1877. As the states were named in alphabetical order, if an objection was raised to its submitted certificate(s), the issue was sent to the commission. Objections were received as the names of Florida, Louisiana, Oregon, and South Carolina were being read. Congress halted its work each time, until the commission had made its decision on the particular state.

All the decisions of the Electoral Commission were on a party-line vote, eight–seven. All the certificates for Hayes were accepted and all the certificates for Tilden rejected. The commission majority refused to investigate the situations, basing their decision on "the face of the returns." In the case of Florida, the commission accepted the certificate signed by a governor who had really been defeated for reelection and rejected the one from the lawful governor because it had been "late." In the case of Oregon, the certificate signed by the lawful governor was rejected.

A strategy of filibuster was considered by the Democrats in the House on February 17. They figured that they still had a chance by preventing the count of electoral votes from being completed by talking nonstop until March 4. The latter date was when the term of office of President U. S. Grant ended and the mandate of the Electoral Commission expired. It was not clear what would happen if there were no president, but the northern Democrats were totally frustrated as the commission inexorably voted for all certificates selecting Hayes.

Southern Democrats would not agree to a filibuster. Their first priority was the removal of federal troops and the "redemption" of the last three southern states. In private discussions with influential Republicans, culminating in a meeting in Washington on February 26, they agreed to go along with Hayes' election if federal troops were withdrawn and the elected Democratic governors were allowed to take office. Finally, many Democrats, including northerners, realized that the choice at this late date was Hayes or anarchy. The electoral count was finished and Hayes was declared to be elected to the presidency in the early morning hours of Friday, March 2.

3.9   THE ELECTORAL COUNT ACT

In 1887, Congress enacted a law (49th Congress, Sess. II, Chap. 90) that addressed some of the ambiguities and gaps in the Constitution and federal law that had been the source of the stalemate in counting the electoral votes in 1876. It may have taken the ten years since the finalization of Hayes' electoral victory to eliminate the bitterness and concern for illegitimacy to generate enough rationality and inter-party cooperation. The first administration of Grover Cleveland was in office.

The first section of the act established the day for the presidential Electors to meet and give their votes as the second Monday in January following their own election. Previously, the day had been the first Wednesday in December (see section 2.5). That day would change again in 1928 to the first Wednesday in January (70th Congress, Sess. I, Chap. 859). In 1934, it would change to the first Monday after the second Wednesday in December (73rd Congress, Sess. II, Chap. 390, Sec. 6(a)).

Section 2 of the act provided that if the final determination of any contest concerning appointment of Electors shall have been made at least six days prior to the time of meeting of the Electors, that determination would be conclusive. The implication of "conclusive" is that no member of Congress, in the counting of electoral votes, could challenge the determination. This stipulation was referred to in the 2000 presidential election controversy as the "safe harbor" provision. A further qualification in the act required that the State law under which the final determination was made was in effect at that time; that is, it could not be a retroactive law.

Section 3 provided that after the final determination of the Electors, it was the duty of the governor of each State and under its seal, to send a certificate containing the Electors' names and votes cast for all the candidates for Elector to a particular office of the federal government from which it would be conveyed eventually to the president of the Senate. In addition, the governor was to send a certificate of election with the State seal to each Elector. The Electors were required to include their certificates when "transmitting . . . to the seat of Government the lists of all persons voted for as President and of all persons voted for as Vice-President." If there were a later determination under State law of a change in Electors, possibly by "judicial methods," it was the duty of the State's governor and the new Electors to repeat the process.

According to Section 4, Congress is to open all the certificates and count them, beginning on the second Wednesday in February at 1:00 p.m. following the meetings of the Electors. [In 1934, Congress changed that date to be January 6 (73rd Congress, Sess. II, Chap. 390, Sec. 7).] The Senate and House of Representatives are to meet together in the Hall of the House with the president of the Senate serving as the presiding officer. Certificates are to be examined in alphabetical order of the states, beginning with the letter "A." Objections to any certificate are to be made in writing signed by at least one member of each legislative body.

There is no clause anywhere in the act that specifies a day beyond which a certificate may be rejected as being late. In fact, the act states that if the certificate has not been received by a specific date, efforts are to be made by federal officials to send a messenger to obtain it. A reasonable implication to be drawn from the verbiage is that a certificate must be in the hands of the president of the Senate soon enough so that objections, if any, may be presented before the certificate is considered by Congress for counting. Conceivably, the certificate could arrive some short time before the name of its state is called in alphabetic order.

When an objection is made by a member of each body, further consideration of certificates will cease until the particular situation is resolved. The House and Senate will separately debate the matter and reconvene together when both have come to a decision. If both bodies agree on either counting or not counting a certificate, the action jointly agreed will be carried out. If the two bodies disagree on a particular certificate, "the votes of the Electors whose appointment shall have been certified by the Executive of the State, under the seal thereof, shall be counted." After the resolution of the issue, the certificate from the next state in alphabetic order will be considered.

Sections 5, 6, and 7 of the act concern maintaining an orderly process in the counting of the electoral votes by the Congress. Particular attention is paid to enforcing time limits on debate and limitations on recesses taken, in order to prevent a filibuster or other delaying tactic. Finally, the "joint meeting shall not to be dissolved until the count of electoral votes is completed and the result declared."

Several changes have been made to the Electoral Count Act since it was first enacted. A major reenactment was completed in 1948 (80th Congress, Sess. II, Chap. 644). The basic substance of the original act remains the same. The date established for the Electors to meet and vote, as well as the date for Congress to be in session to receive the certificates, are those set in 1934.

3.10 THE EXTENT OF ELECTION FRAUD IN THE LATE NINETEENTH CENTURY

Historians of American politics have argued among themselves about whether there was more election fraud in this era than at other times, and if so, how much more. Certainly, there wasn't any less. The problem in arriving at a definitive answer is that the evidence cannot be quantified, and even the boundaries of the category "election fraud" are controversial. Election crimes that have resulted in overturning the true outcome generally will not have been disclosed by the perpetrators (except for occasional boasts when prosecution was not possible). Unlike a crime against property, the victims cannot report missing personal artifacts for which they have records.

Some quantifications are possible. Certainly, a high level of election fraud in the late nineteenth century would be consistent with the low state of public ethics of the era. The Tweed Ring scandal and the 1876 presidential election outrage were more likely to be closer to typical than closer to unique. Historians who have studied the subject have presented some quantified information in connection with their research. For example, Robert Goldman has reported statistics for federal law enforcement activities in the South under the Enforcement Act of 1870 (Goldman, 2001, p. xxiii):

For the years 1870 through 1876: 3,554 election cases were brought to trial, 1,180 convictions were achieved (a 33% conviction rate);

For the years 1877 through 1893: 3,387 election cases were brought to trial, 835 convictions were achieved (a 24% conviction rate).

These statistics show that through 1876, there were, on average, about ten indictments issued every week, but in the later period there were somewhat fewer than four cases brought to trial each week with a somewhat lower conviction rate. The difference may be due to the fact that once the southern white elite redeemed their states, less violence and fraud was needed to maintain control. Also, there was less interest in Washington in providing the necessary resources for prosecutions. Goldman's research did not extend beyond 1893, so that comparison with later activity by the Department of Justice is not possible from his work. To a layperson, the indictment rate of ten per week over seven years, or even four per week over the next seventeen years certainly seems to demonstrate a significant effort unlikely to have been equaled in the twentieth century.

Albie Burke (Burke, 1970, p. 97) presents the costs of the Federal Election Law of 1871, for each year from 1871 through 1894. The total cost of the law was over $4.6 million, but for 1892 alone, the cost was about $0.92 million—about 20 percent of the total. The number of deputy marshals used increased every year, and Burke reports that "In 1890, the number of federal officials at the polls in New York City alone was over 10,000." The activity under the act says nothing about its value, but the increasing requests for deputy marshals each federal election cycle demonstrates that some part of the voting public in the larger cities felt the need for additional assurance of election integrity. As the law was repealed in 1894, no comparisons with other periods can be made. The assignment of federal officials to serve in elections began again in the South under the Voting Rights Act of 1965 (see section 5.5). It had been an interval of more than 70 years before the concept was palatable again to members of Congress and the citizenry that they represent.

Two authors concerned with comparing the amount of election fraud in different periods (Allen and Allen, 1981, p. 177) have reported the number of contested elections for membership in the House of Representatives, from the 1st Congress (began 1789) through the 64th Congress (ended 1917). This data was taken from two public documents of the House, Document No. 510 of the 56th Congress and Document No. 2052 of the 64th Congress. Of the 214 elections contested on the basis of fraud, bribery, or intimidation, 127 or nearly 60 percent occurred in the 30 years between 1869 and 1899. From 1789 to 1869, there were 56 contested elections and from 1899 to 1917, there were 31. In the three decades, 1869 to 1899, the South and Border States had two-thirds of all contested House elections. The authors ascribe this preponderance to issues of Reconstruction. The remaining one-third were primarily in the industrialized Northeast and in the Midwestern states east of the Mississippi River.

Additional evidence of election fraud has been provided by historical research into situations in particular states at particular times. Much of this evidence is supported, in different examples, by judicial transcripts, committee reports of state legislatures, articles from newspapers of the times, or retained correspondence. A categorization, as given here, aids in organizing the descriptions:

The extent of bribery of ordinary voters in the late nineteenth century may be painful to realize for the issue-oriented activist of today. The idealist wants voters to be convinced by the force of political ideas, but that was not necessarily the case at that time. Richard P. McCormick makes the situation quite clear about conditions in New Jersey. He notes that a special committee of that state's legislature found in 1883 that "a large proportion of . . . the voting population depended upon election day as a regular source of income" (McCormick, 1953, pp. 159–162). In 1889, on November 8, the (Trenton) *State Gazette* newspaper wrote that "There was never such open, wholesale bribing of voters as in Tuesday's election. Both parties were equally guilty." In preparation for an election, according to a legislative committee report, "ward workers were given stacks of money at the same time that they picked up stacks of ballots to be distributed among their constituents." The number of bribable voters statewide was estimated at 50,000; about 270,000 votes were cast for governor in that year. Another New Jersey researcher has written that "perhaps as much as one-third of the electorate commonly accepted money for their votes."

New Jersey was not unique. "Money, or 'soap' as it was called, with increasing frequency was used to carry elections after the Civil War" (Evans, 1917, p. 11). Many people, particularly in rural environments, expected their party to pay them for the time to go to the polls and return. A study in 1892 claimed that 16 percent of voters of Connecticut were bribable at prices fluctuating between two and twenty dollars. Other research described massive vote buying that began in 1890 and continued for two decades in rural Adams County, Ohio (which borders the Ohio River some 50 miles east of Cincinnati). In 1910 in that county, a quarter of the electorate, about 1,700 voters, were convicted of vote selling (Argersinger, 1986, pp. 673, 674).

In San Francisco during some years in the 1880s, boss Chris Buckley stood outside the polls wearing an overcoat with his hands in "his pockets filled with quarter eagles." (A $10 U.S. gold coin was known as an eagle. A quarter eagle was worth $2.50 and was about as large as a dime. They were minted at various times from 1796 to 1929.) After a voter had cast his ballot according to his promise, the worker who accompanied him to the polls and watched him cast his ballot would introduce him to the boss. As the boss shook hands with the voter, "the consideration for the vote was easily passed" (Overacker, 1932, p. 33). In Baltimore, there was a tradition of getting out the vote with funds called "walking-around money." Cash was given to functionaries whose job it was to visit neighborhoods on election day. Such cash may have been passed on to neighborhood leaders who promoted voting to their neighbors of similar party affiliation.

Organized bribery at a higher level was not unknown. The 1888 presidential election, described by historian Peter H. Argersinger as "flagrantly corrupt," was won by Republican Benjamin Harrison of Indiana. Harrison lost the popular vote but defeated incumbent Grover Cleveland in his home state of

New York by 13,000 votes. It is believed by some historians that a few Democratic leaders in New York City and Brooklyn (the two cities were still separate at the time) agreed on vote trading (Reynolds and McCormick, 1986, p. 849); that is, they may have agreed to "knife" Cleveland by printing and distributing irregular "Democratic" ballots showing Harrison as their candidate for president. "One leader, it was said, took $25,000 to deliver 3,500 votes in six wards to Harrison" (Josephson, 1938, p. 431). Following Harrison's victory and his pious thanking of Providence for it, Republican national chairman Matt Quay was quoted as remarking to a friend that Providence had nothing to do with it. "Harrison," he said, "would never know how close a number of men were compelled to approach the gates of the penitentiary to make him President."

At the same time as Cleveland was losing, his rival in the Democratic Party, Governor David B. Hill (see also section 3.11), was being reelected by 19,000 votes. One report suggests that "independent" Democratic clubs, at a price, distributed Republican ballots with Hill's name pasted in for governor. *The New York Times* stated at the time that "the electoral votes of the State of New York were sold by Governor Hill" (Josephson, 1938, pp. 430, 431). However, Hill's biographer states that it was not in Hill's interest to have Cleveland lose. If Cleveland had been reelected, Hill would have had a clearer field for the next Democratic presidential nomination (Bass, 1961, p. 123).

Ballot stuffing was widespread. In 1896, the *Dallas Morning News* revealed that Harrison County, Texas, continually produced the largest Democratic majorities in the state, even though two-thirds of its voters were black (and likely to vote Republican in that era). Texas counties were permitted to use two ballot boxes in the late nineteenth century to separate federal contests from state and local contests. The different ballot boxes enabled fraud to be perpetrated on the nonfederal level while national-level contests were kept honest. Fear of federal prosecution was genuine; a state trial was unlikely. It was noted by observers that the Democrats had roughly 2,000 more votes in each election for state and local contests than they achieved in the federal elections. Ballot stuffing of this type in Texas was known as "Harrison County Methods" at that time (Miller, 1995, pp. 111–128).

In 1878 in South Carolina, several Democratic election managers went on trial for permitting the use of "tissue ballots" in order to secure a larger vote. "The use of these ballots, also called 'kiss ballots' was perhaps one of the most widespread and ingenious methods of fraud used . . . in the South generally" (Goldman, 2001, p. 68). The tissue ballot looked like an ordinary ballot, but really consisted of a number of thin identical ballots loosely stuck together. The ballots were voted as one. After the close of polls, the ballot boxes were deliberately and vigorously shaken to separate the tissue ballots. The ballot-box shaking demonstrated that the election officials were in on the fraud. If the perpetrators were not careful, the number of ballots cast would exceed the number of registered voters on the poll lists. Then, some ballots would be randomly discarded by a blindfolded inspector. However, this tactic at least assured that as many voters as possible had voted for the Democratic ticket, even if they were elsewhere at the time.

Tissue ballots were also used in the North (good ideas get around). In an investigation in New Jersey of a State Senate contest in Hudson County in 1887, the ballot boxes in one-quarter of the districts were examined. Over 1,800 illegal ballots had been voted, most of them of the tissue-ballot type (McCormick, 1953, p. 172). The committee investigating the situation admired the expertise of the party workers who had put the ballots together. They opined that the effort had required previous training, implying that this situation was not the first time it was done.

In another type of scam, ingenious ballot boxes were designed to hide extra ballots in secret compartments. To counter the problem of ballot stuffing, redesigned ballot boxes began to be used in some places. They might be made of glass, or they might count the ballots as they were inserted. See section 4.1 for a more extensive discussion.

The use of floaters and voter registration frauds were common. In Maryland in 1880, a Baltimore politician confessed that he had taken nine felons from the Baltimore jail to the rural village of Clarksville. There, each of them voted in turn. They kept going around in a circle, revoting until they had voted all the names on the register. Times change. Now, over 120 years later, Clarksville includes the recently constructed Village of River Hill in the new town of Columbia in overwhelmingly white-collar Howard County. Voter registration requirements are considerably more effective now.

Indiana was a state with loose voter registration laws. The floater vote in Indiana was estimated at 10,000 in 1880, 15,000 in 1884, and 20,000 in 1888 (Josephson, 1938, p. 430). Money needed to be raised to pay these floaters, and that was often done at the state party level or even by the national party. Indiana's reputation for this type of fraud is highlighted by the infamous letter sent from W. W. Dudley, the Republican national treasurer to a local Republican committee leader in that state on October 24, 1888. The letter was leaked and widely republished (Wesser, 1971, p. 1697). Among its contents are the following:

> Your Committee will certainly receive . . . the assistance necessary to hold our floaters and doubtful voters . . . find out who has Democratic boodle, and steer the Democratic workers to them, and make them pay big prices for their own men . . . Divide the floaters into blocks of five, and put a trusted man with the necessary funds in charge of these five, and make him responsible that none get away and that all vote our ticket . . .

It has been reported that in the 1896 election in Indiana, "there were 30,000 floaters reported by watchers as receiving, besides sandwiches and liquor, only $5 a head in this year of depression" (Josephson, 1938, p. 706).

In the ballot-stuffing incident discussed above concerning New Jersey in 1887, it was found that there had been about 10,000 false registrations for the contest in question.

> Scores of voters registered from tugs, canal boats and cheap hotels. The poll lists contained the names of men who had been dead for fifteen years. Gangs of

"repeaters" brought across [the river from New York City] voted as often as ten times in as many election districts. (McCormick, 1953, p. 171)

Intimidation was a common tactic. Top Republican leaders, including the aforementioned W. W. Dudley, importuned corporate leaders to find ways of assuring that their employees would vote for the party. Threats of economic reprisal were made and, in some cases, deposit of ballots were carefully watched at polling places to assure compliance with management's views. In 1885, it was reported in a Congressional inquiry that workers at one of the federal government's own naval yards were required to take ballots in a folded form from a table presided over by one of the foremen and carry them, unopened, to the polls about 100 feet away, where they were required to deposit them without knowledge of the candidates for whom they were voting (Argersinger, 1986, pp. 678, 682).

In the 1888 national election campaign, intimidation of workers was a significant factor:

> The large manufacturers in New York and in the Middle West worked in concert to intimidate their employees. Through them, the [Republican] party organization struck at the pocketbooks of proletarian voters. From Buffalo and Troy in the closing weeks of the canvass came reports that workers in big iron and textile mills were being provoked to panic by threats of unemployment. (Josephson, 1938, p. 428)

This tactic was officially recognized and denounced in 1889 when New York's governor Hill "urged the legislature to punish as a crime the use of pay envelopes which threatened employees with loss of jobs if they should fail to vote as directed" (Bass, 1961, p. 129).

The widespread use of intimidation by employers and creditors was a major reason that the secret ballot was desired by labor organizations. A Philadelphia newspaper, the *Journal of United Labor*, noted in 1889 that the workingman's political preferences "were smothered by the decree of his employer, who dictates what ticket he must vote." A similar sentiment was expressed in *The New York Times* on October 11, 1891, in opposing a lawsuit then being pursued in Ohio to declare the recently adopted Australian ballot unconstitutional in that state. In a column datelined Cleveland, Ohio, the newspaper opined that

> the large manufacturing population of this State has always been more or less intimidated, and it is estimated that about 15,000 voters in the two counties of Hamilton [Cincinnati] and Cuyahoga [Cleveland] alone have been more or less influenced by their employers.

Blatant disregard of election results occurred. Third parties and other independent upstarts were more often the victim of these kinds of frauds than either Republicans or Democrats, the Hayes/Tilden situation excepted. The minor parties, which were newer, did not have members entrenched in powerful offices, and so were more vulnerable. Here are some examples:

Terence Powderly, a Pennsylvania Greenbacker and labor leader of the 1870s wrote that he was defeated by local election judges who, without justification, assigned the Democratic candidate enough extra votes to win. Well-known reformer Henry George (see also section 3.11), running for mayor of New York City on a Labor ticket in 1886, complained that ballots cast for him were counted for his Democratic opponent. In 1893, in Kansas, a Republican candidate was awarded an elected office because of the transposition of voting totals with his Populist opponent, a ploy of the Republican county clerk that the State Board acknowledged but refused to correct. In 1897, the Indiana legislature voted on partisan lines to unseat Populists who, all reports conceded, had received the majority of popular votes (Argersinger, 1986, pp. 675, 676, 683).

Another form of blatant disregard of the results is the replacement of real voted ballots by false ones. In Vincennes, Indiana, in 1889 (Zukerman, 1925, p. 11), the entire contents of a box of ballots were removed and burned, and false ballots substituted.

Corrupt elections over county seats were a feature of settlement of the Great Plains. With the expansion of the railroad network, the prairies began to be populated. Between 1870 and 1890, areas such as Kansas and the Dakotas grew in large multiples of population. A governor would declare that a county had been organized, and officials would be named to govern it temporarily. One of the next major steps would be to establish a county seat—a town selected as the place where the county courthouse would be built, the county governing board would meet, and county officials would have their offices. Banks and a newspaper publisher would be desired, and possibly a library. In many newly formed counties, no settlement had any natural reason to be selected over any other. The prices of land in the selected town might rise significantly over prices in the unselected location, and the decision on selection would be made by a vote of the county residents. Thus, land speculation and dreams of riches drove promoters of particular towns to perpetrate the wildest methods for winning the election.

Much of the trouble in the 1880s occurred in Kansas. James R. Chiles, author of an entertaining article on these altercations, presents this quote from a leading Kansas newspaper in 1889: "Every side of every county seat contest in Kansas is charged with fraud and corruption, and in the majority of cases, the charge is true." One of the worst situation occurred in the election in 1887 in Gray County, Kansas (Chiles, 1990, pp. 100–110, 154). The center of Gray County is about 20 miles from Dodge City, renowned for its gun fights of the era.

Daniel Boorstin has described noteworthy situations that occurred in Grant County and Stevens County, both in Kansas. In Grant County, "voters in [the town of] Ulysses were paid off at the rate of ten dollars apiece as they cast their ballots." In Stevens County, "a county seat war between Hugoton and Woodsdale involved kidnaping, assassination, bribery, the use of militia, and several criminal trials which reverberated for over a quarter of a century" (Boorstin, 1965, p. 167). The men and women of the frontier were used to taking matters into their own hands, and they did so in these cases. As the counties became more settled, most of the violence ended. Hard feelings between some rival places took quite a while to dissipate.

3.11   ADOPTION OF THE AUSTRALIAN BALLOT

The Australian ballot is one that is officially produced, includes candidates of all parties, is available only on election day, and is cast in secret by the voter. Its use began in the Australian state of Victoria in 1856, followed by South Australia later the same year. Two other Australian states began to employ it in 1858 and New Zealand did so in 1870. In Great Britain, there had been proposals in Parliament for the secret ballot since 1830. Oral voting was still being used there in the 1860s. Political leaders of the parties opposed the nonpartisan ballot, as did philosopher John Stuart Mill. The latter's view was that voting "was not a right but a duty and should be exercised publicly in accordance with the voter's most conscientious opinion of the public good" (Fredman, 1968, p. 12). Mill's views would make sense if the only persons granted suffrage were independently wealthy and could not be personally disadvantaged by their votes. A strongly restricted suffrage was the desire of English conservatives at the time. Today, in democratically elected legislatures as well as in other public bodies, voting is generally expected to be open, although legislators may hide behind non-individualized voice votes on some issues. In 1872, a British act requiring the use of the Australian ballot for elections for Parliament and for municipalities was adopted. The method was soon enacted in Canada, Belgium, and Italy.

Pioneers of the Australian ballot in the United States included Henry George (1839–1897). He proposed the concept in an article in the *Overland Monthly* entitled "Bribery in Elections" in December of 1871. The essay countered several of the objections that would be made against the new voting arrangement. George, who was working as an editor in California at the time, noted that an official ballot removed the excuse for party assessments for printing and distributing ballots, and that a truly secret ballot minimized bribery in that it prevented the assurance that a bribed voter carried out his bargain (Fredman, 1968, p. 32). Another article by George entitled "Money in Elections," in the *North American Review* of March 1883 also recommended the Australian ballot. The *Review* was a very influential journal nationwide.

The Philadelphia Civil Service Reform Association advocated the nonpartisan, official ballot in a pamphlet it published in 1882 entitled "English Elections." Robert Schilling, head of a labor union and Greenback party in Cleveland, and later leader of the Knights of Labor and Populist party in Milwaukee, advocated ballot reform in 1881 as editor of the Milwaukee *National Reformer*. He would become, in 1891, national secretary of the

Populist party. That party's statement at their 1892 convention in favor of the Australian ballot is reported later.

The United Labor party, formed in 1886 following Henry George's unsuccessful bid for the mayoralty of New York, put the need for the Australian ballot in their platform of 1888. They were the first national party to do so. Their platform stated:

> We especially and emphatically declare for the adoption of what is known as the Australian system of voting, in order that the effectual secrecy of the ballot, and the relief of candidates for public office from the heavy expenses now imposed upon them, may prevent bribery and intimidation, do away with practical discrimination in favor of the rich and unscrupulous, and lessen the pernicious influence of money in politics. (Fredman, 1968, p. 33)

In New York City, William Mills Ivins (1851–1915) was a champion of election reform, including adoption of the Australian ballot. A well-respected lawyer, he served in a number of highly placed but nonpolitical public offices during his lifetime. He had published two articles on the subject in *Harper's Weekly* in the fall of 1884 and gave three speeches at dinners of the Commonwealth Club of New York in early 1887. Men's clubs were common and politically significant at the time, and the Commonwealth Club had an outlook of reform. It attracted literary and upper-class men of a wide political spectrum. Members included some whose names are still prominently mentioned in histories of political reform, for example, R. R. Bowker, George W. Curtis, E. L. Godkin, and Carl Schurz, as well as Theodore Roosevelt. Roosevelt had previously been a founder of the City Reform Club. Ivins's writings and speeches aroused considerable interest; also, a book of his views was published also in 1887. The book contains the essence of his proposals on the benefits of a publicly printed, all-party ballot (Ivins, 1970 (1887), pp. 65–89).

The credit for the first introduction of an Australian ballot bill in any state legislature goes to George Walthew of Detroit, a Greenbacker and Democrat, in 1885. His bill, submitted to the lower house of the Michigan legislature and based on Canada's legislation, was soundly defeated. Two years later, another bill was submitted to the same assembly by Judson Grenell and was adopted, but failed in the state Senate. Grenell was associated with the Knights of Labor. Away from the East Coast, leading advocates were much less likely to be part of the literary or academic establishments.

The first Australian ballot legislation approved in a state legislature was in Kentucky in 1888, but the act only applied to city elections in Louisville. Advocates for the bill said that they had been influenced by Henry George's 1883 article in the *North American Review*. Strangely, Kentucky was still using oral voting, the last state to do so, and would not end that practice until 1891, when secret ballot legislation was adopted for the whole state.

Massachusetts was the first to adopt the Australian ballot statewide, and the person most responsible for this was Richard Henry Dana III. Dana had old-line Yankee roots, an illustrious father and grandfather, and a degree from Harvard where he excelled in sports. He had helped craft the state's first civil service law in 1883, and also wrote the Australian ballot law, which was enacted in 1888. He began to appreciate the need for the blanket ballot when he observed the tumult at polling stations on election day. A prospective voter was besieged with ticket peddlers each thrusting a separate party's ballot at him. Independent candidates hawked stickers or "pasters." (Pasters were small labels containing the name of an alternate candidate, which could be pasted over the name of the official candidate. Paste pots and brushes were available at some locations to complete the gluing process.) Some of the ballots available were irregular, in that they slyly replaced one or more of a party's candidates with others. Party observers at the polling place could see which ballot the voter had accepted and could follow the voter to the ballot box to assure that he had cast it. Violence at the polling station or nearby was not uncommon. Printing of ballots by the parties and hiring of ticket peddlers resulted in significant campaign costs.

Dana's observations at polling stations were no different than those of thousands of others, but Dana had the will and connections to undertake action. He obtained assistance of friends of civil service reform and of labor organizations. They assisted his crafting of the legislation and managed its progress through the state legislature. When the law was implemented the next year, Dana recalled the new situation:

> I went about the polls, especially in the districts that used to be rough and noisy, where I had seen a man's coat torn off his back, crowds pushing voters away and ballots taken out of men's hands and others substituted . . . All was going on very quietly and in a perfectly dignified manner and that was almost worth the whole of our efforts to obtain the law. (Blodgett, 1966, p. 115)

The Massachusetts Act *to Provide for Printing and Distributing Ballots and the Public Expense, and to Regulate Voting at State and City Elections (1888)* provided for an "office-block" arrangement of candidates (Wigmore, 1889, pp. 58–73). That is, names of all candidates for a single office were presented together in a sequence, in alphabetic order. The voter would record his choice by making an "X" in a box next to his selection. As other states adopted the office-block ballot, the order of the candidates might be determined by a party sequence. In later approvals, the "party column" ballot arrangement, initiated in Indiana, would become popular. In the latter format, all candidates nominated by a particular party were listed in a column under the heading of the party name and party emblem. The latter configuration appeased party leaders who preferred a blanket ballot that looked like the several party tickets in parallel. The party column ballot made it easier for the voter to vote for all candidates of a single party.

In New York, the publication of William Mills Ivins's ideas bore fruit. Representatives of reform clubs and the United Labor party of Henry George joined together to draft a bill for submission to the state legislature in its 1888 session. The bill was introduced by Republican state senator Charles Saxton. Prior to its introduction, *The New York Times* editorialized that

> The need of this reform is most seriously felt in this city, where the use of money to secure votes through the necessity of furnishing and distributing ballots has reached vast proportions. (*New York Times*, December 12, 1887, p. 4)

The bill provided for public printing of the party ballots, distribution of the ballots only by neutral clerks at the polls, a ballot for every party that had polled at least 3 percent of the vote, a ballot for new parties with petitions of 1,000 signatures, and a write-in line for most offices. Documented requests by parties for a ballot would have to be accomplished at least fifteen days before the election. Each voter would make his selections in a private booth, he would have five minutes to do so, and it would be a criminal act for the ballot being cast to be displayed to anyone before being deposited in the ballot box. An exception permitted persons who were illiterate, handicapped, or blind to obtain help from the ballot clerk.

Given that Governor David B. Hill started almost all his political speeches with the sentence "I am a Democrat," it was not surprising that he vetoed the Saxton bill after it had been approved by the Republican-dominated legislature. (The veto was not overridden.) As noted by Hill's biographer Herbert Bass, the real objection to the bill was not in the governor's veto message of 15 pages, but in the character of the Democratic urban vote:

> A substantial part of this vote came from the organized efforts of the machine, especially among the illiterate. The official ballot would severely hamper the organization's ability to poll its full strength . . . (Bass, 1961, p. 101).

In 1889, Saxton reintroduced his bill. Hill vetoed this bill with a 26-page message, and again the veto could not be overridden. Hill's main objection, as before, was the requirement for public printing of the ballot. He wrote that it discriminated against voters who were illiterate or visually impaired.

Saxton's bill was reintroduced in 1890, and events began to force the governor's hand. First, reports of experiences in Massachusetts with the blanket ballot were very positive. Second, there were mass meetings throughout the state that demanded ballot reform. Third, a delegation of Knights of Labor representatives from 34 state assembly districts came to Albany and urged Hill to approve the Saxton bill. Finally, "a gigantic petition weighing one-half ton and bearing 77,000 signatures from New York City and Brooklyn alone, was carried by 14 men to the floor of the legislature, there to rest during the debates" (Bass, 1961, p. 149). When Hill requested that the legislature ask the State Court of Appeals for an opinion on constitutionality and the legislature refused to agree, Hill cast his third veto.

Finally, a compromise was agreed to at meetings among interested parties including Hill, Senator Saxton, and a private group, the Ballot Reform League. The compromise provided for officially printed single-party ballot strips. A straight ticket vote could be cast by depositing the appropriate party's strip. The use of the party strip, headed by a logo, was to assist illiterate voters. Another device to assist voters was the "paster," which could be supplied by parties or private groups. These would become official when pasted by the voters themselves on any party's ballot strip. For the benefit of more independent and literate voters, a blank strip was made available for a voter who wished to write in his own set of candidates. In 1895, after Hill left office, a blanket ballot was adopted (see figure 3.1).

In New Jersey, the scenario played out similarly to that in New York. The New Jersey Ballot Reform Association had been formed in December 1888, and it, together with the Knights of Labor, pushed for a bill in the state legislative session beginning in January 1889. No bill was passed. In the 1890 session, agreement was achieved on a compromise bill put forward by Democratic senator George T. Werts. While ballots were only to be printed by the government, there would be separate ballots for each party, identical in size, shape, and color. These ballots would be obtainable several days before an election by party workers at cost. Then the ballots could be distributed to voters who could cast them as genuine ballots on election day. Before being cast, each voter's ballot was to be placed into an unsealed envelope, also provided by the government. With ballots obtainable before election day, this was not a real Australian ballot system. Of course, it favored straight ticket voting, which was the reason it was acceptable to party leaders. Pasters were permitted (McCormick, 1953, pp. 174–183).

The Werts law was found to be satisfactory, partly because of its provisions establishing a nonintimidating polling station and the official ballot. The law eliminated the chaos around polling stations and prevented much bribery. It also established fairer, more bipartisan procedures for the administration of elections. It was not replaced with a genuine Australian ballot system until 1911.

Many state adoptions occurred through 1891. By that year, all the land in the contiguous United States was organized as 45 states, 3 territories, and the District of Columbia. Enactment by 32 states and 2 territories had occurred. Adoption lagged in the South. Missing from the list of 34 were all the former Confederate states except Arkansas, Mississippi, and Tennessee. Also not included were Iowa, Kansas, New Mexico territory, Connecticut, New York, and New Jersey.

The new Peoples Party met on July 4, 1892, in Omaha to formulate its platform. They were called Populists. They basically represented agrarian interests of the South and West, and some labor interests in the Midwest and East. The preceding two decades had been extremely hard on farmers. In American fashion, they organized a political party to bring their grievances to the people at large and obtain a more amenable federal government in each of its branches.

The "Preamble" of the platform and the first of 10 "Expression of Sentiments" reproduced here demonstrate that the Populists believed that adoption of the Australian ballot was an essential, even though small, part of their overall program. The views expressed make clear that the demand for the Australian ballot was not just a special concern of the Eastern elite.

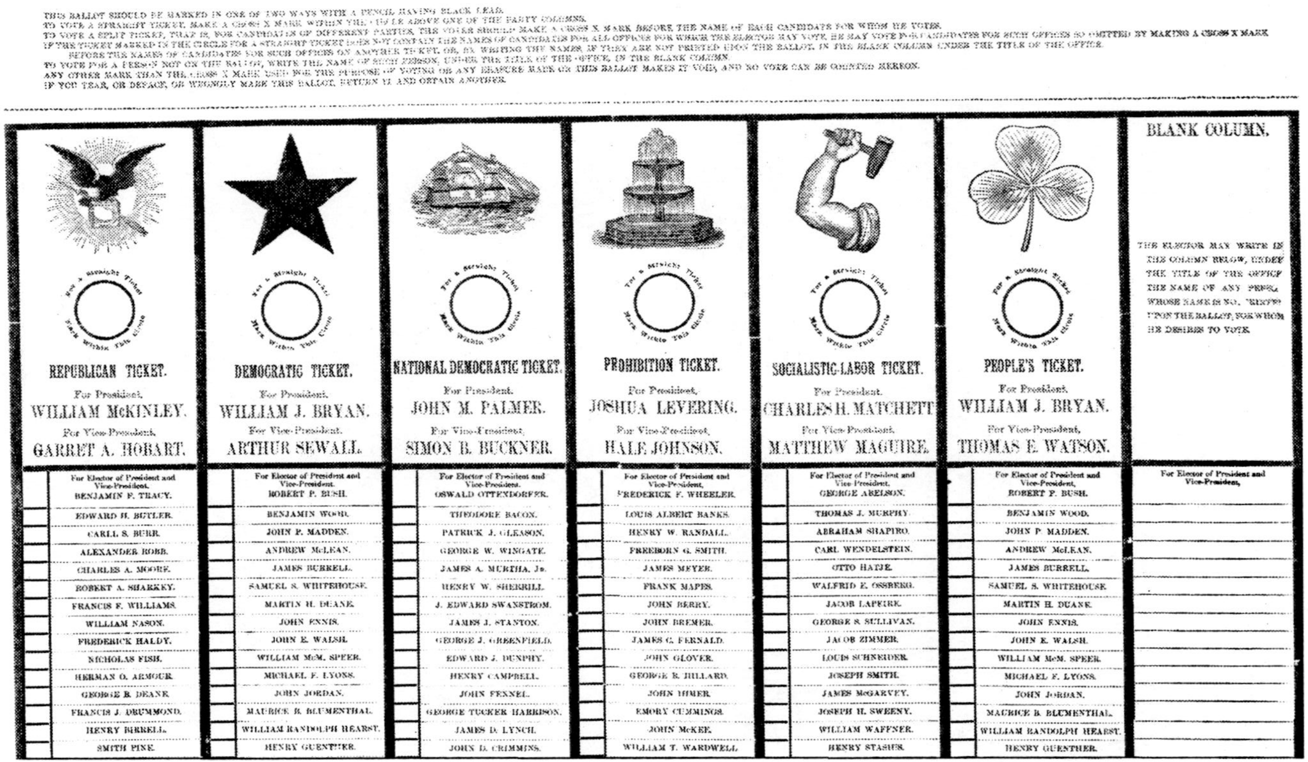

Figure 3.1 Top of an Australian ballot, 1896 general election, Long Island City, NY. Note the party-column form, the party symbols, the voting circles at the top for casting a straight-party vote, and the write-in column at the right.

PREAMBLE

We meet in the midst of a nation brought to the verge of moral, political and material ruin. Corruption dominates the ballot box, the legislatures, the Congress, and touches even the ermine of the bench. The people are demoralized; most of the States have been compelled to isolate the voter at the polling places to prevent universal intimidation and bribery . . .

EXPRESSION OF SENTIMENTS

1 [of 10]. *Resolved*, That we demand a free ballot and a fair count in all elections, and pledge ourselves to secure it to every legal voter without Federal intervention, through the adoption by the States of the unperverted Australian or secret ballot system . . . (Heffner, 1999 (1952), pp. 238, 239)

Through 1896, seven more states adopted the Australian ballot, but there were no more adoptions in the nineteenth century. The overwhelming number of actions by the individual states from 1988 through 1896 demonstrated that the time had come for that particular enhancement to the voting process. The seven recalcitrant jurisdictions failing to adopt at the time were North Carolina, South Carolina, Georgia, Texas, New Mexico territory, New Jersey, and Connecticut. The last listed, as was the case in New Jersey, allowed ballots to be obtained "before election, upon payment of cost" (Wigmore, 1889, pp. 176, 177). In 1897, Missouri regressed and permitted separate party tickets, although officially printed. These eight, except for South Carolina and Georgia, would adopt the blanket ballot statewide by 1930.

3.12   CONSEQUENCES OF ADOPTION

Difficulties for small parties resulted. As ballots were now printed by the government, they could not distribute independent ballots. The major parties created roadblocks for newly formed independent groups by requiring a number of citizen signatures in order to achieve a line or column on the blanket ballot. In some cases, the number of signatures needed was unconscionably large or requirements to be met for acceptable signatures were hard to achieve. In addition, some states passed "anti-fusion" laws. These prevented candidates' names from appearing on the ballot in more than one place. In that case, a small party that wished to endorse a major party candidate could not present that candidate's name on its own ballot row or column. This situation could have contributed to a minor party's inability to poll sufficient votes to automatically qualify for presentation on the next election's ballot.

Several types of ballot frauds could no longer be practiced if the ballots were produced officially by a government agency, included all parties and contests, and were distributed to voters in the polling station immediately before being filled out and cast. For example, bogus ballots, purporting to be official, but presenting nonofficial candidates, could no longer be distributed. The criminal elements, ever resourceful, invented "chain voting" in order to overcome one aspect of the new system.

Many voters at one polling station could be involved in a chain voting fraud. Its purpose was to orchestrate voting a particular way by voters who agreed to be compensated for their actions. To start the fraud, it was necessary to have a single unvoted ballot outside of the polling station. This ballot could be surreptitiously obtained from the election administrators, or it could be obtained by the first voter in the scheme. If necessary, the first voter would enter the polling station, not vote the ballot given, and bring it back outside. That voter would lose the vote. The leader of the scam would mark this unvoted ballot as ordered by higher ups, and hand it to the second voter. The second voter would enter the polling station, pocket the unmarked ballot given out and vote the marked ballot. Again, the unmarked ballot was brought back outside and the process repeated as long as there were voters willing to participate.

A corrective measure in response to chain voting was the production of each blank ballot with a sequentially numbered stub. The purpose was to assure that the ballot cast by the voter was the same ballot initially received. As the voter received a ballot at the polling station, the number of the stub was written down by an election official. After the voter had completed filling out the ballot in a private space and returned to cast the ballot in the ballot box, the number on the stub was matched to the number previously written down. If the number was the same, the stub was torn off and the ballot was cast.

Vote-casting technology would fall off the national agenda for a full century. The adoption of a voting machine not using ballots would be permitted by the Congress in 1899 (see section 4.6) but, after that, there would no federal legislation concerning vote-casting technology until 2002.

Additionally, the adoption of PPCs, marksense ballots, or direct recording electronic machines for voting in public elections would not be listed as significant events in respected volumes of histories of the United States, *even when specific sections of the books were devoted to science and technology*. It would be as if a new type of voting technology was a mere administrative detail no more important than, say, the purchase of new calculators for office workers at the local city hall. The mind-set of both policymakers and the media would change after the close of polls on November 7, 2000.

4

The Late Nineteenth and Early Twentieth Centuries: Mechanization and Political Reforms

Additional developments of the late nineteenth century need elaboration. For one, mechanization would be applied to voting. Second, professional specialization would flower, and this trend would ultimately affect election administration. Third, electricity would be harnessed as a utility, allowing for the development and wide use of devices employing it, such as punch-card-based data processors. In the early twentieth century, additional changes in the voting process would occur, some in response to the corruption of the preceding era.

4.1 Glass Ballot Boxes and Ballot Boxes that Count

Before the voting machine was invented, there were devices developed to store and later to count paper ballots. In earlier times, containers for collecting ballots were casually selected; inverted hats were a typical receptacle. In 1828, in a precinct in Tennessee, a large gourd was used. As elections became more formal and participants were concerned about ballot frauds, the need arose for a more intentional and secure repository. Solid wooden boxes with a hinged lid were used in many cases. The lid of a typical ballot box had a slot or a circular hole allowing entry of ballots, and the lid might have been locked so that two keys, held by representatives of two different factions or parties, were required to open it. A description of a required ballot box was included in a law of 1790 in New Jersey, applying to five counties in which voting by ballot was carried out (McCormick, 1953, p. 92).

Persons intent on fraud applied ingenuity in efforts to circumvent the system. One such example was presented in *Frank Leslie's Illustrated Newspaper* of July 19, 1856 in an article entitled "STUFFER'S BALLOT-BOX." The box that was used, according to the text, "in San Francisco and probably some of our northern cities," had a false bottom just inside the outside panels. Extra ballots already filled out for the favored candidate(s) could be secreted between the inside of the external bottom and the false bottom.

The extra ballots would be released at an appropriate time. This particular fraud would depend for its success on a lack of documentation of the number of voters who came into the polling station to vote; in the nineteenth century, that was a common practice.

Glass started to be used in the construction of some ballot boxes by the time of the Civil War. The purpose was for officials and watchers to be sure the box was empty when polls were opened and to spot the entry of multiple ballots by a single individual. One such box is shown in figure 4.1. Keys to the locks could be held by representatives of competing parties. An example of this type was patented by Alvin Ringo and Amos Pettibone in 1884.

Counting the ballots as well as preventing the entry of multiple ballots was the purpose of a number of ballot-box inventions (see figure 4.2). The issue

Figure 4.1   Glass ballot box, ca. 1880s.

Figure 4.2 Counting ballot box, ca. 1880s. This box has a lever mechanism that accepts one ballot per voter into the box and counts the ballot at the same time. It was manufactured in East Bridgewater, CT.

of ballot stuffing was significant, as the discussions of the previous chapter have indicated. A ballot box with glass sides was required to be used by all counties in New Jersey in 1887. As each ballot was deposited, it was counted, stamped, and punctured, and a bell was rung (McCormick, 1953, p. 172). If more than one ballot was entered at a time, only one of them would be stamped. Also in 1887, Melvin H. Coffin of Boston received a U.S. patent for his "voting machine." According to Coffin's patent disclosure,

> The object of this invention is to furnish an improved ballot box adapted to receive, between two feed-rollers, ballots, one by one, impress upon each by a reciprocating stamp a suitable identifying mark, register accurately the number of ballots cast, and sound an alarm on the deposit of each within the receptacle.

Coffin's machine was operated by turning a crank.

Augustus C. Carey of Boston received a patent for a combination ballot box and ballot counter in 1882, which the U.S. Patent Office classified as a voting machine. Carey's idea was to connect all ballots end-to-end as they were entered into a ballot box. Within the box was a drum on which the ballots were to be wound. A voided ballot was first affixed to the drum and it was wound with a crank until only a half-inch end was outside of the box. Then, the top end of the first voted ballot was attached to it with glue and was wound on the drum, again leaving a half-inch end outside the box. This process of entering ballots was continued while the polls were open. The ballots were entered face down, and if more than one ballot was entered at the same time as a stack, only the one on the bottom would be seen and counted. The number of ballots entered in succession was registered on a counter as the crank was turned. After all the ballots had been entered and the polls closed, a final voided ballot completed the entries. Then, the roll of ballots was removed from the box and placed on a spindle. The ballots were then unrolled and rerolled on a second spindle. As that process was accomplished, the content of each ballot was determined by the election officials (*The New York Times*, June 1, 1883, p. 4).

The use of Carey's machine was supported by U.S. senator George F. Hoar of Massachusetts, who introduced a bill calling for the machine's adoption and purchase throughout all the states and territories at a cost of $50 each. One machine would be used at each precinct throughout the nation (*The New York Times*, January 14, 1883, p. 1). Carey's machine was demonstrated at the Capitol in January 1883, and was later displayed in New York in June of that year. Hoar's bill did not pass, and nothing more was reported about Carey's invention.

John McTammany of Worcester, Massachusetts, received a U.S. patent in 1892 for a "Pneumatic Registering Ballot-Box." Ballots "formed of cardboard or paper having sufficient stiffness to prevent its wrinkling . . ." were to be used. The ballots were to be perforated near the outer edges to indicate choices. Two columns of candidate names were presented on the ballot. Small boxes near the long edges of the ballot were provided for the perforations.

McTammany used compressed air to operate counters that counted holes. There is no evidence that his balloting machine was ever used, but McTammany would be undaunted. He would go on to obtain many more patents concerned with voting machines.

4.2   EDISON'S LEGISLATIVE VOTING MACHINE

A voting machine designed by Thomas Edison (1847–1931) is often confused in general histories with voting machines used by individual citizens for public elections. One such history has a statement that is plainly incorrect. This "revised and updated" history states that "Thomas A. Edison invented the electric voting machine, although it was not used until 1892 because, as a politician kindly explained, it interfered with the patronage system" [Schlesinger, 1993 (1983), p. 315].

Thomas Edison received his first U.S. patent in 1869. He entitled the device "Electrographic Vote-Recorder and Register." It was intended for use in roll-call voting in a legislative assembly and not for voting by the public. There is an essential difference between these two types of elections. In an assembly of elected representatives, voting is generally intended to be public knowledge; the purpose of Edison's voting machine was to openly record how each member voted. Furthermore, for those deciding to vote, the choice is often either "yes" or "no," and just two summing devices are required. On the other hand, in voting by the public to select candidates for offices, secrecy of the votes cast by any voter is to be assured. The choice is often to select one person from several for an office, and there are usually a number of different offices and questions on the ballot. A summing device for each candidate and each yes/no alternative is required. The machines for accomplishing the two disparate tasks are necessarily widely divergent in design.

Edison's device employed a single electric battery that provided direct current (DC) power. Also, each voting member of the assembly was to be supplied with a three-position switch that could close a circuit through the battery with either a YES connection or a NO connection, or leave the circuit open without a connection. An essential component of the invention was a sheet of paper that was "chemically prepared" to respond to electricity. That was the "electrographic" part of the device and, according to the patent, this recording technology was well known. Edison had not yet invented the electric light, so that he could not plan to light up a bulb next to the name of each member on a large display board, as is done in many assemblies now.

The device holding the sheet of paper was to sit on the desk of the recording clerk of the assembly. The sheet would serve as the record for only one roll-call vote; then it would need to be replaced by a fresh sheet. In the device, the sheet sat in a bed between two rails and over the names of voting members of the assembly. The names were in metal type, and the entire list of members was presented twice, in two columns. Each name was separately embedded in nonconducting material. The left column was headed by NO and the right column by YES. Each of the rails consisted of conducting segments, opposite each name, separated by nonconducting segments. The conducting wire from each member's NO switch position was connected to the member's name in the left column; the conducting wire from each member's YES switch position was connected to the member's name in the right column.

When a roll-call vote was to be carried out and members connected their switches to either NO or YES, the recording clerk would roll a roller over the sheet of paper. (Members could abstain if they so chose.) This roller consisted of three parts. The left end and a right end were conducting and were separated by a nonconducting central part. The left end of the roller rolled down over the NO column and the right end of the roller rolled down over the YES column. Each member whose switch was in the NO position was sending electricity from the battery through his name in the NO column, and then through the sheet of paper to the roller. From there, the current traveled through the corresponding conducting rail segment and back to the battery. The sheet would have the voter's name burned into it in the NO column. Similarly, members whose switches were in the YES position would have their names burned into the sheet in the YES column.

Edison had provided, also, for two dials whose pointers were activated by the electricity. One dial would display the number of NO votes and the other the number of YES votes. All the wires from member's switches showing the same choice combined to go through one of two electromagnets. (Some resistance was required in series with each switch to prevent a short circuit.) The current in each electromagnet activated an armature that moved an amount proportional to the current. This armature was mechanically connected to the pointer on the dial.

Edison demonstrated his invention to the chairman of a committee of the U.S. House of Representatives, and was told, "Your invention would destroy the only hope that the minority would have of influencing legislation" (Boorstin, 1973, p. 528). Representatives were using the call of the roll to explain their views at great length. Edison's automated roll-call would prematurely close out debate. The invention was never used. It is now housed at the Henry Ford Museum in Dearborn, Michigan.

4.3   JACOB H. MYERS AND THE "AUTOMATIC BALLOT CABINET"

A device built for use by very many ordinary folks must meet a different challenge than faced by designers of machines intended for scientific or business use. It must be undemanding for almost any person to understand how to use it and to correctly transfer desired choices into actions carried out by the device; that is, the challenge is human usability, not technical complexity. Testing of the device through actual employment determined the public's opinion. Furthermore, reliability under heavy use would be a factor. Experimentation to gain better insight into the factors that minimized human errors in use did not begin until very recently.

Jacob H. Myers of Rochester, New York, was a designer of safes and vaults for banks. He received his first two U.S. patents for voting machines in 1889. It does not appear that the first was ever used. Myers's second patent described a non-ballot machine, similar in some ways to the ones in use today, except that push-keys were used instead of levers. Myers specified the benefits of his machine, as follows:

> By the employment of [my present invention] an honest vote can be had and counted without liability of voters being intimidated [as] the balloting [is] secret, or of their voting more than once for the same candidate or different candidates for the same office; and as the votes are counted as fast as the voter indicates his preference the total number cast for each candidate can be ascertained rapidly and accurately at the close of the polls.

The benefits listed demonstrate the wide concerns about voting in that time period: dishonest counting, voter intimidation due to nonsecret balloting, inadvertent mistakes in balloting that invalidated votes, and slowness of reporting results. Myers must have started to imagine his solution at the same time as others were starting to propose the Australian ballot for New York state. His application for the patent was filed in May 1889 and the patent was issued several years before the Australian ballot was adopted in that jurisdiction.

Even after the Australian ballot was in general use, enthusiasm for well-designed voting machines did not diminish; indeed, it accelerated in areas where their purchase or rental seemed appropriate or cost-effective. Local government officials were pleased to be able to eliminate paper ballots; it took effort to procure them, assure that they were printed correctly, and hire citizens to count them. The results were produced more slowly than the machines' summaries. Hand counts could be incorrect and recounts were time-consuming; issues of "intent of the voter" caused delays and controversy. Many voters were pleased not to have to vote on paper ballots because they might have their votes invalidated due to overvoting or by not following instructions exactly in marking. A ballot might be thrown out due to extraneous marks on it that administrators believed were signals to political operatives that the ballot had been cast as instructed.

In both Myers' patents, a rectangular booth enclosed on four sides, was described. The size of the booth was not given, but it needed to be about nine by nine feet, to allow for entry and exit doors, and the three compartments in it. The entry to one compartment was behind the machine and allowed for servicing. The entry to the second compartment provided access for voting and the third door accessed a vestibule used for the voter's exit. The closing of the outside exit door reset the machine for the next voter.

In voting, the pushing of a key on the machine by a voter advanced a connected counter by one, and there were as many sets of push-keys and counters as there were candidates in all contests. The push-keys were presented to the voter in a rectangular array, with all candidates from one party in a single column, and all candidates for a particular office in a single row (or more than one row if more than one candidate was to be elected to the same office). Each column was displayed with the party name at the top and in a unique color. The latter was used to give illiterate voters a better chance of recording the choices that they had in mind. Each candidate location listed the names of the office and the candidate next to its push-key. It appears that once a voter set a push-key, it could not be reset; the voter had no ability to correct a mistake. The selection of one candidate prevented the selection of all other competing candidates.

The Myers machine was demonstrated in Rochester on November 23, 1889, according to *The New York Times* of the next day. It was reported that Myers and others would petition the state legislature to permit its use. By 1892, the necessary law was passed, and the machine, identified as the "Myers Automatic Ballot-Cabinet" (Ludington, 1911, p. 51) was used in nearby Lockport on April 12 of that year for local elections. In 1893, it was used in a dozen or so small towns in areas surrounding Lockport. According to the report in *The New York Times*, the voters and supervisors seemed "delighted" with the system. The machine was described as having six party columns, with 35 "knobs" in each column. The voter knew that his vote was cast if he pushed the knob in far enough that it could not be pulled out. The machine patented in 1889 was arranged to prevent voting for more candidates than were allowed in each contest, up to two. A later design would expand that number.

Myers obtained two more patents, one in 1890 and another in 1893. Both of these patents made advancements to the non-ballot machine of Myers's second patent. In the 1893 patent, Myers states that the machines' "capabilities are increased and certain alleged objections are overcome." *The New York Times* of May 6, 1894 discussed the revision of the state's "town law" that made it easier for town officials as well as county officials to adopt the Myers machine for elections.

One modification to the Myers machine was to enable voters to write in (or paste in) the name of a candidate not nominated by any party. That was done by providing a roll of writing paper accessible at a slit in the face of the machine. After the name was written or pasted in, the voter pushed in the knob associated with that candidate location. Then, when the voter exited the booth and the knobs were released, the roll of paper was advanced so that the next voter could not know that a write-in candidate had been selected.

Additionally, Myers increased the capability of the machine to allow for "cumulative" voting, that is, "for allowing each voter to cast as many ballots as he may be entitled to, whether for the same or different candidates, and no more . . ." A design allowing a voter to select up to five candidates is given in his 1893 patent, but Myers states that the concept is applicable to a larger number of candidates. Another innovation provided by Myers was a clock that started at zero each time a new voter entered the booth. The clock was to be visible outside of the booth, to indicate the time that the voter had expended. There were rules on the maximum allowable time permitted for voting. Myers states that

> In the event that it is necessary for an officer to enter the booth to eject an unruly or dilatory voter, it is desirable that he [the officer] be prevented from ascertaining what the votes or ballots, if any cast by the voter, are . . .

Therefore, Myers provided a curtain that would fall over the push-keys and hide them from view as such an officer entered the booth. Whether or not the clock and curtain were implemented is not known.

The Myers machine was used in Rochester in the general election of November 3, 1896 and also in that city for the contest for governor in November 1898. It was also used in Syracuse, New York. Connecticut and Michigan approved the use of the Myers machine, but it achieved no success in either state. It was deemed not sufficiently convenient or reliable.

4.4 VOTING MACHINES OF OTHER EARLY INVENTORS

John W. Rhines of St. Paul, Minnesota received a U.S. patent for a "Vote-Recording Machine" in 1890. Rhines' device, which was small compared with Myers's machine, consisted of a keyboard mounted on legs and a cover to that keyboard. The keyboard contained a rectangular array of pushbuttons, like Myers's machine, but there was no surrounding booth.

The Rhines machine employed a strip of paper for each contest to record the total votes. Each strip was divided into columns, one column for the candidate of each party. Numbering wheels served as printing heads to record the total vote for a candidate on the paper strip. The Rhines machine was authorized in Michigan in 1893 but it was unsuccessful in achieving any significant acceptance.

The work of John McTammany, whose Pneumatic Registering Ballot Box was described above, demonstrates that there is no assurance that persistence will pay off. He received eleven U.S. patents on voting machines from 1893 through 1895 and four more in later years. One patent of 1895 provided a counter wheel for each candidate; the voter used a stylus pushed into a hole to activate the turning of the wheel to the next count.

Several of his other patents involved the use of a tally-sheet instead of counters. His next-to-last patent of 1895 provided the design of a "Pneumatic Vote-Counting Machine" whose function was to automatically count holes in a tally-sheet.

A test of McTammany's machine was made in Worcester, Massachusetts, on October 10, 1896. In that test, the holes made by voters to indicate selections were counted by McTammany's pneumatic counting machine and were transmitted by telegraph to the city hall, a short distance away. Certainly, this electrical communication of data was an innovation to be widely used much later.

The voting machine was used again in Worcester in the general election of November 3, 1896. *The Washington Post* editorialized on November 9 that "the secret ballot is one of the greatest reforms of modern times," and that the display of candidates on a voting machine "simply hangs the blanket ballot on the wall." The newspaper opined further that:

> The expense of printing ballots, the annoyance and delay of folding them, and delays and mistakes in the counting are all eliminated by the machine. The counting becomes automatic and instantaneous. The result is ascertainable with unquestionable accuracy within a few minutes after the closing of the polls. There can be no tampering with the count, and no disputing of the returns; for there are no ballots in existence to be altered or wrangled over, nothing but the registered figures of the voting. No bribed voter can leave a trace or sign of any kind as evidence to his briber that he has kept his bargain.

The Washington Post's enthusiasm for a perfected voting machine was misplaced on the device tested in Worcester. Unfortunately for McTammany ("a fearfully suggestive name," according to the newspaper), Worcester didn't approve his machines and abandoned them. The city returned to the use of the Australian ballot. Despite the fact that the first voting machine laws of Connecticut, Rhode Island, and Massachusetts permitted use of the machine, no further deployment appears to have occurred. McTammany's two additional patents of 1897 and one each in 1913 and 1914, the latter two assigned to his company in Portland, Maine, did not result in renewed interest.

Sylvanus E. Davis, also of Rochester, New York, received a U.S. patent in 1894 and a second one in 1895. His machine was also a non-ballot device (except in voting for write-in candidates) like Myers's machine, indicating the sum of votes for each nominated candidate on counters. Selection of candidates by the use of push-keys was very similar to the operation with Myers's machine but all candidates for a particular party were listed in a row rather than a column. The Davis voting machine was used in Jamestown, New York, in the general election of November 1898. Jamestown is about 140 miles southwest of Rochester in the far western corner of the state. Many other inventors and business concerns were attempting to get approval from New York and other states to allow the use of their machines. New York permitted the "Boma Automatic Ballot-Machine," the "Standard Automatic Voting Machine," and the Myers and Davis machines to be used, by revisions of law, at various times through 1898 (Ludington, 1911, pp. 52, 53). A list of numbers and dates of issuance of patents for ballot boxes and voting machines referenced in this chapter are given in table 4.1.

Alfred J. Gillespie of Atlantic, Iowa, received his first patent for a voting machine in 1897. Atlantic is a small town about 80 miles west of Des Moines in the southwestern part of that state. His machine was different than those previously described in that the voter could change his mind before the vote was finalized. This was a significant improvement.

Gillespie received four additional patents in the next several years. Two were dated in 1899 and the other two in 1900. In the 1899 patents, a curtain was provided that was connected to the handle of a lever that started and

Table 4.1 Some significant patents for ballot boxes and voting machines

Patentee	Residence	Date of issuance (year/month/day)	Patent number
Carey, Augustus C.	Boston, MA	1882/10/31	266,950#
Coffin, Melvin H.	Boston, MA	1887/11/29	373,814#
Cooper, Henry C. H.	Jamestown, NY	1898/11/15	614,419
Davis, Sylvanus E.	Rochester, NY	1894/9/25	526,628
Davis, Sylvanus E.	Rochester, NY	1895/11/12	549,631
Dean, James H.	St. Paul, MN	1899/3/28	622,191**
Dean, James H.	St. Paul, MN	1899/11/7	636,730
Edison, Thomas A.	Boston, MA	1869/6/1	90,646
Gillespie, Alfred J.	Atlantic, IA	1897/2/9	576,570
Gillespie, Alfred J.	Rochester, NY	1899/7/11	628,792
Gillespie, Alfred J.	Rochester, NY	1899/7/11	628,905
Gillespie, Alfred J.	Rochester, NY	1900/4/17	647,657
Gillespie, Alfred J.	Rochester, NY	1900/5/8	648,944
Gillespie, Alfred J.	Rochester, NY	1913/9/9	1,072,939
Gillespie, Alfred J.	Atlantic, IA	1914/3/3	1,088,816
McTammany, John	Worcester, MA	1892/9/13	482,691#
McTammany, John	Spencer, MA	1893/8/8	502,743**
McTammany, John	Spencer, MA	1894/5/29	520,609
McTammany, John	Spencer, MA	1895/9/10	546,076
McTammany, John	Spencer, MA	1895/11/19	550,052***
McTammany, John	Spencer, MA	1897/4/6	580,140*
McTammany, John	Spencer, MA	1913/6/24	1,065,703
McTammany, John	Spencer, MA	1914/8/25	1,108,384
Myers, Jacob H.	Rochester, NY	1889/11/19	415,548*
Myers, Jacob H.	Rochester, NY	1890/3/25	424,332
Myers, Jacob H.	Rochester, NY	1893/4/4	494,588
Rhines, John W.	St. Paul, MN	1890/3/4	422,891
Ringo, A. & Pettibone, A.	Chicago, IL	1884/6/17	300,512#
Shoup, Samuel R.	Wilmington, DE	1907/5/7	852,911
Shoup, Samuel R.	Wilmington, DE	1907/5/7	853,127
Shoup, Samuel R.	Hoboken, NJ	1909/8/31	932,915
Shoup, Samuel R.	Hoboken, NJ	1914/1/13	1,084,585
Shoup, S. R. & Ransom F.	Weehawken, NJ	1936/9/15	2,054,102*

Notes
* Includes one additional patent number in sequence for each asterisk.
\# Ballot box.

terminated the voting process. The curtain was closed by the voter in preparation to vote, and was opened on completion of the vote. It provided complete privacy for the voter and is another feature included in today's machines. (Myers's voluminous booth was no longer needed.) One 1899 patent also shows small levers associated with each candidate's name. These levers are also seen on contemporary machines; their positions may be changed before the voting session is ended. The first patent of 1900 provided improvement in the method for voting for write-in candidates while the second of that year supplied a method for "group" voting, that is, "to permit the voter to cast a ballot for any predetermined number of candidates for a particular office whether nominated by the same or different parties."

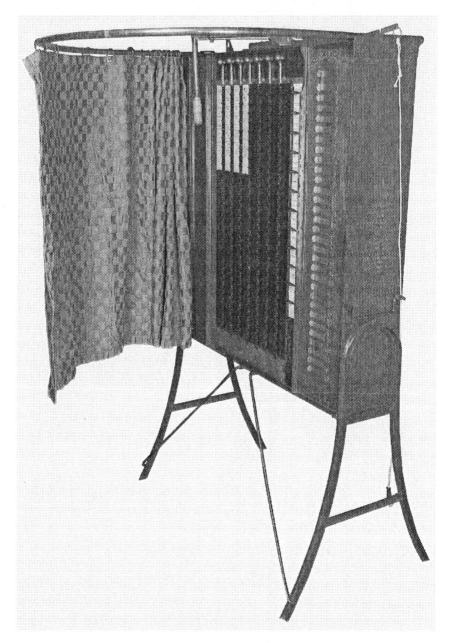

Figure 4.3   Lever voting machine, ca. 1899. Manufactured by the Standard Voting Machine Company of Rochester, NY. Alfred Gillespie invented the procedure in which the large "vote" lever first closes the curtain for privacy and opens it while registering the votes at completion of voting.

4.5   Consolidation of Companies

Gillespie and his work came to the attention of an office equipment supply company of Rochester, New York. He was persuaded to come to that city and join in the formation of the Standard Voting Machine Company (Standard VMC). Gillespie's patents of 1899 and 1900 identify the inventor as residing in Rochester and assigning his patents to that company. The "Standard Automatic Voting Machine" approved for use in New York state in 1898 is, with high probability, the machine of that company. It was manufactured in Rochester from 1898 to 1900. A particular Standard Voting Machine, no. 983, is in the possession of the Smithsonian Institution, National Museum of American History. (This machine is shown in figure 4.3). The machine records on its surface the dates of patents and some patent numbers used in its design and construction. These patents are those of both Myers and Gillespie. Apparently, Myers's original firm, the Myers Ballot Machine Company, was merged into the Standard VMC.

The Smithsonian is also in possession of U.S. Voting Machine no. 408. That machine records patents of Sylvanus E. Davis and two other individuals, Henry C. H. Cooper and James H. Dean. Cooper resided in Jamestown, New York, and his patent was finalized in 1898. Dean, of St. Paul, Minnesota, obtained his patent in 1899. Dean's patent cites three previous patents of his, obtained earlier the same year. The machine had been manufactured in Jamestown, where it had been used. Both the Standard model and the U.S. Voting Machine model were constructed about 1899 or very soon after, since all the patents listed are from that year or before. Both machines were donated to the Smithsonian by the Automatic Voting Machine Division of Rockwell Manufacturing Company of Jamestown, New York, in 1961.

By 1900, the U.S. VMC had merged with the Standard VMC and all manufacturing was consolidated in Jamestown. The new organization was called U.S. Standard VMC. Production would remain in that city for the next 80 years, until technological change ended the demand for new machines.

4.6   Conflict over the "Written" Ballot Requirement

Laws in all states but Kentucky were adopted by 1872 requiring that voting was to be by written or printed ballot. One purpose of these laws was to ensure the elimination of oral voting. The federal government had done the same in 1871. As reported in section 3.7, the federal law required "that all votes for representatives in Congress shall hereafter be by written or printed ballot . . ."

In western New York, a contest for the House of Representatives in 1896 eventually led to a new law of Congress. Henry C. Brewster had defeated William E. Ryan by 25,399 to 17,109, but Ryan complained that 31,354 votes cast in Rochester had been by voting machine. These, said Ryan, were invalid under the requirement of the federal law mentioned earlier. A committee of Congress investigated the matter and decided that Brewster would have won anyway if machines were not used. Therefore, he should have the seat (Zukerman, 1925, p. 24). However, in view of the problem created by the advance of technology, a law was adopted on February 14, 1899 (55th Congress, Sess. III, Chap. 154) stating:

> All votes for Representatives in Congress must be by written or printed ballot, or voting machine the use of which has been duly authorized by the State law; and all votes received or recorded contrary to this section shall be of no effect.

One effect of the new law was that it ensured that each state government would be in charge of the approval of voting machines. Typically, a local jurisdiction can use or procure voting equipment only if it is of a model approved by the state.

4.7   USE OF VOTING MACHINES: 1900–1938

The "written ballot" requirement of state constitutions required legislatures to wrestle with the legal language that would permit non-ballot voting machines to be used. The Massachusetts Supreme Judicial Court had thrown out the use of voting machines on this basis in 1907, the Ohio Supreme Court had done the same in 1909, and so had the Kentucky courts in 1938. In many states, new phrasing had been devised and it was permissive. Any type of machine would be allowed "provided secrecy be preserved."

State legislatures and the public that had ratified the necessary constitutional changes realized that secrecy in voting was an essential requirement of the democratic process. Oral voting had been eliminated for this reason, and party-produced ballots were similarly rejected. It had taken a very long time to achieve the benefits of the Australian ballot, and no change in technology would be allowed to undo the successful struggle to attain secrecy for each and every voter. In several states, the highest courts permitted the use of voting machines without a change in the legal language. The basis of those decisions was that the new technology would preserve secrecy, and that was the underlying intent of the law requiring a written ballot. Among these states were Illinois and Michigan in 1905, Minnesota in 1906, Montana in 1907, Washington in 1914, and Maryland in 1935.

Voting machines began to be adopted in a variety of cities between 1900 and 1910. Cities in which they were installed, because of state permission, and which did not discontinue their use later, included Buffalo, Hartford, and Indianapolis. Michigan and Illinois permitted their use, but Detroit and Chicago did not adopt them for several decades. It might be expected that cities would be attracted to the machines because of the likelihood of the reduced time for producing the first results of an election, and the elimination of the large number of ballots that would otherwise have to be counted. Larger cities could more likely afford the costs than smaller places; the latter would lack cost-effectiveness in their use.

Use of the machines would be opposed in some large cities where political organizations believed that their adoption would be detrimental to their maintenance of control. Interestingly, some "good government" groups also opposed voting machines because they believed their use would encourage straight-party voting. The desire to eliminate straight-party voting was for reduction of the power of political machines. This demand was strongly made at the Conference for Good City Government held in Buffalo, New York, in 1910 (Zukerman, 1925, p. 29). The remedy proposed was the elimination of the straight-party lever, through the use of which a voter could vote for all candidates of a single party with a single motion. As a result, in the next few years, efforts to eliminate the straight-party lever were made in a number of state legislatures.

Some revocation of use occurred in the following decades, although some adoptions continued. New Jersey discontinued the use of the machines in 1911. In 1917, Utah legislated against them; California, Colorado, and Rhode Island did the same in 1921. Cities that had initially adopted them but later threw them out included Denver, Milwaukee, Minneapolis, Jersey City, Newark, Salt Lake City, and San Francisco. The reasons for rejection are varied, but one common motivation appeared to be congestion at the polls. Unlike the situation with ballots, where several voters may privately fill out their ballots simultaneously, only one person can use a voting machine at one time. Along with permission for adoption, states established a limited time for voting on a machine, often one or two minutes. Even with that restriction, queues began to form before people went to work or after they came home. As the machines were expensive, an insufficient number of machines were available to be used at many locations.

A second motivation for machine rejection was a requirement to supply paper ballots in case the machines were not functioning or in use when a voter reached the polling station. The confusion inherent in the use of two types of voting processes at the same time in the same place caused some cities, such as Minneapolis, to abolish use of the machines. A third motivation for eliminating the machines resulted from the adoption of preferential voting in Wisconsin. The machines could not handle the situation; their use was dropped in Milwaukee.

By 1930, such states as California (again), Ohio (again), Florida, Georgia, Pennsylvania, Texas, and Washington had allowed their use. This made the machines available for use in all those states' larger cities.

Chicago's early experiences with voting machines are worthy of note. Citizens approved voting machine use by referendum in 1904. In 1911, 200 machines were delivered and were used in a primary election in 1912. Much difficulty was encountered. In some city wards, a major political party organization told its voters not to use them and to ask for paper ballots instead, which was permitted. A very large machine was required due to the long Chicago ballot and the cumulative voting system required for candidates for the state legislature. The machines needed an exactly level floor to work properly, and that had not been planned for nor achieved in most cases. In an investigation of the situation by the state legislature, it was alleged that more than $200,000 had been spent by the successful vendor to secure the contract. That accusation was denied by others. Chicago did not attempt to again use voting machines for many years (Harris, 1934, pp. 252, 253).

New York City's experiences are similarly interesting. The state of New York, in 1921, required New York City to adopt the machines but, by various means, the city was able to delay. The Tammany organization opposed them. With ballots, control of the election could be exercised in several ways, for example, through the release of false counts of ballots, with the addition of pre-marked extra ballots, and with the fraudulent elimination of properly cast ballots voted for the opposition. The latter could be caused to occur by "losing" or replacing ballots from precincts where the opposition was strong, or with invalidating marks surreptitiously placed on those ballots with concealed leads under the fingernails of a manual counter. Without ballots, these frauds could not be perpetrated. The actual counts would be read off the machines.

An 80-page report to evaluate voting machines and support their adoption was prepared at the request of the Republican County Committee of New York (i.e., Manhattan). The 1925 report by T. David Zukerman, previously cited, was expectedly laudatory. Zukerman's report countered objections raised by opponents of voting machines. Two of these objections are pertinent today, 80 years later. One of these objections was the "lack of voter's assurance that [the] vote will be counted in accordance with [voter's] desires." This objection is understandable with a non-ballot voting device. Zukerman responds with an interesting statement:

> Presumably the voting machine does require an act of faith on the part of the voter in a mechanical contrivance whose workings he cannot see. No more so, however, than is required in the case of the automobile in which he drives up to the polls. Indeed, he has even less assurance that the paper ballot on which he has seen the marks beside the names and followed with his eyes as it was deposited in the box will be counted as he intended; for neither does he in this case actually see his vote recorded, nor does anyone else. That is one of the elements of the secret ballot . . . (Zukerman, 1925, p. 63).

The concern expressed and the reasoning of the response will be revisited in the discussion of public confidence in electronic non-ballot voting machines in section 7.6.

A second objection considered by Zukerman is the frequency of breakdowns and the necessity of repairs. This question will always be faced when machines are furnished for public use. The issue of contingency planning was as important in the twentieth century as it will continue to be in the twenty-first. An election administrator ignores or minimizes this concern at his or her peril. Public confidence is closely connected to smoothly run elections, including successfully functioning machines.

The voting machine industry's leader in 1900 was U.S. Standard VMC. With the combination of the inventions of Myers, Gillespie, Davis, Cooper, and Dean as assets of the merged organization in Jamestown, the design and manufacture of machines that met the needs of a wide variety of state requirements became a reality. National sales became possible and the general diffusion of use began. U.S. Standard retained its lead in manufacturing for as long as the machines were produced. It produced 330 machines in 1911, 500 in 1920, and 1,000 in 1930.

In 1907, Samuel R. Shoup of Wilmington, Delaware, received two U.S. patents for voting machines. One claim made by Shoup in both patents was that he could "reduce the number of operating parts" required to carry out the voting functions. In 1910 and 1914, Shoup obtained two more patents and listed his address as Hoboken, New Jersey. No manufacturing seems to have occurred at that time.

The company involved in the Chicago contract in 1912 was the Empire Voting Machine Company of Rochester, New York. In 1913, Alfred J. Gillespie received another patent and assigned it to that company. It is likely that, about 1910 or so, Gillespie decided to form a new company and compete with his former one. An interesting point is that, in 1914, in a final patent, Gillespie gave his address as Atlantic, Iowa, his original hometown. He had specified his residence as Rochester, New York, for all patents from his second through 1913.

Zukerman mentions four voting machine companies as submitting bids in 1922 to satisfy the requirements of New York state that New York City must use voting machines. One of these companies was Automatic Registering Corporation of Jamestown, New York. This was the new name adopted in 1914 by U.S. Standard after it had absorbed some other companies. In 1925, the name was again changed to Automatic VMC, generally known as AVM (Automatic Voting Machine Corporation, 1958, p. 4). Two other companies submitting bids in 1922 were the Progressive VMC of Dayton, Ohio, whose machine was called the "Yoe," and the Cummings VMC of Knox, Indiana.

The fourth bid submitter was Shoup VMC of Weehawken, New Jersey, formed by Samuel R. Shoup and his relative Ransom F. Shoup. An evaluator of the bids said that the Shoup machine was equal in quality to the machine from Jamestown, still called the U.S. Standard, and superior to the other two. However, the Shoup company had submitted only drawings, indicating that its machine was not yet available. By the 1930s, Shoup was manufacturing machines in Brooklyn. The U.S. Standard machine was chosen by New York in 1922, even though its unit price was the highest. The latter company's reputation for experience and reliability had won out (Zukerman, 1925, pp. 8, 9).

Use of voting machines continued to increase as the twentieth century progressed. In 1928, AVM advertised that 1 of every 6 voters (16.67 percent) would vote on a machine in the forthcoming presidential election. That would have been roughly 6 million out of 36 million voters. A large majority of the machines were sold or rented by AVM. If a voter required 2 minutes to vote and the polls were open for 13 hours on election day, then a voting machine could service 390 voters. On this basis, the 6 million voters using the machines in 1928 would have required fewer than 20,000 machines, including some in reserve. This number is quite small when compared with the number of radio receivers or telephones then in use (see section 4.10 for the number of telephones). Voting equipment has a very specialized market. Local governments are the ultimate buyers, even though they are not the end users.

Interestingly, mechanical lever voting machines have never required the use of electricity for their basic function. Power was only applied to provide lighting helpful to the voter to better see the information on the face of the machine. When Myers designed his first machine, DC could have been used but it was not employed. By the turn of the century, electricity was available as a public utility. However, no manufacturer chose to apply it before World War II.

4.8   PROFESSIONALIZATION

A significant trend in the late nineteenth century, extending into the twentieth, was the professionalization of complex lines of work. This important sociological change was an aspect of what historian Robert H. Wiebe has identified as the development of "A New Middle Class" (Wiebe, 1967, pp. 111–132). Professions relevant to election equipment are, of course, engineering and the physical sciences, but other professions applicable to the general voting process are business management, political science, and public administration.

Professionalization implies, first, the existence of an extensive category of knowledge that is well understood by the practitioners, including the relationship of the field to society as a whole. Members of the profession, who are typically credentialed, should be able to undertake purposeful analyses involving the collection and processing of real-world data, contribute to the solution of relevant problems of clientele or employers, advance the field with new knowledge, and educate new entrants to full competence. The development of professionalization in the late nineteenth century and in the next century paralleled the implementation of civil service reform. The need in all levels of government for professionals whose knowledge was apolitical, for example, in accounting and budgeting, contract management, engineering, statistics, earth sciences, physical sciences, and biological sciences, made politically based hiring and firing wasteful and self-defeating.

Engineering, as an occupation, is very old, if it is limited to the building of roads, structures, ships, weaponry such as catapults, and mechanisms for using water. Egyptian pyramids, Khmer and Maya temples, Roman aqueducts, European cathedrals and Inca precision stonework indicate its worldwide application in construction. In the United States, engineering did not suddenly arise in the late nineteenth century, but it became much more significant. Its importance rose with the increasing pace of inventions and applications. In addition to applications in construction and transportation, engineers designed machines for industrial processes and manufacturing, and installed the applications. They designed machines, also, to generate motive power, first steam, and then electricity.

The military Corps of Engineers was established in 1794. Civil engineering as a profession was an outgrowth of military engineering, hence the distinguishing name. Opened in 1825, "the Erie Canal proved to be a great school for engineers, training through practice a whole generation of American practitioners" (Pursell, 1995, p. 101). It was appropriate at the time that the world's first private engineering school, Rensselaer Polytechnic Institute, should be established in 1824 in Troy, New York, near the canal's eastern terminus at the Hudson River. Harvard's program was started in 1842 and Yale's in 1847. The American Society of Civil Engineers was formed in 1852. The federally funded land-grant college system, set up under the Morrill Act of 1862, provided for each state and territory to establish an institution to teach the offspring of "farmers and mechanics" the science and practice of agriculture and the use and design of machines.

Lehigh University began its engineering program in 1865. Columbia University set up a School of Mines in 1867 and a professional society for mining engineers was started in 1871. A graduate of Columbia's program will be prominently featured for his inventions and entrepreneurship. His efforts to mechanize the processing of data would be appreciated and well utilized, not only in engineering, but also in other professions whose research would be grateful for the ease with which data could be reduced for analyses.

Yale and Massachusetts Institute of Technology (MIT) graduated their first mechanical engineers in 1868, and MIT and Cornell began their electrical engineering programs in 1882. The American Society of Mechanical Engineers was started in 1880 and the American Institute of Electrical Engineers in 1884. The application of electricity and then electronics eventually would make possible the invention of the electronic digital computer and its use in the voting process.

Business management became a profession as businesses became more subject to deliberate planning in the era. Businesses provided a platform for the introduction of new techniques of organization and effective applications of technology. Organizations were helped toward those goals with the ideas of the first industrial engineer Frederick W. Taylor (1856–1915) and his promotion of "scientific management." Interestingly, the transcript of testimony by Taylor on that subject before the U.S. House of Representatives on January 25, 1912 is reprinted in a book entitled *Classics of Public Administration* (Taylor, 1978 (1912), pp. 17–23). Taylor was followed by others such as Frank Gilbreth (1868–1924), who invented the concept of time and motion study, and Frank's wife Lillian Gilbreth (1878–1972), who applied the concept of an efficiently designed workspace to the kitchen. "Efficiency" and "systematizing" became important concepts used by business managers in the pursuit of a more effective company. "Project management," a process of systematization used both in business and government, can be an important tool in preparations for elections.

Political science began as a specialization within social science. The American Social Science Association was formed in 1865. Its charter was very inclusive, covering many concerns of ordinary lives, for example, sanitation, employment, education, crime, relief (welfare), mental health, and "numerous matters of statistical and philanthropic interest." The inclusion of "statistical . . . interest" in the charter was a recognition, even at that early date, that the use of that mathematical method of analyzing human societies was essential. In 1879, those interested in charities and social welfare dropped out to form their own society (Trattner, 1989 (1974), pp. 212, 213). During the 1880s, academicians interested in history, economics, and statistics also departed to begin their own groupings. Finally, the American Political Science Association (APSA) and the American Sociological Association were established in 1903 and 1905, respectively. There was already a journal on the subject of interest, *Political Science Quarterly*, begun in 1886.

In the twentieth century, there was some political science research on the voting process. The quantity was small in comparison to the number of studies of the electorate itself, electoral participation, and election issues and outcomes. A subject hardly covered at all was the effect of various types of voting technology on different socioeconomic groups. That omission would be corrected after the Florida debacle of 2000.

Public and election administration started as outgrowths of activities concerned with the governance of cities. During the early years of the twentieth century, nonprofit organizations called "bureaus of municipal research," as well as other citizen-based good government organizations contributed to efforts to improve city management. Among their concerns were the administration of elections. Their activities were based on the belief that more honest elections might reduce the corruption that was a significant attribute of "boss" rule. In the decade 1925 through 1934, Joseph P. Harris (1896–1985), who in 1962 invented the PPC ballot system, undertook detailed studies of voter registration and election administration. He carried out research with the aid of a fellowship from the Social Science Research Council in the 1920s. He also served as secretary of the Committee on Election Administration of the National Municipal League. (The league was one of the good government groups that were derisively called "goo-goos" by some supporters of machine politics.)

Harris had received his doctorate in political science at the University of Chicago, where he was a student of Charles Merriam. According to a recent article on the "Chicago School of Political Science," "Merriam joined the progressive call for good government and the creation of public agencies administered by trained experts, not political hacks" (Monroe, 2004, p. 95). Clearly, Harris' work demonstrates that he learned that lesson well. An associated article on the same subject mentions that "The scholars trained in the Chicago department, and their students, have enriched the entire corpus of political science—in American politics . . . [and] public administration . . ." (Almond, 2004, p. 91). Many well-known academic scholars are mentioned in that paper, but not Harris.

Harris authored *Registration of Voters in the United States* in 1929. The book described the results of his work in planning a comprehensive system of voter registration for local governments. There was, in many election offices at that time, a requirement for equal division of employees between the two major political parties. Nonpartisan civil service hiring was not in effect in many election offices before World War II and employees were not hired because of competence:

> In most cities the office force is recruited from the ranks of professional politicians with little attention to clerical ability. . . . No private organization would attempt to get along with the type of employee usually found in election offices (Harris, 1929, pp. 136, 137).

Harris quotes from a letter sent to him by an election official reminiscing about the situation before administrative changes were made:

> It would be difficult to imagine a more incompetent and drunken lot of loafers anywhere than the nondescript outfit that was put on registration and election work, with a few exceptions (Harris, 1929, p. 137).

With regard to professionalization, election administration, a special type of public administration, would not be considered by academicians of the time as a suitable candidate for that type of improvement. No significant effort to provide academic training for those engaged in the field would occur until well after World War II. Harris would attempt to start the process of improving the field with his book *Election Administration in the United States* in 1934. He would begin the text with the following:

> There is probably no other phase of public administration in the United States which is so badly managed as the conduct of elections (Harris, 1934, p. 1).

His work had been recognized soon after his books were published. He had been appointed in 1936 as a member of the newly formed President's Committee on Administrative Management; the president in this case being Franklin D. Roosevelt. The committee was headed by Merriam and two other outstanding practitioners Louis Brownlow and Luther Gulick (Pugh, 1988, p. 14). A recommendation of the committee which was implemented was the establishment of the Bureau of the Budget (later renamed Office of Management and Budget) in the Executive Office of the President.

In more recent times, Harris' early work seems to have been forgotten or ignored. His books have never been updated with new data to demonstrate how the situations that he discussed have changed or not changed. Harris' concerns were not considered to be important issues for the academic aspects of political science or public administration. The milieu of his interests was the real world and down-to-earth practicality in a government function that provided the essential machinery of democracy. Some academicians would refer to these issues as "housekeeping," as there was no connection shown with theories of the governmental process.

A relevant professional organization, the American Society for Public Administration (ASPA), was founded in 1939 at an annual meeting of APSA. Public administration practitioners claim the often-cited article by the young Woodrow Wilson in *Political Science Quarterly* in 1887, which made the essential distinction between politics and administration, as the intellectual beginning of the profession [Wilson, 1978 (1887), pp. 3–17]. The bureaus of municipal research and other nonprofit citizens' leagues of the early twentieth century also are claimed as forerunners (Pugh, 1988, p. 9). Brownlow and Gulick, mentioned earlier, were among its founders. Much later, the society formed sections on several important subject areas of governmental involvement in national life, for example, human services, transportation, and environmental regulation, but not election administration. Consistent with the views of its academic members, ASPA would not carry forward the work on elections of the early nonprofits, or elaborate and extend Harris' contributions. Without the support of an academic discipline, election administration would struggle and flounder with professionalization only a hope for the future. In the late twentieth century, election officials of state and local governments would form professional societies of their own (see section 6.12 for the development of two of these organizations that have become especially important).

4.9   HERMAN HOLLERITH AND PUNCH-CARD DATA PROCESSING

The use of PPCs in Florida in 2000 resulted from the work of Herman Hollerith (1860–1929), more than a century before. Born in Buffalo, New York, Hollerith exemplified the inventiveness and entrepreneurship of the late nineteenth century. He entered the Columbia School of Mines in 1875 and graduated in 1879. He would use his engineering training extensively, but would never employ the specialty of mining. He received no formal instruction in electricity, but nearly all his inventions would employ that form of power.

In 1880, he went to Washington, DC, to work for the U.S. Census Office. While there, he met Dr. John Shaw Billings, a physician and head of the Division of Vital Statistics. Billings served as a mentor to Hollerith and, years after, the latter quoted Billings as stating that "There ought to be a machine for doing the purely mechanical work of tabulating population and similar statistics . . ." (Austrian, 1982, p. 6). Billings aided Hollerith's effort to collect and use health data. These data would be processed and aggregated with his devices to generate statistics useful for decision making in public heath policy.

Census managers realized that the large number of clerks required to process the 1880 census had exhausted the funds supplied before all the data collected could be turned into useful statistics. Some radically new processing method was required for the census of 1890, the 11th since the first census of 1790. Population increases and the desire to determine more details about individuals would require an even larger quantity of data to be collected and more statistics to be calculated.

Hollerith got his idea for punched cards from seeing a train conductor punch holes in a railway ticket, using particular areas of the ticket to record a "punch photograph" of the passenger. Train conductors used this method to prevent a new passenger from using someone else's punched ticket to claim that the fare had already been paid. If two individuals involved in the fraud were physically different in some way and that difference had been punched into the ticket, the scam would be prevented.

In September 1884, Hollerith filed his first patent application for his data processing device and would file two others in the next few years. He described his inventions as improvement in the art of compiling statistics. His first patents would be issued on January 8, 1889. The first in the sequence of three on a row was no. 395781.

In 1886, he went to Baltimore where he had received a contract to reduce data to generate statistical results. He recorded and summarized vital statistics for the city's Health Department with his punch-card machines. To produce the Baltimore statistics, he made holes in the cards himself, using a train conductor's punch. The holes were fully punched through with the tool. There were no "hanging" chads. Later, when Hollerith designed mechanical punches, the same result obtained, that is, the holes were unambiguously and fully punched through. This condition would pertain for all punched cards used over the years in their business or statistical applications.

The two machines he used in Baltimore were a tabulator and a sorting box. The tabulator included a counter for each usable location in a card. A particular location indicated an answer to a yes/no question. A hole indicated one of the binary possibilities and no hole indicated the other. The operator of the tabulator entered each card in the machine, one at a time. Wherever the machine found a hole, an electrified stylus would poke through the hole into a small cup of mercury. That action would close an electric circuit fed from a battery and increment the associated counter.

The sorting box was divided into a number of compartments with lids. The use of the sorter enabled a succession of tabulations to be done, each based on a smaller number of records.

After a successful contest of his machines pitted against two manual data reduction systems, he was awarded a contract for the 1890 census. His headquarters were in the Georgetown section of Washington, DC, near the old C & O canal. His machines were run with batteries, recharged each day from Thomas Edison's DC lighting circuits, which had been made available recently in Washington. Some of Hollerith's machines were being manufactured in Boston at a Western Electric facility. It turned out that this location was the same place used by Alexander Graham Bell and by Edison for his early work. (Note Edison's residence in table 4.1.)

Further experimentation allowed Hollerith to add to his inventory of different types of machines. He designed an electric adding machine, a keypunch machine, and an automatic feeder for the keypunch. His sorter was redesigned to use electricity and was made more automatic. He invented the plugboard to more easily change connections in the sorter and tabulator.

Later, Hollerith sold his equipment to health departments of other cities and states, to other nations for their censuses, and to private corporations. The Prudential Life Insurance Company was his first private customer and he sold equipment also to railroads. In about 1896, he incorporated as the Tabulating Machine Company. In 1911, he sold out in a merger of several organizations, including his own, that formed the Computing-Tabulating-Recording Company. In 1914, the new company hired Thomas J. Watson (1874–1956) as its general manager. In 1924, Watson, as president of the firm, changed its name to International Business Machines, known in brief as IBM.

4.10   MORE DEVELOPMENTS USING ELECTRICITY

A patent for the telephone was obtained by Alexander Graham Bell (1847–1922) in 1876. By 1880, there were already 54,000 telephones in use in the United States. New inventions soon improved voice quality, but an essential breakthrough was the invention of telephone switchboards. The first was installed in New Haven, Connecticut, in 1878. These provided the facility for one of a large number of subscribers to select another for a one-to-one conversation that was bidirectional. The number of telephones grew rapidly; in 1890, there were 228,000. In 1896, presidential candidate William McKinley was able to call his state campaign chairmen from his own home. In 1900, there were over 1.3 million telephones in use and, in 1915, there were over 10 million (Fischer, 1997, p. 274).

The use of electric power as a utility was foreseen by Thomas Edison as he worked on the development of the electric light bulb in the 1870s. The bulb's use in homes required a power source in a form that did not yet exist. DC current was available from batteries and was used with the first telephones. It was not yet supplied as a utility from a central generating station.

Edison received a patent in 1880 for his light bulb that could be used indoors. With the backing of financier J. P. Morgan (1837–1913), he built an electric power station generating DC at Pearl Street in New York City in 1882. Generating stations were soon installed in other cities. At the value of voltage needed for the lights, DC could be efficiently transmitted over short distances. It was not, however, the final word. Edison had backed the wrong horse in this race.

The first practical alternating current (AC) motor was patented by Nikola Tesla (1856–1943) in 1888. Tesla was an immigrant, educated in the Austro-Hungarian empire. He came to the United States to find backing for implementing his ideas about the use of AC and obtained financial aid from George Westinghouse (1846–1914), inventor of the air brake.

AC has significant advantages. It could be used (and is used today) to transmit power at very high voltages but low levels of current over long distances in its three-phase form invented by Tesla. The low current level minimizes the losses in the transmission process. At application points, the voltage is stepped down, as it was stepped up for transmission. The change in voltage levels is accomplished with a "transformer." Tesla was one of the developers of these devices.

AC began to be widely available as the basic power source for almost all home and business uses. It was used to power the Chicago World's Fair in 1893. In the same year, contracts were awarded to Westinghouse to provide AC as the electricity generated from the force of flowing water at Niagara Falls (Hanson, 1982, p. 21). If DC was needed locally, it could be obtained from AC through a simple process called "rectification."

4.11 VOTING PROCESS CHANGES IN THE EARLY TWENTIETH CENTURY

During the first decades of the new century, there were several strong efforts made to obtain changes in the voting process. Reformers, many of who supported Theodore Roosevelt in his unsuccessful Progressive Party challenge of 1912, were certain that additional and altered voting procedures would make governmental bodies more responsive to the citizenry. They believed, as a result of their understanding of conditions in the late nineteenth century, that elected governmental officials were far too often the tools of big business or political bosses.

Selection of U.S. senators by state legislatures had been, in many cases, the result of private deals that ignored the public at-large. Recognition of this fact created a demand for their direct election. This was achieved through a modification in the Constitution (17th Amendment, ratified 1913). Implementing legislation required that elections for senators would occur on the same day as elections for members of the House of Representatives and Electors for president and vice president.

The direct primary for nomination of candidates was another subject for reformers. They campaigned to implement, in the states, individual citizen voting for candidates instead of conventions or caucuses of insiders. There had been attempts in the nineteenth century through state legislation to control primaries, but the laws were limited in effect. In 1903, Wisconsin enacted the first comprehensive direct-primary law. Oregon passed such a law in 1904 and nearly all states (except in the South) adopted similar requirements by 1920. These laws further regulated political parties and made any claim that they were private clubs not subject to open enrollment impossible to sustain. In the South, only Supreme Court decisions would open primaries to all citizens.

The processes of citizen ballot initiatives and recall of elected officials were promoted in states and cities. Success in these latter endeavors varied from place to place. California adopted these measures, and the recall was successfully used to replace its governor in 2004.

Women were given the right to vote in all federal and state elections under another Constitutional alteration in this period (19th Amendment, ratified

1920). With that action, the size of the electorate was nearly doubled. Some states and territories, particularly in the West, for example, Wyoming, Utah, and Colorado, had previously granted women the voting franchise. There was a belief among some that giving women the vote would tend to reduce violence and rowdiness during elections, as their presence at the polls would have a civilizing influence.

American Indians were categorically enfranchised at about the same time. Following World War I, Congress granted citizenship to the Indians who had honorably served (66th Congress, Sess. I, Chap. 95). In 1924, Congress conferred citizenship on all American Indians who had not yet received it (68th Congress, Sess. II, Chap. 233). Some had previously obtained citizenship in the nineteenth century by law or treaty. Even after 1924, some states were recalcitrant in permitting Native Americans to vote. Indians at that time were thus in the same position as blacks, legally enfranchised by federal law but, in some states, unable to exercise the right of suffrage.

Constitutional permission for a direct federal income tax on individuals was achieved through the 16th Amendment, ratified 1913. The imposition of a personal income tax provided the means for obtaining additional revenue necessary to carry out the national regulatory functions that, increasingly, were being demanded. This burden had no immediate impact on the voting process, but it did enable the federal government to obtain a source of funding roughly correlated with an individual's ability to pay. (In 1913, customs duties provided 45 percent of all federal revenue. Now the percentage is minuscule.) The income tax gave each citizen a larger personal stake in the income of the federal government; every taxpayer was more directly involved in how much the government took in and what it did with its money. That arrangement provided an increasing awareness of national citizenship as contrasted with state citizenship.

An impact on the voting process would occur much later. The Florida fiasco of 2000 generated the impetus for federal financial assistance under the Help America Vote Act of 2002. That assistance would not have been possible without the deep pockets that Uncle Sam had acquired as a result of the 16th Amendment and the legitimacy of additional tax legislation that it has allowed.

Additional territorial expansion and new states were established during this period. Alaska, which had been purchased from Russia in 1867, became an organized territory in 1912. Hawaii was annexed in 1898; its territorial government was established in 1900. The last three territories in the contiguous United States, Oklahoma, New Mexico, and Arizona, became states, the first in 1907 and the latter two in 1912; the U.S. Senate was augmented accordingly. Alaska and Hawaii became states in 1958 and 1959, respectively.

The House of Representatives was increased in size to 435 members in 1911 (62nd Congress, Sess. I, Chap. 5). Seats were apportioned to the states under the 13th census of 1910. Allowance for one seat each was made for the expected needs of Arizona and New Mexico. In the same act, a requirement for House districts based on the 13th census to consist of "compact territory" was adopted. In 1921 and later that decade, during the terms of Presidents Harding and Coolidge, Congress failed to reapportion the House on the basis of the 14th census (1920); that neglect had not occurred with respect to any previous census nor has it occurred since. In 1929, the requirement for compact territory expired. That situation occurred by virtue of a new law of that year (71st Congress, Sess. I, Chap. 28) concerning the forthcoming 15th census in which the requirement was not renewed. Gerrymandering of district boundaries, which could not be instituted under a strict requirement for compact territory, was too powerful a partisan tool to be denied. House size has remained at 435 as of 2005; it was temporarily 437 after the admission of Alaska and Hawaii, until the reapportionment due to the 18th census of 1960.

Extension of the Australian ballot to other states occurred. Three of the eight jurisdictions listed that had failed to adopt the Australian ballot in the nineteenth century, Texas, Connecticut, and New Jersey, did so, respectively, in 1905, 1909, and 1911. Delaware, in 1913, backtracked and "permitted distribution of ballots by party chairmen prior to the day of election, voters being able to mark the ballots in advance" (Albright, 1942, p. 29). Three of the states previously listed as lacking the official blanket ballot, Missouri, New Mexico, and North Carolina, legislated it in the 1920s. Georgia, in 1922, permitted its counties to adopt the Australian ballot, but not all did so immediately. In addition to Georgia, Delaware, and South Carolina did not have a truly secret statewide ballot system in the 1930s and 1940s. South Carolina adopted the Australian ballot in 1950 (Schlesinger, 1993, p. 365). Delaware eliminated paper ballots and switched to mechanical lever machines, statewide, in 1953.

The presidential short ballot, eliminating the names of Electors, was promoted with the increasing adoption of lever voting machines. Although Massachusetts, in 1892, had provided a single square on its paper ballot to indicate a vote for all Electors for president of a single party (the Electors were still named), other states started to simplify the presidential ballot in 1900 and later. Minnesota similarly specified a single square in 1901. The advent of the voting machine, with its limited space, induced Iowa, Indiana, New Jersey, and Illinois to eliminate the names of the Electors in 1900, 1901, 1902, and 1903, respectively. They provided a single lever for "Presidential Electors" of a particular party on the machines. Later, New York and Rhode Island would do the same.

Where paper ballots were still used, the process of eliminating the names of the Electors began later. Nebraska eliminated the Electors' names in 1917 and Iowa accomplished that change in 1919. Iowa's law on this subject specified that "a vote for the candidates of a party for president and vice-president shall legally be regarded and counted as have been cast for the list of candidates of that party for electors" (Aylsworth, 1930, p. 967). This wording assured that the Electors would be named on the day specified under federal law. The elimination of Electors' names significantly reduced the size of ballots, particularly in the larger states that adopted the procedure. These included Illinois, Michigan, and Ohio. By the 1940 presidential election, 17 states had done so (Albright, 1942, pp. 99–113).

Under the 20th Amendment of 1933, terms of senators and representatives end and new terms begin on January 3 at noon; terms of president and vice president end and new terms begin on January 20 at noon. Now, the count of electoral votes would be carried out by the new Congress, not the old one. The last time that Congress had visited this issue was in 1872 (see section 3.7).

In 1934, as noted in section 3.9, Congress changed the dates for the Electors to give their votes in each state and for Congress to receive and count them.

4.12   ELECTION FRAUD IN THE EARLY TWENTIETH CENTURY

Rural areas were subject to frauds, as were urban areas. In some Southern states, precinct registration officials had wide discretion to disqualify prospective voters. An applicant's failure to give "a reasonable interpretation" of the Constitution to the satisfaction of the precinct official could result in denial of registration. African Americans were routinely denied registration in this manner. Additionally:

> In Pennsylvania, the formidable Republican state machine built by Matthew Stanley Quay gained its victories in part through multiple voting and illegal registration in small upstate cities and rural townships. Vote buying and stealing were also common in the rural areas of southern Ohio and southern Indiana. . . . Various sources have reported general acceptance of election fraud in Kentucky and West Virginia. In Texas, V. O. Key found evidence in the 1940s that party workers in many parts of the state continued a long tradition of manipulating ballot box results. (Goldberg, 1987, p. 183).

V. O. Key's research in Texas would seem to be validated by Ronnie Dugger's review of conditions resulting in Lyndon Johnson's U.S. senate primary victory in 1948 (Dugger, 1982, pp. 322–341).

The far West was not immune. A fraudulent election in 1914 associated with a prolonged coal miners' strike in Huerfano County, Colorado, is reported by Keyssar (Keyssar, 2000, p. 160). In that case, seven precincts were totally on coal company land; company guards refused admittance to the polling stations to anyone that they thought would vote against candidates supporting the company. Furthermore, illiterate scabs were assisted by precinct officials to vote the company way. The election was voided by the Colorado Supreme Court following a protest.

In larger cities, significant parts were, at that time, controlled by a ward boss. These wards were typically those in the transient part of the city, where certain kinds of crimes might be tolerated. Bipartisan representation on election boards, as a practical matter, might be nonexistent in these wards. As noted by Joseph P. Harris,

> The graft, corruption, and protection of vice and crime in many cities can be traced directly to the influence exercised by the corrupt and unscrupulous politicians who control these wards (Harris, 1929, p. 9).

Harris has given examples of election fraud during Prohibition, that is, following passage of the 18th Amendment in 1919 and prior to ratification of the 21st Amendment in 1933 (Harris, 1929, pp. 362–377, 1934, pp. 340–369).

In Philadelphia, returns from a transient ward in 1923 showed a highly unlikely 91.5 percent turnout while a typical stable ward had a 65.5 percent turnout.

In Louisville, a municipal election in 1925 was set aside by the Kentucky Court of Appeals. The local Republican party had paid volunteers to vote while impersonating dead or moved individuals.

In Chicago, the Republican primary in 1926 was cited as possibly one of the most corrupt elections ever held. Violence, intimidation, kidnapping, repeating, ballot stuffing, and other felonies occurred.

In Pittsburgh, following the 1927 election, a number of precinct officials were found guilty of ballot stuffing and changing the selections on ballots properly cast.

In Cleveland, an investigation of elections in 1928 resulted in indictments of precinct officials for votes cast in the names of persons who were dead or out-of-town and for deliberate miscounts of ballots.

4.13   PROGRESS IN SYSTEMS OF VOTER REGISTRATION

The concern here is not the set of requirements for suffrage, but the establishment of administrative systems. Lists of qualified voters were originally generated through the use of landholder and taxpayer records, when there were these types of requirements for voting. After such requirements were eliminated, there was no record system easily adapted for registration purposes. In Massachusetts, in 1800, a law was adopted requiring assessors of each town or plantation to prepare lists of qualified voters. These lists were then given to the selectmen, that is, each town's political leaders, posted, and revised for each election. Citizens not on the list could not vote. Those not listed but who believed that they were qualified could approach the selectmen on the day of election to request their addition to the list. The constitutionality of compulsory registration in Massachusetts was challenged and upheld in 1832 in a case called *Capen v. Foster*. Other New England states adopted similar laws in the early nineteenth century.

In Pennsylvania, the first registration law was enacted in 1836, but it applied only to Philadelphia. As in Massachusetts, assessors were assigned to produce the list and no person whose name was not listed could vote. The process was vigorously debated at the Pennsylvania constitutional convention of 1837. Supporters said that the law significantly reduced fraud and violence, while opponents stated that the law discriminated against the poor; the same arguments, for and against registration regulations, are used today. Opponents stated that data was collected by a house-to-house canvass, carried out during the day when workingmen were away at jobs, whereas at the homes of the rich, "the gold and silver door plate with name was enough" to verify the occupant's residence. The continuation of the law was approved, and opponents' amendment to extend the law throughout the state was defeated.

National interest in voter registration started to increase after 1860, and by World War I, most states had adopted some form of an administrative system. Indiana adopted its first registration law in 1911, which is one reason that the state was a hotbed of fraudulent activity before then. It later repealed that law. As of 1929, according to Harris, some form of registration was found in every state except in Indiana, Arkansas, and Texas. In the latter two, poll tax payment records served as a substitute.

In general, registration laws applied more stringent requirements to cities; the larger the city, the more stringent the requirement. The intent of the laws was to prevent election fraud, but the laws were, for the most part, ineffective. At first, the voter was not required to submit an application; the registration officers were authorized to prepare lists of qualified voters from their knowledge and from canvasses. Politicians often handed in long lists of names to be registered, and these were likely filled with names of persons who had moved or died or were fictitious. The purpose of these fraudulent lists was to provide opportunities for repeaters, impersonators, or ballot stuffing by precinct officials.

Then, personal registration began to be required. The burden was put on the voter rather than on the government to initiate registration. In many places, the attempt to assure a registration list having integrity was coupled with a requirement for reregistration every year. In other places, reregistration was required every two years and in some places, four years. The necessity of reregistration was considered onerous by many citizens. The movement to permanent registration began with Boston in 1896. In that city, the job of an annual canvass was carried out by the police, and this action made it possible to purge a centralized list every year. A similar process began to be carried out in Milwaukee in 1911 and in Omaha in 1913. The centralized list under control of a single election commissioner eliminated control of ward politicians over registration. Centralization was of significant value in the prevention of fraud. Minnesota adopted a permanent registration law for cities having a population of over 50,000 in 1923. New Jersey did so in 1926 for cities with population over 15,000. Permanent registration was adopted in Ohio and Michigan in 1929.

Joseph P. Harris strongly made the point in 1929 that permanent registration can only work if purging of the list is well carried out (Harris, 1929, pp. 214–239). If there is no effective procedure for purging, the knowledge that registration lists are filled with names that be fraudulently used is a detriment to public confidence in elections. A method that he proposed, cancellation of registration for failure to vote, became controversial with the increasing interest in voter registration as a component of civil rights in the 1960s. The National Voter Registration Act of 1993 eliminated purging solely for failure to vote (see section 5.11). As a result, concerns have risen again (see section 7.10).

Harris' discussion about record keeping by election administrations presents an incredulous situation, even for 1929. Harris states:

> Most of the existing records belong to the days when the typewriter had not been invented and loose-leaf or card records were unknown. Practically all of the clerical work at present is laboriously written out in longhand . . . (Harris, 1929, p. 159).

For purposes of efficiency, Harris recommended a loose-leaf page or file card for each voter, but the possibility of the application of punched cards was not proposed. In 1929, that would have been a distinct possibility in the larger jurisdictions. It had been 43 years since Hollerith had put each of his subject's data on one punch card. In 1928, the 80-column IBM card, continually used since then, had been devised. Punch-card data processing was in wide use in business.

By 1936, punch-card data processing was used in the operations of the federal Social Security Administration. The records of employees covered by social security were each entered on a punch card. Coverage extended to 26 million workers employed by 3 million employers. By comparison, the failure of election administrations to use any punch-card data processing in 1929 demonstrates the backwardness of its operations. In many places, administration of elections would continue to remain behind standard business practices for the remainder of the century.

5

THE MIDDLE AND LATE TWENTIETH CENTURY: MOVEMENTS FOR EQUALITY, ENFRANCHISEMENT, AND VOTING FACILITATION

5.1 THE EFFORT TO END RACIAL DISCRIMINATION

It is not possible in this presentation to graphically detail the events of the 1950s and 1960s that led to the passage of the Civil Rights Act of 1964 (Public Law 88-352, July 2, 1964) and the Voting Rights Act of 1965 (Public Law 89-110, August 6, 1965). The high level of public emotion can be cited, but not explicitly described with the literary flavor that it deserves. An initiating factor was the heightened demand on the part of the black community of the South that their second-class citizenship be brought to an end. The sympathetic response by many whites throughout the nation, except in the South, made it possible. The problem of African Americans in the South was not only their inability to vote; it was the pervasive segregation that resulted in inferior treatment in almost every aspect of life. Despite the Supreme Court ruling in *Brown v. Board of Education of Topeka* in 1954 that school segregation was inherently unequal, little had changed in the years immediately afterward. The Birmingham, Alabama, bus boycott, triggered by Rosa Parks's refusal to give up her seat to a white man, had occurred in 1955. The following years were filled with demonstrations—"sit-ins" that attempted to desegregate restaurants and restrooms, demands for "try-on" privileges in clothing stores, and violent reactions by some whites. Some blacks who had attempted to register to vote were summarily dismissed, others were shot down, and little was done by local white authorities to pursue justice. While the Civil Rights and Voting Rights Acts were intended to end the unconscionable discrimination against African Americans, the elimination of voting restrictions due to race would apply also to American Indians, Alaskan Natives, and Asian Americans.

5.2 EQUALITY OF POPULATION IN LEGISLATIVE DISTRICTS

At about the same time, a different demand for equality was being pursued through the federal courts. This was the concern of some citizens that legislative districts, both state and federal, were skewed so that, in some districts, significantly fewer citizens could elect a representative than in other districts. In general, rural districts were favored. One of the first efforts to redress this grievance was in *Colegrove v. Green* in 1946. In this case from Illinois, the plaintiff charged that that states' Congressional districts "lacked compactness of territory and approximate equality of population." The U.S. Supreme Court denied the plaintiff's complaint, holding that there was no existing federal law that imposed any requirements "as to compactness and equality of population of districts."

The viewpoint of the Court began to change with *Gomillion v. Lightfoot* in 1960. In this case, Alabama had redrawn the boundaries of the city of Tuskegee, originally an approximate square, to a multisided figure that excluded nearly all black residents from the city. The unanimous Supreme Court held that the state's actions violated the 15th Amendment and that the state was unable to identify any "countervailing municipal function" that would justify the changed boundaries.

In the landmark decision of *Baker v. Carr*, 1962, plaintiffs complained that Tennessee had failed to reapportion its state legislative districts in over 60 years, thereby ignoring shifts of population that should have markedly revised district boundaries. The Supreme Court agreed that legislative redistricting in this case was a justiciable issue. The question of "equal protection," required under the 14th Amendment, merited evaluation. Thus, the opinion in *Colegrove* was not followed.

In the closely following case of *Gray v. Sanders*, 1963, a resident of Atlanta, in Fulton County, Georgia, filed a suit against officials of the Georgia Democratic Party and the Georgia Secretary of State because of the manner in which the results of the Democratic Party primary were computed. At issue was the Georgia county unit system, under which each county was given the same weight regardless of population. Justice William O. Douglas delivered the eight–one opinion of the Court and ruled for the plaintiffs. Perhaps one of the most memorable statements of the U.S. Supreme Court was within this opinion:

> The conception of political equality from the Declaration of Independence, to Lincoln's Gettysburg Address, to the Fifteenth, Seventeenth, and Nineteenth Amendments can mean only one thing—one person, one vote.

Soon after, another case from Georgia, *Wesberry v. Sanders*, was decided early in 1964. This situation concerned Congressional districting. The plaintiff's fifth Congressional District had a population at least twice as large as some of the other districts in the state. The Court held that Georgia's apportionment scheme was discriminatory. The Court recognized that "no right is more precious" than that of having a voice in elections. It held that

> to say that a vote is worth more in one district than in another would not only run counter to our fundamental ideas of democratic government, it would cast aside the principle of a House of Representatives elected "by the People."

Reynolds v. Sims was another in the series of cases that would require relative equality in apportionment. This case, decided in 1964, originated in Alabama. In another eight–one decision, the Court upheld the challenge to the Alabama state legislative scheme, holding that the equal protection clause of the 14th Amendment demanded "no less than substantially equal state legislative representative for all citizens . . ." The Court held that both houses of bicameral state legislatures had to be apportioned on a population basis. States were required to employ "honest and good faith" efforts to construct districts as nearly of equal population as practicable.

5.3   VOTING RIGHTS ADVANCED IN CONSTITUTIONAL AMENDMENTS

The District of Columbia achieved some federal voting rights in 1961. In Article 1, Section 8 of the Constitution, it is stated that:

> Congress shall have Power . . . To exercise exclusive Legislation in all Cases whatsoever, over such District (not exceeding ten miles square) as may, by cession of particular States, and the acceptance of Congress, become the Seat of the Government of the United States . . .

Thus, DC was formed from parts of Maryland and Virginia, but the part taken from Virginia was later given back to that state. The District had never been given official representation in Congress or the right to vote for president before 1960.

The composition of DC began to change after World War II, as more affluent residents moved to the adjacent states, Maryland and Virginia, and were replaced by blacks moving up from the South. Congress believed it was right for citizens of the District to be able to vote for president and vice president, even if the area did not have representation in that body. The question was now associated with the national issue of racial segregation. The result was the 23rd Amendment, proposed by Congress June 16, 1960 and ratified by the states on March 29, 1961. The amendment provided that the District could appoint and elect the same number of Electors that it would have if it were a state, but no more than the least populous state. As a practical matter, the District would have three electoral votes, beginning with the 1964 presidential election.

In 1970, Congress approved a nonvoting delegate from DC in the House of Representatives. In 1978, Congress adopted a proposed constitutional amendment by the necessary two-third majority in each House, which would give the District two seats in the U.S. Senate, as well as a voting seat in the House of Representatives. That proposal would not be ratified by a sufficient number of states (38 were needed) in the allotted time of seven years and would not go into effect. It is very possible that if Congress had adopted a limited measure only assigning a seat in the House for DC, it would have been ratified.

The imposition of a poll tax, common in states in the South, had the function of preventing the poor from voting. Many of them were black, but certainly not all. Thus, the 24th Amendment was proposed by Congress on August 27, 1962 and ratified by the states on January 23, 1964. It eliminated poll taxes in elections for president and vice president, for presidential Electors, and for members of Congress. The law did not prevent the imposition of a poll tax in state or local government elections. That would come soon after.

Later, during the Vietnam War, it was realized that American soldiers could die fighting at age 18 but could not, in most states, vote at that age. The result was the proposal by Congress on March 23, 1971, to require states to lower the voting age to 18, if they had not done so already. The 26th Amendment with this requirement was quickly ratified on June 30, 1971.

5.4   EVENTS LEADING UP TO THE VOTING RIGHTS ACT

Activism and violence marked the struggle for civil rights in the1960s. On August 28, 1963, Dr. Martin Luther King, Jr. delivered his famous "I have a dream" speech from the steps of the Lincoln Memorial in Washington before an estimated crowd of 200,000. However, 1963 would see several murders in response to civil rights demands. (King himself would be murdered in 1968.) Among those assassinated were Medgar Evers, a black community organizer on June 12, 1963, in front of his home in Mississippi. Four young girls were killed on September 15, 1963 in a bombing at the Sixteenth Street Baptist Church in Birmingham, Alabama. On November 22, 1963, President John F. Kennedy was shot and killed in Dallas, but no connection with black civil rights was ever demonstrated. Vice President Lyndon Johnson of Texas was sworn in as president later the same day; his support for voting rights legislation would be important and effective. Another long-term result was the recapture of the South by the Republican party.

Three civil rights workers, James Chaney, Andrew Goodman, and Michael Schwerner, were slain on June 21, 1964 in Mississippi. On March 7, 1965, peaceful marchers were set upon by state police with fire hoses and vicious dogs in Selma, Alabama, a scene widely seen throughout the country through photos and films. The Rev. James Reeb was attacked on March 8 in the same place, which resulted in his death two days later, and Viola Liuzzo, a mother of five from Detroit, was deliberately shot and killed while lawfully driving in Alabama on March 25.

There were legal assaults on the denial of voting rights prior to 1965. In 1915, in *Guinn v. United States*, the Supreme Court invalidated voter registration requirements containing "grandfather clauses." These made voter registration in part dependent upon whether the applicant was descended from men enfranchised before enactment of the 15th Amendment. The court found that the Oklahoma law at issue had been adopted to give illiterate whites, but not blacks, a way to avoid taking the state's literacy test for voting. In 1944, the Supreme Court held, in *Smith v. Allwright*, that the Texas "white primary" violated the 15th Amendment. This decision began the elimination of enforcement of Southern laws, which held that political parties were private clubs and therefore exempt from equal protection provisions.

Congress passed civil rights legislation in 1957 and 1960. The first of these (September 9, 1957) created the U.S. Commission on Civil Rights as well as the Civil Rights Division within the U.S. Department of Justice (DOJ). The attorney general was given authority to intervene in and institute lawsuits seeking injunctive relief against violations of the 15th Amendment. The 1960 Act (Public Law 86-449, May 6, 1960) permitted federal courts to appoint voting referees to conduct voter registration following a judicial finding of voting discrimination. The 1960 Act, in its Title III, required retention of all documentation of federal elections for 22 months, a provision that would prove to be important in auditing of registration rolls and of vote-casting and vote-counting records.

The 1964 Civil Rights Act concerned elimination of discrimination in places of public accommodation, in public education, and in employment. (It concerned voting rights, also, but most of those provisions were superseded by the Voting Rights Act of 1965). It specifically identified religion and national origin, as well as race and color, as categories that required nondiscrimination.

The strategy of litigation on a case-by-case basis would prove to be of very limited success in the jurisdictions that had been sued. It did not prompt voluntary compliance among jurisdictions that had not been sued. Literacy tests, poll taxes, and other formal and informal practices combined to keep black registration rates minimal in Alabama, Louisiana, and Mississippi, and well below white registration rates in other Southern states.

5.5 PROVISIONS OF THE 1965 VOTING RIGHTS ACT AND AMENDMENTS OF 1970

The original act of 1965 was prefaced with the explanation that it was "An Act to enforce the 15th Amendment to the Constitution of the United States, and for other purposes." An important function was to end the use of "tests or devices" as mechanisms for disfranchisement. This phrase meant:

> any requirement that a person as a prerequisite for voting or registration for voting (1) demonstrate the ability to read, write, understand, or interpret any

matter, (2) demonstrate any educational achievement or his knowledge of any particular subject, (3) possess good moral character, or (4) prove his qualifications by the voucher of registered voters or members of any other class. (PL 89-110, Sec. 4 (c))

Sec. 4 (a) made clear the elimination of tests or devices. This section stated that:

> To assure that the right of citizens . . . to vote is not denied or abridged on account of race or color, no citizen shall be denied the right to vote in any federal, state, or local election because of his failure to comply with any test or device. . . .

The demographics of voting were referenced in the law. Sec. 4 (b) required that:

> The provisions of subsection (a) shall apply in any state or in any political subdivision of a state which (1) the Attorney General determines maintained on November 1, 1964, any test or device, and with respect to which (2) the Director of the Census determines that less than 50 per centum of the persons of voting age residing therein were registered on November 1, 1964, or that less than 50 per centum of such persons voted in the Presidential election of November, 1964.

Under Section 5 of the Act, no voting changes were legally enforceable in "covered" jurisdictions unless approved either by a three-judge federal court in the District of Columbia or by the attorney general. If the latter's opinion were requested, he or she would have 60 days to object and, if no objection were received, the changes could go forward. Nevertheless, the changes could still be challenged in a court. Section 5 initially applied to all of Alabama, Georgia, Louisiana, Mississippi, South Carolina, and Virginia, and parts of North Carolina and Alaska. The latter was able to get itself removed from coverage within a few years under provisions of the Act conditionally permitting that to happen. Of North Carolina's 100 counties, 39 were covered.

The appointment of federal examiners was an enforcement mechanism for assurance of equality in registration and voting. The examiners are to prepare and maintain lists of persons eligible to vote in federal, state, and local elections and to examine applicants concerning their qualifications for voting. Any person who an examiner finds "to have the qualifications prescribed by state law not inconsistent with the Constitution and laws of the United States shall promptly be placed on a list of eligible voters." The list is to be closed 45 days before the next election. In addition, the examiners may:

> (1) enter and attend at any place for holding an election in such subdivision for the purpose of observing whether persons who are entitled to vote are being permitted to vote and (2) enter and attend at any place for tabulating the votes

cast at any election held in such subdivision for the purpose of observing whether votes cast by persons entitled to vote are being properly tabulated. (PL 89-110, Sec. 8)

Section 11 of the Act prevented anyone "acting under the color of law" to refuse to permit any person to vote who is qualified to vote, or "willfully fail or refuse to tabulate, count, and report such person's vote." Intimidation, threats, or coercion of persons attempting to vote and of those urging others to vote was specifically forbidden.

The use of languages other than English was recognized in the law. Section 4 (e)(1) stated that:

Congress hereby declares that to secure the rights under the 14th Amendment of persons educated in American-flag schools in which the predominant classroom language was other than English, it is necessary to prohibit the states from conditioning the right to vote of such persons on ability to read, write, understand, or interpret any matter in the English language.

The process to end poll taxes for state and local government elections was begun in the Act. The Congress declared in Section 10 (a) that "the constitutional right of citizens to vote is denied or abridged in some areas by the requirement of the payment of a poll tax as a precondition to voting." It authorized the attorney general to seek the judgment of the district court as to whether the imposition of the poll tax was Constitutional, that is it had some legitimate purpose other than denying persons who could not afford it the right to vote.

The Voting Rights Act was upheld in 1966 by the Supreme Court in *South Carolina v. Katzenbach*. Virginia's poll tax (and by implication, poll taxes in all state elections) was found unconstitutional in *Harper v. Virginia State Board of Elections*, also in 1966. The effect of the 1965 Voting Rights Act was, over the next two decades, an enormous increase in the percentage of black voter registrations in Southern states. It would rise to approximate the percentage of white registration.

The amendments of 1970 (Public Law 91-285, June 22, 1970) extended the reach of some of the provisions from five years to ten years. The limitation of five years had occurred in several places in Section 4 (a) of the 1965 Act, relating to the concern of the courts and use of tests or devices. The demographics of voting were extended from the 1964 presidential election to the 1968 presidential election. Other states or subdivisions that used tests or devices were added to the purview of the Act, even if their voter registration demographics could not be cited by the director of the census as having less than 50 percent registered.

In the 1970 Amendments, Section 6, Congress provided for the ability of citizens who changed their residences between states just before a presidential election to vote for president and vice president or their Electors. Such citizens would be allowed to vote for those offices if they applied 30 days or more before the election, regardless of other residence requirements.

5.6   Amendments of 1975: Bilingual Elections

In the amendments of 1975 (Public Law 94-73, August 6, 1975), provisions of Section 4 (a), in which the time of "five years" had been replaced by "ten years" in 1970, would contain a new replacement of "seventeen years." References to the 1968 election were replaced by references to the 1972 election.

A new section, "Bilingual Election Requirements," was added to the Voting Rights Act in 1975. The Act defined new terms:

> The term 'language minorities' or 'language minority group' means persons who are American Indian, Asian American, Alaskan Native or of Spanish heritage.

As a result of this enactment, whenever any political subdivision of a state provides:

> any registration or voting notices, forms, instructions, assistance, or other materials or information relating to the electoral process, including ballots, it shall provide them in the language of the applicable minority group as well as in the English language: *Provided*, that where the language of the applicable minority group is oral or unwritten . . . the . . . political subdivision is only required to furnish oral instructions, assistance, or other assistance relating to registration and voting.

This requirement for ballots and other materials in the other language would pertain only if:

> (1) more than 5 percent of the citizens of voting age of such subdivision are members of a single language minority and (2) that the illiteracy rate of such persons as a group is higher than the national illiteracy rate . . . Illiteracy means the failure to complete the fifth primary grade.

The impact on larger political subdivisions with several different language minorities, such as Los Angeles (LA) County, could have been severe. LA County, the nation's largest local jurisdiction, was using the Votomatic PPC system when the law was passed, and continued to use it through 2000. (By 2004, the county needed to be concerned with five Asian languages as well as Spanish: Chinese, Japanese, Korean, Tagalog, and Vietnamese.) Conny B. McCormack, registrar-recorder of LA County, has said that, by agreement with the U.S. Department of Justice, the county did not have to implement all precincts with ballots in all languages. County officials, using data from the U.S. Bureau of the Census, determined particular precincts where significant numbers of minority-language speakers were present. Voting materials and sample ballots in those languages were distributed to residents. Minority-language speakers who were not in a targeted precinct could call the office of the registrar-recorder (later, use its website) and ask to be put on a list to

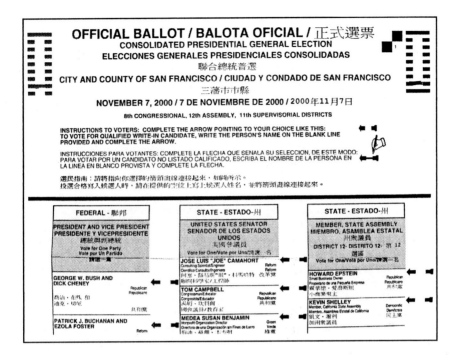

Figure 5.1 Top of a 9¾-inch-by-18-inch optical-scan ballot using three languages, San Francisco, CA, 2000.

permanently receive voting materials in their language. Minority-language speakers could take the sample ballots in their language into the voting booth, where they could match the sample ballot against the Votomatic vote-recorder pages. The latter were only in English.

If LA County had wished to change its voting system from Votomatic PPCs to marksense ballots, it might have had to provide ballots in all of the other languages. The county could not easily change its voting system at reasonable cost until it could do so by providing ballots in other languages on demand. The latter could occur only with a direct-recording electronic (DRE) voting system.

San Francisco (City and County) accepted the challenge of multilingual marksense (optical scan) ballots, even though it made them larger and much heavier to transport in bulk. (See figure 5.1 for the top part of the city's three-language ballot.)

5.7 AMENDMENTS OF 1982: MINORITY PARTICIPATION

Minority participation in the election process was a primary subject of voting-rights amendments of 1982. In 1973, in *White v. Regester*, the Supreme Court had decided that at-large election arrangements were unconstitutional if they diluted the voting strength of minorities. The Court required that some districts should be created in which minorities could more easily elect their own candidates. However, in *City of Mobile v. Bolden* (1980), the Court decision was that the Voting Rights Act "prohibited only election procedures with a racially discriminatory *intent.*" Procedures that did not have a discriminatory intent were Constitutional, even though their *result* might be discriminatory (Yarbrough, 2002, p. 1).

In response to that decision, Congress agreed to add a section to Section 2 of the Voting Rights Act, which would negate *Bolden*, but would result in significant litigation regarding redistricting:

> Sec.2. (a) No voting qualification or prerequisite to voting . . . shall be imposed or applied . . . in a manner which results in a denial or abridgement of the right . . . to vote on account of race or color . . .
>
> A violation of subsection (a) is established if, based on the totality of circumstances, it is shown that the political processes leading to nomination or election in the state or political subdivision are not equally open to participation by members of a class of citizens protected by subsection (a) in that its members have less opportunity than other members of the electorate to participate in the political process and to elect representatives of their choice. The extent to which members of a protected class have been elected to office in the state or political subdivision is one circumstance which may be considered: *Provided,* That nothing in this section establishes a right to have members of a protected class elected in numbers equal to their proportion in the population.

Opponents of this section in Congress were able to add the final clause beginning with *Provided.* The opposition was concerned that without this proviso, the section would result in a quota system for group representation. In addition, the 1982 amendments (Public Law 97-205, June 29, 1982) replaced seventeen years in Section 4 (a) with "nineteen years." The provisions of Section 5, concerning "preclearance" by states or their political subdivisions to make changes in voting procedures, were extended for 25 years. Thus, portions of the Voting Rights Act require reauthorization in 2007.

5.8   Impact of the 1982 Voting Rights Act Amendments on Redistricting

An end to discriminatory at-large representation was one effect of the 1982 legislation. Hundreds of at-large schemes of legislative representation in cities, counties, and states were eliminated and replaced by systems with single-member districts. With an at-large process in a white-majority jurisdiction, black candidates are very unlikely to be elected in a situation where voting is polarized to the extent that, overwhelmingly, whites will not vote for blacks. With single-member districts, each district may be designed to take into account its demographic composition. Some of these changes occurred voluntarily and some were forced by federal lawsuits against the at-large arrangements.

An important case in the series before the Supreme Court was *Thornburg v. Gingles* (1986). The issue concerned the 1982 redistricting of North Carolina's legislature. Several black voters of that state charged that several multimember districts impaired their ability to elect candidates of their choice. Justice William Brennan, writing for the Court's majority, affirmed the plaintiff's contention for all but one of the districts. His opinion established conditions for a "vote dilution" violation to prevail. Two of these conditions were that "the minority group must be able to demonstrate that it is sufficiently large and geographically compact to constitute a majority in a single member district," and that "the white majority votes sufficiently as a bloc to enable it . . . usually to defeat the minority-preferred candidate."

The effect of the replacement of multimember with single-member districts was a considerable increase in minority representation in state and local government.

Legal conflict over majority–minority districts (MMDs) was another effect. Congressional districts were already single-member and contiguous because of the Congressional requirement of 1842 (see section 2.4). The conflict was fostered because of the responsibility assigned to the U.S. Department of Justice for preclearance of electoral changes in any covered jurisdiction under Section 5 of the Voting Rights Act. Beginning with the administration of Republican President George H. W. Bush (began in January 1989), the DOJ demanded an increase in Congressional MMDs over what certain covered states proposed for redistricting under the 1990 census. (An MMD is a district in which the population majority is nonwhite.)

It was believed by some that the Republican intention was to pack blacks, who were almost all Democrats, into a small number of districts to benefit Republican representatives in the rest of the state. Furthermore, they argued, the effect would be a return to the "separate but equal" doctrine that was enunciated in *Plessy v. Ferguson* (1896) and used as the basis for school segregation until *Brown v. Board of Education of Topeka* (1954), and other types of segregation until passage of the Civil Rights Act of 1964. Opponents of MMDs further believed that they were conducive to continued intergroup animosity. However, when Democrat Bill Clinton replaced George H. W. Bush as president in January 1993, the DOJ continued to support additional MMDs because that tactic was promoted by liberal interest groups, such as the American Civil Liberties Union (ACLU) and the National Association for the Advancement of Colored People. Their priority was election of more minority members of Congress, even if it reduced the total number of Democrats in the House of Representatives.

The use of computer software that was able to accept and use several types of demographic data about every census tract or political precinct in a state enabled state legislatures to consider many variations of redistricting plans. The plans could favor the party in power or protect incumbents of both parties, whichever was wanted by the leaders of the legislature. With the use of computers, the shapes of districts could be considerably more varied than could be designed manually.

In North Carolina, the state's first plan following the 1990 census included one MMD in the eastern lowland part of the state. It was primarily a poor, rural district. The DOJ rejected the plan and demanded a second MMD. The second such district approved by the state legislature was a bizarre shape that violated any reasonable definition of geographic compactness. This second MMD was appropriately described as "a long snake that winds its way through central North Carolina for 190 miles, scooping up isolated precincts with nothing in common save a large number of minority voters" (Yarbrough, 2002, p. 21, quoting the *Wall Street Journal*). There were several locations at which parts of the district were connected by a single point; that is, the district continued on opposite sides of an X. This was necessary, for example, because District 12, the second MMD district, split District 6 (not an MMD) in two parts. At the crossing point of the X, if District 12's two parts met the federal requirement to be "contiguous," then District 6's two parts were also contiguous.

The district was challenged in federal court as an unconstitutional racial gerrymander. The Supreme Court reviewed the situation twice. In the first review, in *Shaw v. Reno* (1993), the Court was attempting to determine if a valid Constitutional issue had been raised. They agreed that it had. A full trial was scheduled. After the trial of *Shaw v. Hunt* (1996), Justice William Rehnquist's majority opinion agreed that since no compelling state interest had been shown other than race-based districting, the second MMD was unconstitutional and violated the 14th Amendment's requirement of equal protection.

In *Miller v. Johnson* (1995), the Supreme Court turned down a similar scheme in Georgia, where an MMD had been designed that ran from Atlanta to the ocean, 260 miles away. Again, it had been the redesign urged by the DOJ that prompted opponents to file a lawsuit.

There have been other cases of this type that have come before the Court, and the Court has not been of one mind. According to Tinsley E. Yarbrough, "only Justices Antonin Scalia and Clarence Thomas were on record as considering every intentionally created MMD a forbidden racial gerrymander." Generally, Justices David Souter, Stephen Breyer, and Ruth Bader Ginsburg were on the other side. Furthermore, Justice Sandra Day O'Connor in a separate concurrence in *Bush v. Vera* (1996), a similar case from Texas, concluded "that a state's attempts to avoid a Section 2 vote dilution suit constituted a compelling governmental interest that justified MMDs" (Yarbrough, 2002, pp. 162, 163). In *Easley v. Cromartie* (2001), Justice O'Connor would join the more liberal justices in a majority ruling that North Carolina's redrawn 12th district might have been created to assure a safe Democratic seat, an allowable constitutional ploy, rather than for the unconstitutional purpose of racial gerrymandering.

In this continuing saga, let Justice Anthony Kennedy, at this time considered to be in the middle of the Court's political spectrum, have the last word, from his opinion in *Miller v. Johnson*:

> The essence of the equal protection claim, recognized in *Shaw*, is that the State has used race for separating voters into districts. Just as the State may not,

absent extra-ordinary justification, segregate citizens on the basis of race in public [facilities] . . . so did we recognize in *Shaw* that it may not separate its citizens into different voting districts on the basis of race . . . Race-based assignments embody stereotypes that treat individuals as the product of their race, evaluating their thoughts and efforts—their very worth as citizens— according to a criterion barred to the Government by history and the Constitution. . . . They also cause society serious harm . . . Racial gerrymandering, even for remedial purposes, may balkanize us into competing racial factions; it threatens to carry us further from the goal of a political system in which race no longer matters—a goal that the Fourteenth and Fifteenth Amendments embody, and to which the Nation continues to aspire.

5.9   Voting Accessibility for the Elderly and Handicapped

Concerns for another group with voting issues would arise in the 1980s. The Voting Accessibility for the Elderly and Handicapped Act (VAEHA) (Public Law 98-435, September 28, 1984) would be adopted. Section 2 of the Act stated that "it is the intention of Congress . . . to promote the fundamental right to vote by improving access for handicapped and elderly individuals to registration facilities and polling places for federal elections." Section 3 of the Act required that each political subdivision responsible for conducting elections assure that all polling places for federal elections are accessible to handicapped and elderly voters. There were allowances in case no accessible place was available. An advance request by such a voter could result in reassignment to an accessible place or provision for an alternate means of casting a ballot on election day.

According to the Act, each state or political subdivision responsible for federal elections "shall provide a reasonable number of accessible registration facilities" or provide an opportunity for registration by mail. Instructions printed in large type, conspicuously displayed, are to be posted for the benefit of handicapped individuals in each registration and polling location, and telecommunications devices for the deaf are to be made available for the reception of information by individuals so handicapped. As with the Voting Rights Act, no funding was provided to assist in the process of assuring the presence of the required facilities or implementation of the administrative needs.

In 1990, the Americans with Disabilities Act was adopted (Public Law 101-336, July 26, 1990). This law was very comprehensive, but did not specifically mention any application in registration and voting, although requirements for places of public accommodation were described in detail.

5.10   Overseas Absentee Voters

Concern over assurance that this group could easily vote was considered in "The Federal Voting Assistance Act of 1955" (Public Law 84-296, August 9, 1955). The law provided a number of recommendations to the states on this subject. It required also that the U.S. administrator of general services print and distribute postcards to be made available outside of the United States not later than August 15 before a federal election. Such postcards would serve as an application for voter registration. The cards would not require U.S. postage.

The next Congressional action on this subject was the "Overseas Citizens Voting Rights Act of 1975" (Public Law 94-203, January 2, 1976). The substance of this act was to state unequivocally that each citizen residing overseas is entitled to register and vote by an absentee ballot in any federal election in the state or any election district of such state in which that citizen was last domiciled immediately prior to departure, "even though he does not have a place of abode or other address in such state or district and his intent to return to such state or district may be uncertain . . ." The voter would have to have met all voting qualifications in the applicable state or district, except minimum voting age. Furthermore,

> Each state shall provide by law for the casting of absentee ballots for federal elections by all citizens residing outside the United States who . . . have returned such ballots to the appropriate election official of such state in sufficient time so that the ballot is received by such election official not later than the time of closing of the polls in such state on the day of such election.

A decade later, Congress extended the requirements for assuring the right to vote by overseas citizens in the "Uniformed and Overseas Citizens Absentee Voting Act" (Public Law 99-410, August 28, 1986), known in brief as UOCAVA. There was a specific emphasis in this law on the "uniformed services" and members of their immediate families who may be with them at their overseas locations. The uniformed services are defined as all the military services, the Coast Guard, and the commissioned corps of the Public Health Service and the National Oceanic and Atmospheric Administration. Under this Act, the president is to designate the head of an executive department to have primary responsibility for its federal functions. The president named the Secretary of Defense to that position and an office in the Department of Defense called the Federal Voting Assistance Program (FVAP) was established to carry out the obligations.

The presidential designee is to prescribe a federal write-in absentee ballot, including a secrecy envelope and mailing envelope, for use in federal elections by overseas voters who make timely application for, but do not receive, absentee ballots from their states. The law then describes procedures, if both a federal and a state absentee ballot are received, in order to prevent the submission and counting of both ballots. Additionally, the law made recommendation to the states to maximize access to the polls by all overseas voters. The law makes clear that military authority is not to be used to influence the vote of, or require attendance at the polls of, a member of the Armed Forces, but that "nothing in this section [of the law] shall prohibit free discussion of political issues or candidates for public office."

5.11   THE NATIONAL VOTER REGISTRATION ACT

The movement to adopt methods of voter registration that would allow more inclusivity partly resulted from the decline in participation in national elections by the voting public. In 1988, turnout was about 51 percent of the electorate, close to the lowest ever (which was 49 percent in 1924), having fallen for several quadrennial election cycles in succession. Civic-minded organizations that had no political bias, for example, League of Women Voters, supported increasing registration. Other organizations supported additional registration because they believed that if turnout could be augmented, it would benefit the liberal wing of the Democratic party. One of those latter organizations was called Human Service Employees for Registration and Voting Education or HumanSERVE. Closely associated with HumanSERVE were two professors, Frances Fox Piven and Richard Cloward, who wrote a book on the subject of voter registration. In the Preface, they stated:

> Of the nearly 70 million Americans who are not registered to vote, two out of three have family incomes that fall below the median, and the opinion polls show that their preferences lean toward the Democrats (Piven and Cloward, 1989, p. xi).

However, registration drives carried out in 1984 during the administration of Ronald Reagan did not support this contention, if actual increases in registration are a measure. The same authors note that:

> the religious Right's registration campaign (together with the Republican campaign) overwhelmed black registration increases in the South (Piven and Cloward, 1989, p. 192).

Nevertheless, the election of Democrat Bill Clinton to the presidency in November 1992, along with a Democrat-majority Congress, gave liberals the chance they needed to have relevant legislation adopted. The main idea for implementation was to require voter registration applications to be available at (1) offices of each state's motor vehicle agency and at (2) public service agencies frequented by lower-income individuals. These agencies would be required to forward the applications to the appropriate election administrators. Thus, the National Voter Registration Act (NVRA) (Public Law 103-31, May 20, 1993) became known as the "motor–voter" act.

The idea of motor–voter registration was not new to this Act, nor was it particularly controversial. The legislature of Michigan had adopted such a program in 1975. Other states implementing the idea in the next few years included Arizona, Maine, Ohio, and Oregon. In Colorado, in 1984, a statewide referendum adopting the program was passed, after legislation proposing the idea had failed on several occasions. Proponents could point out that "Colorado had no postcard registration, no deputization, registration was only permitted at county election offices between the hours of 9 and 5;

people could be purged for missing a single election . . ." (Piven and Cloward, 1989, p. 221). The idea for voter registration at public service agencies other than for motor vehicles was being promoted by HumanSERVE.

NVRA applied only to elections for federal offices. The federal government has no administrative jurisdiction over state elections unless, as with the Voting Rights Act, a provision of the Constitution can be cited. None could be identified with NVRA. Nevertheless, states, even Southern ones, have adopted requirements for state and local elections that were originally imposed for federal elections. The administrative difficulties that would result from the maintenance of two separate election systems were not acceptable. States not covered by the NVRA were only those that required no voter registration whatsoever for federal elections (North Dakota) or permitted election-day registration at a polling place under laws enacted before March 11, 1993 (Minnesota, Wisconsin, and Wyoming).

Under the law, each state driver's license application, including any renewal application, is to serve as an application for voter registration, unless the registrant declines to permit it. The voter registration application may include information that serves to prevent duplicate voter registrations and enables election administrators to assess voter eligibility, including citizenship. The application must include the signature of the voter attesting, under penalty of perjury, the truthfulness of the information provided. Once a registration application is accepted at a motor vehicle office, it must be transmitted to an appropriate election official within 10 days, or within 5 days if the close of registration is less than 10 days away. The incomplete implementation of this data interchange requirement was demonstrated by the example of Florida in 2000.

States may utilize mail registration under the law. They may require a first-time voter to vote in person, that is, not by absentee ballot, if he or she has registered to vote in a jurisdiction by mail and has not previously voted in that jurisdiction. This provision may not apply to persons entitled to vote by absentee ballot under UOCAVA or under VAEHA.

In addition to motor vehicle bureaus, state agencies that *must* provide voter registration materials are to include "all offices in the state that provide public assistance" and offices that provide services to persons with disabilities. Other offices that "may" be designated to serve as voter registration agencies include public libraries, fishing and hunting license bureaus, and unemployment compensation offices; other possibilities are listed. A recruitment office of the Armed Forces of the United States must serve as a voter registration agency.

A most important provision of NVRA is that:

> Any state program . . . to protect the integrity of the electoral process . . . shall not result in the removal of the name of any person from the official list of voters . . . by reason of the person's failure to vote.

This alteration in rules for purging registration lists was a priority of the proposers. Under NVRA, a registrant's name may be removed from the official list of registered voters upon request of the registrant directly, or because the registrant has reported a new address that is outside of the registrant's current jurisdiction. This new address may have been reported to a motor vehicle agency or to any other official voter-registering agency. Thus, these other agencies must develop procedures for data transmission of change-of-address to an appropriate election administration agency. The latter may use the National Change Of Address process of the U.S. Postal Service as a tool to help identify registrants who may have moved. A registrant may be removed from the official list for mental incapacity or criminal conviction, as provided under state law, or because it has been determined that the registrant has died.

The process for removal from the official voters' list of a living registrant may follow from the return of any correspondence to the registrant as "undeliverable" by the Postal Service. Then, the election administrator may send a forwardable confirmation notice with an enclosed postage-paid reply card. If no reply is received, and the voter does not attempt to vote in the jurisdiction in two successive federal general elections, the registrant's name may be removed from the official list of registered voters (Sims, 2001, pp. 1, 2).

Continuing monitoring of the operation of the legislation was provided for in the NVRA but no plans were put into place for corrective legislation if defects were uncovered. The states were to be informed as to their duties and Congress was to be sent a report every two years on the effectiveness of the Act. A paper form for mail-in voter registration was to be designed by the FEC.

The requirement of assurance that the registrant really and truly no longer lives at the address previously given, which depends in part on the effectiveness of the U.S. Postal Service, has added administrative steps to the process of maintaining a correct list of registrants. In many cases, election officials do not possess the diligence, the necessary administrative systems, or the resources to fully carry out these procedures. The NVRA provided no authorization of funding with its imposed requirements.

6

THE MIDDLE AND LATE TWENTIETH CENTURY: ELECTION ADMINISTRATION AND COMPUTING TECHNOLOGY

An issue considered here is one that very few people in political leadership positions understood or cared about in the late twentieth century: the effectiveness of election administration. It was a public activity with very low priority. An important problem of election administration was constantly changing technology as the use of computers became possible. The bottom line in this era was whether the voting public had confidence in the accuracy and integrity of the new systems. If the results were provided quickly, and there was little question about who won, the issue of public confidence typically would not arise. In some early uses, very delayed results were produced and serious public concerns were raised.

The ability of election administrators to select and implement computerized voting equipment, which the voting public was able to effectively utilize, was a question little understood. Two U.S. representatives and a few technical specialists kept interest alive. Efforts to assist election administrators to deal effectively with the new technology in terms of comparative resources applied, were minimal.

6.1   CONTINUED USE OF LEVER MACHINES

At the end of section 4.7, it was noted that lever machines were used by about one of every six voters in 1928 and that, in the early 1930s, the Shoup company had begun to compete with AVM. By 1944, 29 percent of voters used lever machines and in 1948, the usage was about 30 percent nationwide (*The New York Times*, November 3, 1948, p. 5).

In 1946, Mayor Curley of Boston asked MIT to undertake a study of the two contenders. MIT's report from the dean of engineering compared the Shoup and AVM machines. It noted that both machines were well designed and that either would be capable of giving good service over a long period of years. As a result of the MIT report, Boston bought 718 Shoup machines at a slightly higher price than equivalent AVM machines.

Human usability turned out to be a distinguishing factor between the machines. Possibly, that was the reason that the Shoup machines had been purchased initially. The 1946 MIT report had stated:

> We feel that the vertical arrangement of the ballot on the Shoup machine is of considerable advantage because confusion on the part of the voter is less probable. With the horizontal ballots [of the AVM machine], it is conceivable that the voter may not be clear as to whether he should move the lever above or below the strip on which the candidate's name is printed . . .
>
> We prefer the Shoup machine, mainly because (a) there appears to be less chance of confusion and incorrect balloting on the part of the voter and (b) less chance of error on the part of the persons delegated to read the machine count and report vote counts.

In the 1950 competition, AVM's sales manager Frank P. Stone, admitted that there was some loss in the vote due to the horizontal ballot arrangement, but nowhere near 15 percent, as had been charged by competitor Ransom F. Shoup. Stone claimed also that in voting for slates of candidates, the Shoup machine was less capable, in that

> the names run close to the floor and people have to stoop over to read them, and short persons have difficulty reading the names on the top.

Despite its criticality in this situation, human usability in design of voting equipment was considered hardly at all by social scientists or other investigators in the next half-century. In a professional article published in 1998, Susan King Roth, an associate professor of industrial design, wrote:

> The human use of voting equipment and voters' perceptions of the voting experience have largely been overlooked. (Roth, 1998, p. 29)

In the same article, Roth described an experiment concerning usability of voting machines in Franklin County (Columbus), Ohio. It was noted that average American female eye height is 60.3 inches, but that the top of the printing of the "issues" section of the machine (running horizontally) was 67 inches off the floor. In the experiment, "several subjects who were observed to stand well below the top of the ballot interface did not vote at all on this section. One subject stated that she did not see any issues on the ballot" (Roth, 1998, p. 33).

In 1956, an important issue was not human factors, but the financial health of the two manufacturers. AVM's sales in the early years of the century "were bolstered by campaigning reform groups who wanted to do away with the easily corruptible paper ballots" (*Wall Street Journal*, May 1, 1956, p. 1). Production had slowly climbed from 1,000 machines in 1930 to 1,750 in 1940, 3,100 in 1950, and 4,000 in 1955. AVM had outsold Shoup by two-to-one each year in the past ten.

In an article later that year, it was predicted that 50 percent of the national total of 62 million voters would use voting machines in the forthcoming presidential election (*New York Times*, November 1, 1956, p. 39). They would be used in some places in 41 states, up from 32 states in which they were used in 1952. It was expected that between 90,000 and 100,000 machines would be used, indicating that between 310 and 344 voters would use each machine. By the time the article was published, Shoup VMC was a division of Republic Steel Corporation, located in Canton, Ohio.

AVM did not remain independent for long. In 1958, it became a division of Rockwell Manufacturing Company. In the 1960 general election, voting machines were used in all or some parts of 44 states. In Connecticut, Delaware, Kentucky, Louisiana, Maryland, New York, and Rhode Island, they were used in every precinct. Among large cities, only Los Angeles and Milwaukee were cited as not using them (*New York Times*, November 1, 1960, p. 58). Newer users included Cleveland, Kansas City, Minneapolis, Oklahoma City, St. Louis, and Toledo. Voting machine use was expected by 55–60 percent of all voters (*Wall Street Journal*, November 8, 1960, p. 4).

Use of lever machines increased to 65 percent of all voters in 1964. All other voters (except the very small number pioneering in use of the PPC system) were still using hand-counted paper ballots. Machine sales increased partly in response to disputes over "intent of the voter" that is, the interpretation of ambiguous ballots filled out by hand. "Rhubarbs over recounts" delayed the naming of the governor of Minnesota for 4-and-a-half months in 1962, it was reported.

By the 1960s, AVM could include an optional printer with its machines. The printing facility would be enabled after the close of polls and would provide, in quintuplicate, the number of votes cast for each candidate or issue alternative on the machine. This did not prevent the replacement of its aging machines in New York City with Shoup machines in 1962. Shoup was now a subsidiary of General Battery & Ceramic Corp. Frank P. Stone, the former AVM sales manager, was now its president (*Wall Street Journal*, July 20, 1964, p. 1).

After 1964, the percentage use of lever machines would begin to decrease as the deployment of the new computer-based balloting devices became significant. In 1978, Shoup would end production of the machines and, in 1982, AVM would do the same. Nevertheless, some 43 percent of all voters used them in 1980. AVM would soon be purchased by Sequoia Pacific. After production stopped, older machines, which were being replaced, were scavenged for parts when needed. Small companies arose, functioning to refurbish and maintain machines still in use. New York City would continue to service the machines as a municipal function. In 1988, lever machines were still being used by one-third of all voters (Saltman, 1988, p. 49) and in 1996 by about 23 percent (Brace, 2004, Attach. 6). In the 2004 general election, New York City continued to use its lever machines.

6.2   DEVELOPMENT OF COMPUTERS THROUGH THE MID-1970S

Digital computers differ from calculators in that they can perform a sequence of mathematical and logical operations based on a "program" developed by their human operators. The most essential breakthrough in concept was the storage of the program within the computer.

Electrical relays, used in office machines and telephone switching devices in the early twentieth century, were the first logic devices adapted for use in computers. Among the first designers were George R. Stibitz of Bell Telephone Laboratories. His computer was completed in 1939 (Ifrah, 2001, p. 209). Harvard physicist Howard Aiken proposed construction of a machine based on relays and punch-card technology. This machine was constructed by IBM for Harvard and was completed in 1944 (Cohen, 2000, pp. 107–120). Grace Murray Hopper, whose name would become closely associated with the art of programming, worked with this computer.

Vacuum tubes were the next type of technology employed. The first vacuum-tube arithmetic unit, using 300 of the devices, was built by Prof. John V. Atanasoff of Iowa State College, with the assistance of Clifford Berry. The machine was able to carry out work by 1940 (Gustafson, 2000, pp. 91–106). The Electronic Numerical Integrator and Calculator (ENIAC), a machine containing 18,000 vacuum tubes, was constructed at the University Of Pennsylvania's Moore School of Electrical Engineering in Philadelphia by engineer J. Presper Eckert and physicist Dr. John W. Mauchly (Shurkin, 1996, pp. 117–138). It was completed in late 1945. The stored-program concept was developed there, with consultation by mathematician Dr. John von Neumann.

Eckert and Mauchly began the commercialization of computers in 1946 and eventually constructed the Universal Automatic Computer (UNIVAC). This first of these was delivered to the U.S. Bureau of the Census in 1951. Another model was used successfully by the Columbia Broadcasting System (CBS) in 1952 to predict the outcome of that year's presidential election with returns from a few selected precincts. Sensational publicity resulted.

IBM was involved in commercial development also. It began deliveries of its 700-series machines in the late 1940s, but concentrated primarily on business applications. By 1956, IBM had more installations than the UNIVAC company, then a division of Remington Rand (Cordata, 1987, pp. 281–287).

The transistor, a solid-state triode, was invented at Bell Telephone Laboratories in Murray Hill, New Jersey, in 1947. An improved type was invented in 1950. The developers were John Bardeen, Walter Brattain, and William Shockley (Hanson, 1982, p. 78). The original developments employed germanium but later improvements used silicon; both elements are of a class called semiconductors. "Integrated circuits" using silicon were developed at Texas Instruments (TI) by Jack Kilby and at Fairchild Semiconductor by Robert Noyce.

Large-scale integration (LSI) of transistor circuits was pioneered at Intel Corporation, formed in 1968. By 1970, 1,000 transistors could be designed into a single chip (Campbell-Kelly and Aspray, 1996, p. 227). In 1971, Intel produced a new product called the MSC-4, which consisted of four chips. These chips included a central processor, a short-term register store, a random access memory, and a read-only memory. Thus, the microprocessor was born. The year 1974 saw the announcement of several single-chip microprocessors. These included the Motorola 6800, the TMS 1000 from TI, and the Intel 8080. Chip manufacturers continued to improve their processes, packing more and more transistors into a single chip.

The effect of computer development on vendors of voting equipment was dependent on the types of equipment available at any particular time. From the mid-1960s through the mid-1970s, central processors with readers for marksense or punch-card ballots were available for centrally counted ballots. Once LSI made microprocessors available, full-function computer chips could be purchased and employed in precinct-located voting equipment. Then, either central-count or precinct-count was possible. Precinct-count equipment would not be identified as being supplied by a computer manufacturer, but rather by the vendor of the voting device. The invisibility of the chip in the special-function equipment would cause a leading chip-maker, Intel, to want its users to specify "Intel inside."

6.3   SOFTWARE

The first computer programs were handwritten by the users, instruction by instruction, in a code in which the command part of each instruction was in English, for example, "add," while the storage register addresses were in decimal numbers. This procedure was just one step above machine code, that is, instructions using only the "0s" and "1s" that were needed by the hardware. Since each machine had its own unique instruction set, each person using the machine needed to be trained to use it. The incompatibility of machines required that any program written for a particular machine be rewritten to be used on any other machine.

In 1953, at IBM, John Backus obtained internal funding to begin a project in "automatic programming" for the IBM 704. He argued that much of the cost in running computers was due to programming writing, testing, and "debugging." Therefore, productivity would be improved with a method that would allow the use of instructions that were closer to human language. Backus and his team produced the 18,000 instructions required to enable the use of the new programming language called FORTRAN (for Formula Translation) by April 1957. The program that was developed was called a "compiler." Its second version, containing 50,000 lines of code, was released in 1959. At about that time, a new noun—"software"—began to be used.

Since then, a large number of programming languages have been developed, each supported by a compiler or compilers as necessary. The real crunch in programming development began when the need to write very extensive and complex programs arose. The development of an operating system for IBM System/360, called OS/360, demonstrated the problem. Operating systems manage the flow of work in a computer; the more complex the work, the more difficult is the writing of such a program. This particular program would consist of over one million lines of code and was to support the function of "multi-programming." The development of OS/360 began in the spring of 1964 and the program was not released until the middle of 1967. Some 5,000 staff-years had gone into its development and its cost was three times the original budget. The difficulty began a movement to professionalize the writing of programs with the techniques of "software engineering."

The issue of software correctness began to become known to the general public as computers started to be used to control machinery. Errors in software could result in human injury or death, or could cause the destruction of the devices the computer was controlling. In some cases, machinery, for example, a missile being launched, would have to be deliberately destroyed if it ran amok and threatened lives or property. An extensive written discussion of the issue as part of the more general problem of the failures of modern technology has been undertaken by Peter G. Neumann. He has made a speciality of identifying "risks" and proposing methods of assuring reduction in the incidence of dangerous or costly errors due to technological failures. Examples presented by Neumann concerning software errors are "The 1990 AT&T system runaway," the "DO I = 1.10 bug in Mercury software," and the "Therac-25" computer-based radiation therapy system (Neumann, 1995, pp. 14, 15, 27, 68–70). He also discussed software engineering and computer-based voting systems (Neumann, 1995, pp. 231–255). The problem has not gone away; software engineering techniques and software testing may not be effectively applied. An example, in 2003, of a software error not caught before a chip-using device was sold to customers is indicated by the following statement on a circular contained in a purchased package of diabetic test strips to be employed with a blood-glucose testing meter:

> [The manufacturer] has identified a situation that can occur no more than once every seven days, during a ten-minute time period, which can cause an individual test result to be stored incorrectly in the memory of the [name of test meter].

6.4   INCREASING USE OF COMPUTERIZED VOTING, 1960–2000

It is an interesting commentary on changing tastes, along with changing technology, that county after county adopted computer-readable ballots in the 1960s and 1970s, given that earlier in the century the public was eager to eliminate hand-counted ballots by replacement with lever machines. Local governments were responsible for system implementation and, for computer-based voting, it would be found that some were not up to the task. The unit costs of the mechanical lever devices and their storage and transportation costs were contributing factors in the drive to replace them, as well as the desire to be up-to-date. While the use of lever machines significantly reduced the time for determining results over hand-counted ballots, and also reduced the number of citizens needed for hand counting, there were not equivalent reductions with use of computer-readable ballots.

It was not realized that the issue of intent of the voter, eliminated with the adoption of lever machines, would return with a vengeance when computer-readable ballots were adopted. Similarly, overvotes, which were eliminated with lever machines, would reappear again. Ignored also was the difficulty in implementing electronic ballot-sensing and vote-tallying technologies. Reductions in labor costs of human ballot counters, which had loomed large in the minds of decision makers as lever machines were adopted, were replaced with costs of equipment maintenance and repair by much more highly paid technicians. Furthermore, while it is true that the gross fraud possible in ballot counting by hand was nearly eliminated, it was replaced with card-reader malfunctions, voters' difficulties in using punch-card ballots, and the floating fear that unseen software manipulation, not possible to be detected, was responsible for lost elections.

Marksense ballots and machines for reading them and summarizing the result appeared concurrently with developments with punched cards. Los Angeles County had never adopted lever machines because the number of contests and issues on its ballot were greater than could be serviced by one unit of that type of machine. In addition, for the approximately 5,000 precincts in the nation's largest local election jurisdiction after New York City in 1960, the cost would be about $14 million for two machines per precinct. The machines weighed about 800 pounds each, and the large number needed would be reflected in the storage space required (with floors able to support the load) as well as in the difficulty in transporting them back and forth in the county's large area. Without machines, it took about two weeks for the county to manually count all of its 2.8 million ballots.

Los Angeles County funded one of the very first attempts to develop a computer-readable ballot system. According to a newspaper article (*Wall Street Journal*, November 8, 1960, p. 4), the county spent $900,000 for development of the device by Norden Data System Division of United Aircraft, located in Gardena, a city in the county. The Norden system was not adopted, although a "test election" was held on November 16, 1960.

Coleman Engineering Company of Los Angeles produced the first marksense system that was actually adopted and used in the 1960s and early 1970s. It was later marketed by the Gyrex Corporation, also of California. The Coleman/Gyrex machine was similar to the Norden device proposed for Los Angeles County. Voters inked squares on paper ballots with a stamper that formed a fluorescent mark that could be sensed by ultraviolet light. Operation was based on central counting of ballots by a single computer unit. The system was used in Hamilton County (Cincinnati), Ohio, in 1964. It was also deployed in Orange County (Anaheim), California, in the same year, and later in Kern (Bakersfield) and Contra Costa (Concord) counties in the same state, as well as in Multnomah County (Portland), Oregon.

Cubic Corporation of San Diego also produced a marksense system deployed in the early 1960s. Its "Votronic" vote counter was used in several counties in California: Alameda (Oakland), Santa Clara (San Jose), Riverside, and San Diego. With the Cubic system, the voter marked squares with a heavy dot and automatic reading was accomplished with an infrared sensor.

The first punch-card voting system was the Coyle Ballot Marking Device, produced by Martin A. Coyle of Ohio. The device was approved for use in January 1960 by the Ohio secretary of state. Coyle's device was used in 1961 in two small Ohio counties, Butler and Greene. The Coyle ballot card listed the names of the candidates and the ballot questions. The ballot, containing the names of candidates and issue choices, was rolled into the voting unit by the voter. It could be seen through a glass window, where it was magnified for better viewing. The voter used colored knobs to pick out choices. Pressing a button caused a hole to be punched in the card next to the name of the selected candidate or issue choice. When finished, the voter rolled the ballot from the machine and deposited it in a ballot box. Remington Rand tabulating equipment was used to summarize the choices made by all voters.

The Votomatic PPC system was invented by Joseph P. Harris in 1962. Harris invented the brand name Votomatic, taking the "omatic" part from the name of an existing commercial product. The idea for the adaptation of the IBM "Port-a-Punch" had been given to Harris by the chief election officer of Alameda County, California (Nathan, 1983, p. 131). Each Votomatic "vote recorder" weighs only a few pounds and its size is only 16 inches long, 13 inches wide, and 2 inches deep.

Harris was able to get Oregon to test the device by letting the public use it at the Oregon State Fair. The first purchase from Harris Votomatic, Inc. was by De Kalb County, Georgia, in the Atlanta metropolitan area. The unit cost just $150, and De Kalb county bought 500 of them for use in the September 1964, primary election. De Kalb's alternative was to buy 25 more lever machines each year at about $1,500 apiece to keep up with the county's growth. In the general election of November 1964, the Votomatic device was used in Fulton County (Atlanta) as well as in De Kalb, and it was used also in Lane County, Oregon, and Monterey and San Joaquin Counties, California.

It would become apparent that the Votomatic system was not easy to use for write-ins. The names of write-ins would have to be written on an envelope in which the punched ballot was placed for privacy. In some Votomatic systems, a special hole location for write-in votes was not provided. In such cases, precinct officials would have to remove the ballot from its envelope and examine the ballot to determine whether or not the voter had voted for any of the listed candidates as well as the write-in. If so, there would be an overvote. The limitation did not inhibit the system's sales appeal.

IBM bought the system from Harris in 1965. When the counties that were considering purchasing the system learned that IBM was going to manufacture it and put it on the market, IBM's reputation provided the impetus to buy. In 1969, however, IBM decided that the investment had not been a good one; it sold the system. There had been some elections in which the system had been criticized, and that was unacceptable to IBM (Nathan, 1983, p. 136). A fundamental fact of election administration is that, often, the best that an administrator can achieve is not to receive any media publicity at all about how an election was run. Almost always, publicity is negative. Similarly, if the operation of the computerized voting equipment was subject to public discontent, that fact was certain to be widely reported by the media. That was a lesson that IBM needed to learn. As it was a very large company involved in many industries, IBM's exposure from bad publicity was not worth the very small increase in gross revenue that the Votomatic system brought in.

In 1969, IBM sold the rights to produce the system to five separate companies. The company that did the most with it was Computer Election Systems (CES), established in Berkeley, California. The company was founded by several former IBMers who left the computer giant to produce and market the voting device.

Soon, the Votomatic system achieved significant acceptance. The early marksense systems, that is, Coleman/Gyrex and Cubic Votronic, would be displaced by Votomatic PPCs. More than 30 states had adopted legislation permitting its use. Among the largest cities in the nation, 16 of the top 100 were employing it in the 1972 election (Council of State Governments, 1973, p. 31). The initial use of these systems typically was in conjunction with business computers that were being employed for a variety of applications by governments or nearby corporate facilities. Use of the Votomatic system increased continually until 1988. In that year, it was being used by just about 40 percent of the voting public (Saltman, 1988, p. 49). After 1988, the percentage of use of the Votomatic system would decrease. It was used by about 37 percent of voters nationally in 1992 and 34 percent in 1996. After a number of sales and consolidations, what was CES became part of Election Systems and Software (ES&S).

At first, counting ballots had to be done at night, after the end of daytime operations that needed to be accomplished by the owners of the computers. In the mid-1970s, minicomputers began to be produced, and there was a greater likelihood that election operations could be run on computers solely dedicated to those needs. Administrators of Votomatic systems would, in almost all cases, continue to use central counting. The first use of precinct counting with the Votomatic system would occur in 1976. The user was suburban Cook County, Illinois (all of Cook County except Chicago). Chicago itself would eventually adopt precinct counting for its Votomatic system, but only in 1984.

The Datavote punch-card system started to be sold a few years after the Votomatic. The idea for the system had been developed by Curt Fielder and some associates who were employed in southern California by an aerospace firm. Fielder found that, in order to successfully market the idea, he needed the backing of a substantial company. Working with Diamond International Corporation of San Diego, he was able to sell the system to the state of Hawaii in 1968. By the early 1970s, it was being used in several additional jurisdictions, and in 1988, it was used by about 4 percent of all voters. In 1992, it was used by about 7 percent of voters and in 1996 by 8 percent or so.

The Datavote system provided a much easier arrangement for write-in candidates and for absentee voting than Votomatic. On the Datavote ballot, a blank line could be made available for a write-in, but the hole next to that line would need to be punched in order to inform the computer. A prescored Datavote ballot card with candidate names on the card could be sent to an absentee voter, who could easily punch out the chad.

Marksense systems became important again when precinct-located reading and counting equipment started to be sold in 1976 and later. Percentage use by voters continually increased through 2004 (see figure 6.1). Most of the systems sold are precinct-count, requiring a reader and computer at each polling station. Operation with central counting is possible and less expensive. Poorer, rural counties used central-count in Florida in 2000. To indicate a vote, an ordinary pencil may be used by a voter to fill in a small oval or square or to connect the head and tail of an arrow. Optical scanning is the most widely used sensing method. The fact that ballot size is not constrained to a standard punch card is advantageous. By 1980, use was about 2 percent of all voters. In 1988, use had risen to 7 percent, in 1992 to 15 percent, and in 1996 to 24 percent. In the latter year, marksense use would exceed the use of lever machines. In 2000, more voters used marksense systems than PPCs (Brace, 2004, Attach. 6). An advantage of precinct-count systems is that they can be programmed to return the ballot to the voter if an overvote has been cast. The process may or may not specify which contest has been overvoted.

DREs were a natural replacement for lever machines. An initial and unusual example of DREs was the Video-Voter, built by the Frank Thornbur Company of Chicago, introduced in Illinois experimentally in 1975. In 1988, less than 3 percent of voters used DREs. By 1992, use was up to nearly 5 percent of voters, and in 1996, they were used by more than 7 percent. In 2000, about 13 percent of voters used them, although none was used in Florida. The continuation of use of non-ballot systems seemed advantageous to some election administrators and elected officials of local jurisdictions. The cost and transportation of paper ballots were eliminated, overvotes were prevented, and there was never a problem of intent of the voter. Elimination of the latter prevented contentious recounts. Some DREs may be easily implemented for operation with headphones providing voiced instructions, allowing vision-challenged individuals to vote independently.

Full-face DREs are similar in appearance to lever machines but much lighter in weight. The full face is covered by a translucent, flexible, coated-paper material serving as a ballot. Under the coated-paper surface are micro-switches. When a voter pushes a small blank square with his or her finger next to the name or description of a selected alternative, the micro-switch is activated and its associated light shines through the ballot. A very recent development is the replacement of the paper surface with a large flat electronic screen developed for TVs. The screen may use plasma or liquid crystal display (LCD) technology, and may be operated as a touchscreen or with a cursor or mouse.

Multiple-screen DREs, based on electronic displays but not touchscreens, began to be introduced around the late 1980s. These present the voter with

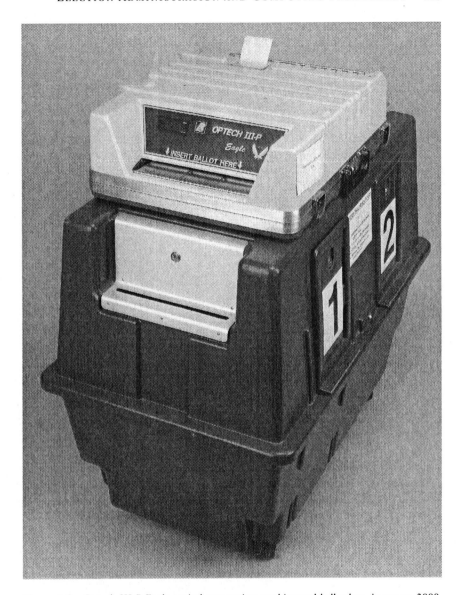

Figure 6.1 Optech III-P Eagle optical scan voting machine and ballot box, in use ca. 2000. Manufactured by Sequoia Voting Systems, Oakland, CA.

a succession of screens on a single terminal, each displaying only part of the ballot. An early type provided buttons around the edge of the screen that could be used to make or change selections. A more recent machine provides the voter with a cursor operated with knobs, which can successively select choices on each screen.

Multiple-screen DREs, using touchscreens, become widely available in the late 1990s. These allow selections to be made directly on the screen with the touch of a finger (see figure 7.1). The screen may respond by changing the type size, typeface, intensity or color of the candidate's name, or by placing an "X" or check mark next to the candidate's name. Changing one's mind is possible, typically, by repeating the selection action; the repeat serves to des-elect the candidate.

Vendors of voting equipment have been varied. In 1997, the International Foundation for Election Systems (IFES), headquartered in Washington, DC, began to publish a Buyer's Guide for Election Services, Supplies, and Equipment. The guide has been published yearly or once every two years and is generally available.

6.5   FEAR OF SOFTWARE FRAUD—ROUND I (1969)

With the 1968 general election in California, a significant number of com-puter-readable ballots began to be counted in an electronic machine whose internal activities could not be seen. Suspicion of software error arose. The same process when done by lever machines did not raise equivalent concerns, even though the counting and summing mechanisms could not be seen, either. Zukerman's report (section 4.7) had mentioned the problem, but the issue was never considered by the public with the intensity that would be demonstrated with regard to computerized voting.

The possibility of election fraud through computer software manipulation was raised in a page-one story in *The Los Angeles Times* on July 8, 1969. Los Angeles County had begun to use computerized voting the previous year. The article began:

> Recently, six computer experts met . . . and devised their own form of war games: how to rig an election, using computer techniques. Three of the men formed the offensive team—the group trying to find ways of rigging the machines. The other three went on defense trying to devise ways of detecting fraud. In each test, the offensive team won. Highly sophisticated techniques were devised for the computers which were not detected or prevented by coun-termeasures . . .
>
> Officials of both major parties are interested in updating security provisions to safeguard against any future fraud. When so much power and sometimes money rides on the outcome of an election, they say, someone sometime is going to be tempted to try to "buy" a victory by rigging the machines that count the votes . . . (Bergholz, 1969, p. 1)

The article went on to describe methods of rigging that it said could be made undetectable. Votes could be moved from one candidate to another in small quantities, for example, one of every ten, not in wholesale amounts that would be obvious. The malicious computer subroutine, which was written to carry this out, would not go into operation until counting began and would destroy itself, eliminating any sign of its presence, before the counting ended.

The story in *The Los Angeles Times* created an enormous stir in the metro-politan area. The county's registrar-recorder (director of elections) appeared in a television interview to deny the possibility of vote rigging by means of the computer program. The county's Board of Supervisors created a five-member Election Security Committee "to investigate computer rigging of elections." Stories on the controversy were carried by major East Coast newspapers (*The New York Times*, July 13, 1969, p. 64, *The Washington Post*, July 24, 1969, p. F6). A study of the Los Angeles vote-tallying system was undertaken by a consultant hired by the California State Commission on Voting Machines and Vote-Tabulating Devices. The security committee would report, in March 1970, that:

> No evidence came to the attention of the committee to indicate that fraud has been attempted or perpetrated with the system in the county . . . Qualified experts have testified that while computer rigging is technically possible, the chances of it are extremely remote . . . Election fraud by computer rigging would not be possible without collusion and deliberate intent among several persons having access to the election computer and programs.

Concern lingered, however, and following the June primary and November general elections of 1970, the county hired consultants to undertake reviews of the computerized voting system. A summary of the recommendations of the various consultants to improve system security has been published (Saltman, 1975, pp. 35–38). As a result of the concern about software correctness, California adopted a regulation stating that 1 percent of the precincts chosen randomly, but no fewer than three, must be recounted manually to verify computer counts. A mathematical analysis has shown that the closer the election, the higher the percentage of ballots that should be recounted to retain the same level of confidence (Saltman, 1975, pp. 113–119). In the limit, as the difference between the candidates narrows toward zero, all the ballots should be recounted. Rounds II and III on the issue of software fraud will be discussed in their chronological sequence.

6.6   EXAMPLES OF DIFFICULTIES IN COMPUTERIZED VOTING, 1968–1971

A variety of counties and cities reported administrative and technological difficulties in adopting new computerized techniques for voting. In all cases, the public's demand for the quick reporting of results and administrators' concerns for costs drove the selection of voting equipment and the design of the ballot processing system. If these arrangements began to come apart on election night due to poor planning, insufficiently considered contingency plans often made the situation worse. In addition to the examples cited here, others could have been presented, also.

In Los Angeles County, the June 1968 primary was the first election in this county in which the Votomatic system was used. There were some difficulties, but the problems were studied following the election. "Changes made included improved perforations on the ballot cards so that the chads punched by the voter would separate from the ballot completely" (American University and National Scientific Corp., 1973, pp. VI–27).

In Los Angeles County, after the June 1970 primary, a Los Angeles newspaper headline read "New Computer Snafu: Final Vote Unknown." Due to the large number of incorporated areas within the county, the myriad boundaries of various special districts and the requirement for ballot rotation, over 1,600 different ballot types were required. Chad continued to be a problem, despite the fix following the June 1968 election:

> Approximately one-half of one percent of all ballots had failed to read in the card readers on initial processing. Observers noted that when the ballot inspectors would fan a two-inch deck of ballot cards after receiving them, clouds of chad would fall out. Investigation of this phenomenon showed that it was due to the voters failing to completely remove the chad in the voting process. Many of the card reader jams were due to chad. (Saltman, 1975, p. 17)

In Fresno County, California, in June 1970, the notable difficulty was that the computer program needed to count the punch-card ballots was not completed before the election. In fact, it was not completed until several days after the election and counting could not begin until 87 hours after the polls closed.

The primary election in Detroit in August 1970 saw the first use of punch-card voting in this city. The elapsed time from the close of polls to the completion of the final count was 73 hours.

A study by the local chapter of the Association for Computing Machinery stated that poor construction of the devices promoted extra punctures in the ballot cards and hanging chad. Furthermore, said the study,

> since the ballot labeling was always on the left side of the ballot card, it was natural for a left-handed voter to position his hand above rather than to the left of the ballot card. In this position, the temptation to angle the stylus is strong . . .

Angling of the stylus might have been responsible for some of the failures to fully punch out chad. City clerk George Edwards was quoted as saying:

> We had far too many card jams in the computer. Experience has shown us that the ballot cards used are too frail. First, they are susceptible to changes in the weather in that they absorb moisture and thereby cause computer jams. Secondly, we have found that running a given precinct four, five, or six times through the computer, there may be a tendency for one or more chads to "pop out." This, of course, would change the vote total in that precinct. (Saltman, 1975, pp. 18–20)

The election process in Hamilton County, Ohio, broke down completely on the night of November 2, 1971. A hand recount of a precinct already tabulated revealed that the Coleman/Gyrex electronic vote-counting equipment was crediting votes to the wrong candidates.

It was determined that the program tapes that controlled the Coleman/ Gyrex device had been incorrectly prepared. Dedicated staff members working day and night were able to reprogram the tapes in five days. The count was completed at 11:00 p.m. on November 7. Although in prior elections with the system, results had not been obtained until 4:00 a.m., the next day, too late for the morning newspapers, the current situation was unacceptable. A congressman opined that "what's really at stake is the public's confidence."

6.7 Federal Offices Established to Respond to New Technology

With increasing use of computers in the federal government, the need for management of their use seemed clear to Congressman Jack Brooks (D-TX), chairman of the House of Representatives Committee on Administration in 1965. His concern resulted in the passage of amendments to the Federal Property and Administrative Services Act of 1949. The 1965 amendments would be known as "The Brooks Act" (Public Law 89-306, October 30, 1965). This law established three agencies for controlling the use of computers. The agency later called the Office of Management and Budget would set policy; the General Services Administration would procure the equipment and the National Bureau of Standards (NBS) would set standards for their use. NBS was tasked also to assist other federal agencies in the application of computer technology.

The need for standards was demonstrated by the inability of some early computers to connect to peripheral equipment, for example, a printer or tape drive, made by a different company. Coding and electrical interface standards were needed. Additionally, standards for high-level programming languages needed to be made available within the government to enable programmers to work with more than one computer without having to be retrained. Communications and security standards were needed also. NBS established the Center for Computer Sciences, later given other names, in the late 1960s.

The Clearinghouse on Election Administration (CEA) was established in 1972 as a result of difficulties in elections using computers. In late 1971, the Congress was considering legislation that would become the Federal Election Campaign Act (FECA) (Public Law 92–225, February 7, 1972). That law would set limits on expenditures for election campaigns for the office of president. Responsibility for administering the act would be given to the comptroller general, head of the General Accounting Office (GAO), the auditing arm of the Congress. (In 2004, the name of the GAO would be changed to the Government Accountability Office.) In the course of debate in the House of Representatives, Congressman William J. Keating (R-OH), from the Cincinnati area (Hamilton County!), introduced an amendment that was included in the adopted legislation in Section 308 (c). The relevant part of the act is as follows:

It shall be the duty of the Comptroller General to serve as a national clearinghouse for information in respect to the administration of elections. In carrying out his duties under this subsection, the Comptroller General shall enter into contracts for the purpose of conducting independent studies of the administration of elections. Such studies shall include, but not be limited to, studies of:

1. the method of selection of, and the type of duties assigned to, officials and personnel working on boards of elections;
2. practices relating to the registration of voters;
3. voting and counting methods . . .

Mr. Keating made clear his reasons for submitting the amendment in a statement on the floor of the House on November 30, 1971.

> Election day is the most important day to any democratic nation. When the Government fails to function efficiently on this day, a tremendous credibility gap occurs between the Government and the people. All the sections of the bill are meaningless if we are unable to properly execute the election itself.
>
> In Cincinnati this past election the citizens woke up the morning after the election to read in the paper "There are no election returns to report. There won't be any for three days". . . Research into this problem shows there have been numerous difficulties across the Nation.
>
> In Detroit during the primary election the newspaper headline was: "Computers Foul Vote Count". . . Similar stories have appeared in San Francisco, Atlanta, Los Angeles, and indeed in other cities across the Nation . . . This amendment will allow for State and local officials to turn to a national center or clearinghouse for information on good and bad ideas in voting systems . . . (Congressional Record, p. 43392)

6.8   GAO-CONTRACTED REPORTS RECOMMEND ACTIONS

As a result of the passage of the FECA, the Office of Federal Elections (OFE) was established in the GAO. The OFE was led by Phillip "Sam" Hughes, later assistant comptroller general and then undersecretary of the Smithsonian Institution (*The Washington Post*, June 20, 2004, p. C11). The CEA was set up in the OFE and consisted of just five civil servants; Gary Greenhalgh became its chief in 1973.

Two contracts to be cited were issued by the OFE/CEA while it was part of the GAO. The first of these, published with authors specified as American University and National Scientific Corporation, was actually written by Professor Richard G. Smolka of the university and by W. Edward Weems, Jr., president of the corporation. The second was written by Roy G. Saltman, a computer scientist with NBS, in support of that bureau's requirement to assist other agencies. The commencement of the latter project resulted from a fortuitous meeting of Saltman and Greenhalgh in 1973 at a conference of computer professionals interested in applications in local governments. The GAO was amenable to the study because it had received a communication, said to be from Senator John Tunney of California, that requested an evaluation of the problems of computerized voting in that state. The GAO paid

NBS in an inter-agency transfer of funds for the undertaking of the effort, which took 14 months. The NBS received and continues to receive a significant fraction of its operating income from consulting activities in support of other federal agencies. Additionally, NBS, similar to a university, allowed its scientists to put their names on their work issuing from the agency. Its name change in 1988 to National Institute of Standards and Technology (NIST) made no dent in these practices.

The Smolka/Weems report of 1973 reviewed election difficulties that had recently occurred in several larger local jurisdictions. Two were named specifically by Congressman Keating in his presentation reported earlier. Six of the seven local governments studied had recently adopted computerized voting. The report provided 8 long-term recommendations and 26 short-term ones. One of the long-term recommendations was that the number of constitutional offices elected should be reduced and that greater flexibility in the scheduling of elections should be applied to reduce the number of concurrent contests. A second long-term recommendation was that funding from state sources should be provided to meet specified election costs. A third was to eliminate the requirement for ballot rotation, as it significantly increased complexity in administration of the election. The report stated that:

> The circumstances under which a candidate in the first or any other position obtains an advantage have never been documented by empirical research . . . Since the expense and complications of ballot rotation are known, much can be said for a consistent ballot format which permits the voter to locate his choices among the candidates prior to entering the voting booth. (American University and National Scientific Corporation, 1973, pp. VIII–5)

Short-term recommendations concerned methods of improving administration, assurance of system operability through preelection testing, review of ballot layouts for clarity of presentation, manual recounting of a sample number of precincts when automatic tabulation was used, improved training for election workers, and education of voters in use of the voting equipment.

The report by Saltman in 1975 also described a number of elections using computerized methods in which difficulties had occurred. Many recommendations of this report proposed administrative and technical changes to improve system security and assure accounting for all ballots printed, whether used, unused, or spoiled. Inclusion of audit trails, separation of duties, and use of non-multi-programmed computer operations were among the measures proposed. Some findings and conclusions concerned institutional factors, such as the need for increased state leadership of its local governmental efforts. Other findings included the following:

> There is little, if any, research being carried out systematically on the human engineering of voting systems. Therefore, no organized data are available on the effects of different kinds of voting systems and ballot arrangements on voting patterns and voting errors due to the human response to the equipment.

> A National Election Systems Standards Laboratory would serve a valuable function for all states if established to set national minimum standards for federal election procedures assuring accuracy and security, and similar standards for election equipment and systems performance . . . (Saltman, 1975. p. 9)

While the two reports discussed here were widely disseminated to election administrators, they had little impact in causing change. There was no force of law behind them. The total disaggregation of the U.S. election system to thousands of counties, cities, and townships would, in any event, prevent any unified response.

6.9   The Clearinghouse is Retained in the FEC

By 1974, there appeared to be general dissatisfaction with the FECA as originally written. Additionally, it was said that Elmer Staats, the comptroller general, was uncomfortable with having been assigned campaign finance oversight responsibilities. That was an issue too politically charged for a supposedly nonpartisan agency. The House Administration Committee was busy rewriting the FECA legislation and, as drafted, the CEA was eliminated. However, Congressman William E. ("Bill") Frenzel (R-MN) objected. He had supported Congressman Keating's amendment of 1971 and he wanted the CEA continued. In debate in the House on July 2, 1974 (Congressional Record, p. 22143), Frenzel is recorded as stating:

> The bill, by abolishing the elections clearinghouse in the General Accounting Office, eliminates the only good thing the federal government does to help the state and local governments run their election administration systems.

Frenzel got his way in the House version, and the Senate version had not abolished the CEA. Thus, the CEA was retained in the FECA Amendments of 1974 (Public Law 93-443, October 15, 1974). This act established the FEC and located the CEA within it. There were additional amendments to the FECA in 1976 and 1979. Although the wording of the Clearinghouse's responsibilities was altered in 1979 to eliminate specific enumeration of subject matter, its duties were not substantially changed.

The CEA, now called the National Clearinghouse on Election Administration (NCEA) within the FEC, continued to contract for studies. It began to publish reports on innovations in election administration, on election statistics and the administrative structure of state and local election offices, and other useful documents. Through fiscal year 1979, the NCEA's budget was more than 10 percent of the FEC's appropriation. This may only indicate the minimal funding of the FEC.

The NCEA under Gary Greenhalgh, still having a personnel count of just five, proposed that national standards for election equipment be developed as a follow-on to Saltman's recommendation. It was supported in this effort by the Advisory Panel that it had created. The panel, consisting of election officials from state and local governments, represented a wide range of jurisdictional types and sizes, and both major political parties. During its June 1977 meeting, the panel recommended unanimously that the Clearinghouse immediately undertake a program leading to the development of voluntary engineering and procedural performance standards. These could be used by state and local governments in procuring, testing, operating, and retesting voting systems and all associated support hardware and software. Members of the panel stated that while they appreciated the potential difficulties arising from federal entry into the voting equipment field, the problems were serious enough to warrant federal action.

In their discussion of this recommendation, the panel members noted the lack of technical expertise in most state and local governments, which would prevent those jurisdictions from individually testing sophisticated voting systems and support equipment. They stated, also, that the lack of adequate financial resources to hire technically trained individuals required government officials to rely on the vendors for technical information and support. In such situations, a problem of conflict-of-interest could arise. Assigning responsibilities for problems and assuring that they were identified and fixed could be difficult and confusing. Another issue brought out was that vendors often specified the reliability of their equipment for ideal laboratory conditions and did not appreciate the variety of environments in which the equipment would be placed during use.

Finally, panel members stated that there was a need to look at related human engineering standards. It was asserted that neither the manufacturer of voting systems nor most state and local election offices paid much attention to how the voter interacts with the various voting devices. Evidence was cited suggesting that not only ballot design, but the equipment itself, can have a great impact on minorities, minority language, handicapped, and visually impaired voters (National Clearinghouse on Election Administration, 1983, pp. 20–22).

6.10   THE FEASIBILITY STUDY AND STANDARDS DEVELOPMENT

NCEA efforts eventually succeeded. In the 1979 amendments to the FECA (Public Law 96-187, January 8, 1980), Section 302 stated that:

> The Federal Election Commission, with the cooperation and assistance of the National Bureau of Standards, shall conduct a preliminary study with respect to the future development of voluntary engineering and procedural performance standards for voting systems used in the United States. The Commission shall report to the Congress the results of the study, and such report shall include recommendations, if any, for the implementation of a program of such standards (including estimates of the costs and time requirements of implementing such a program). The cost of the study shall be paid out of any funds otherwise available to defray the expenses of the commission.

The preliminary study called for in this bill was contracted to the late Robert J. Naegele, an engineer resident in California doing business as Granite Creek Technology. Naegele had assisted the California state authority on voting machines by developing methods of testing voting equipment proposed for certification in that state. He was one of the few people in the country having that type of experience. Naegele's 83-page report was completed and submitted to the Congress in 1983 (without any indication of its authorship). Its conclusion was that:

> Performance standards for voting system are both needed and feasible. (National Clearinghouse on Election Administration, 1983, p. 1)

The study reviewed the Advisory Panel's adoption of its recommendation and its reasoning. It pointed out that the standards would concern "performance," and therefore would not inhibit design or innovation. Approval by an authorized body testing election equipment against the standards would allow new vendors to more easily enter the market. A certification that equipment meets requirements would benefit vendors and give election officials more confidence in equipment procurement.

Standards development was begun after the NCEA received funding in 1984. There was no federal legislation in place that could require the standards to be mandatory. Consequently, if they were to have any effect, they would have to be adopted by the states, one-by-one. An Advisory Panel consisting of vendor representatives and election administrators was appointed to assist in standards development, but Robert Naegele did most of the writing. In 1985, Gary Greenhalgh resigned as chief of the NCEA and he was replaced by Penelope Bonsall, who had previously served as election administrator for the state of Alaska.

In time, the NCEA received a smaller percentage of the FEC's budget, eventually going down to less than 2 percent. A total of just $225,000 was separately assigned to the development of the standards between the years 1984 and 1990.

6.11   FEAR OF SOFTWARE FRAUD—ROUND II (1985–1988)

In the middle 1980s, national concern again surfaced about the possibility of malicious software manipulation. The issue had never really gone away, but it awaited events to cause it to bubble up to the surface.

A Dallas, Texas, mayoralty contest in April 1985 was the starting point for a situation that eventually involved the Texas attorney general and the state legislature. Terry Elkins, campaign manager for defeated candidate Max Goldblatt, collected data from the election that she believed documented fraud. Some months later, she approached the office of the Texas attorney general with her concerns. She claimed that while the tabulating machine was down, during the counting, the computer program was changed to the detriment of her candidate. Much information about this controversy has been documented (Saltman, 1988, pp. 16–22, 58–64). In 1987, Ms. Elkins coauthored an article in *Campaigns & Elections*, a magazine for political operatives. The piece concerned the general problem of incorrectness of election-counting software. If the technical publications of others were too esoteric for individuals whose concern was practical politics, Elkins's article was right in their faces (Elkins and Waskell, 1987, pp. 20–25).

On November 25, 1986, the Texas House of Representatives Committee on Elections, chaired by Clint Hackney, held a hearing on possible changes in the state's election laws. The hearing was held as a result of the Dallas election controversy. The result was a revised statute on requirements for the voting process when computers are involved. The law was adopted on September 1, 1987, and some of its provisions were as follows:

- *Auditing*: A voting system may not be used unless it is capable of providing records from which the operation of the system may be audited.
- *Deposit and Availability of the Program*: Copies of the "program codes" and related documentation must be filed with the Secretary of State . . . The software on file is not public information, although it may be made available to the Attorney General for investigation of irregularities.
- *Use of Remote Terminals*: "No modem access to the tabulation equipment" must be available during tabulation.
- *Testing of Equipment*: Each unit of tabulating equipment shall be tested "using all applicable ballot formats."
- *Discrepancies in Ballot Totals*: If, in the use of a precinct-located computer, a discrepancy of more than three exists between the number of ballots recorded by the computer and the number of ballots written down by the precinct officials, the final count of that precinct shall be done centrally.
- *Manual Count*: A manual count of all the races in one percent of the election precincts, but in no less than three precincts, shall be conducted at the local level. The Secretary of State also may conduct a manual or automatic count of any number of ballots. No specific ground for obtaining an initial recount is required.

A second signal event was that The New York Times *published a series of articles* concerning possible fraud in computerized elections. The first article, beginning on page one of the July 29, 1985 issue and written by freelance author David Burnham, was entitled "Computerized Systems for Voting Seen as Vulnerable to Tampering" (Burnham, 1985, p. 1). The piece in *The Times* included the following:

The computer program that was used to count more than one-third of the votes cast in the Presidential election last year is very vulnerable to manipulation and fraud, according to expert witnesses in court actions challenging local and Congressional elections in three states . . .

The vote-counting program that has been challenged in Indiana, West Virginia and Maryland was developed by Computer Election Systems of Berkeley, Calif. In Indiana and West Virginia, the company has been accused of helping to rig elections. The computer program has been challenged in Florida, but so far experts have not been permitted to examine the program in connection with the challenge . . .

Two computer experts were cited in the article who were quoted as supporting the possibilities of easy manipulation. One was Howard Jay Strauss, associate director of the Princeton University Computing Center. Their full statements, not reported in the article, significantly qualified the ease of fraudulent changes by indicating that there were methods with which such malicious activities could be prevented. Furthermore, said one, there was no evidence that such criminality had actually occurred (Saltman, 1988, pp. 12–15). None of the challenged election results identified in the article were overturned, but the effect of the article was to increase public unease about computerized voting. Foundation funds for additional studies of the question would be made available.

The John and Mary R. Markle Foundation, headquartered in New York City, would fund a number of projects as a result of the 1985 articles in *The New York Times*. The foundation had an interest in the field of public communications and decided that the accusations made in the first article, as well as the general concerns reported in subsequent articles about the lack of knowledge of election administrators, deserved additional review.

A workshop on Captiva Island, Florida, for 26 invited experts, was sponsored by the Markle Foundation in February 1987. The attendees included election administrators, election equipment vendors, computer security experts, journalists concentrating on election reporting, lawyers who had engaged in election litigation, and researchers. Presentations were given by Marie Garber, head of the Maryland State Administrative Board of Election Laws, Richard H. McKay, president of the Election Services Division of Business Records Corporation (formerly CES), Robert J. Naegele, president of Granite Creek Technology, Richard G. Smolka, publisher of *Election Administration Reports*, and Willis H. Ware, senior scientist at The Rand Corporation. A report of the meeting was written by Prof. Lance Hoffman of George Washington University (Hoffman, 1988, pp. 1–93).

A guide to computerized voting systems was also supported. The project was carried out by ECRI, a scientific testing laboratory of Plymouth Meeting, Pennsylvania. The guide was intended for election administrators. The 50-page document, authored by project leader Malin Van Antwerp and staff, included a description of various equipment then available as well as useful trade-off information for considerations in the selection process. Among its statements was:

we recommend strongly that jurisdictions not purchase new vote recorders that require prescored cards. (ECRI, 1988, p. 4)

Roy G. Saltman's report of 1988 was paid for by the foundation. In early 1986, foundation program officer Larry Slesinger approached NBS and asked the agency to accept enough money for Saltman to undertake a two-year study of the current problems of computerized vote tallying. As the need for external funding was vital to NBS and the proposed project was consistent with the agency's mission, Saltman was made available for the work.

The administration of some 12 elections in 11 states, which had encountered difficulties between 1980 and 1986 were analyzed. Additional information was provided in a report that had been undertaken by the Illinois State Division of Voting Systems, directed at the time by Michael L. Harty. Administrative problems were categorized as follows:

1. insufficient preelection testing;
2. failure to implement an adequate audit trail;
3. failure to provide a partial manual recount of ballots;
4. ballot reader malfunctions;
5. non-reproducible results due to the use of PPC ballots;
6. loss of management control, due to the use of borrowed equipment and computer operations by outsiders;
7. inadequate contingency planning; and
8. inadequate systems acceptance procedures.

Examples of elections demonstrating non-reproducible results due to use of PPC ballots were Palm Beach County, Florida, November 1984; Dallas, Texas, April 1985; Stark County, Ohio, May 1986; and Gwinnett County, Georgia, November 1986 (Saltman, 1988, pp. 58–80). These examples, demonstrating the inability of PPC systems to reproduce counts, suggested to Saltman an inherent condition in the voting method that could not be easily repaired. An essential tenet of the scientific method is that experiments can be replicated to demonstrate the correctness of the deduced results. Although elections are not experiments, the importance of reproducible results (through retention of original documents) to verify the original assertions pertains also. As a result, Saltman proposed that:

> The use of pre-scored punch cards contributes to the inaccuracy and to the lack of confidence. It is generally not possible to exactly duplicate a count obtained on pre-scored punch cards, given the inherent physical characteristics of these ballots and the variability in the ballot-punching performance of real voters. It is recommended that the use of pre-scored punch card ballots be ended. (Saltman, 1988, p. 5)

As with other recommendations, this proposal had no immediate impact. After the 2000 Florida brouhaha, it was remembered by the media (e.g., Whoriskey, 2000, *Miami Herald*).

The vulnerabilities of non-ballot voting systems have been extensively discussed by Saltman (Saltman, 1988, pp. 26–29, 39–42).

The essential problem of mechanical lever machines is that there is not, nor can there be, an audit trail of each voter's choices. The correct recording of the sum of voters' choices depends on the proper mechanical connections within the device, the zero setting of its initial values, and its correct operation throughout election day. There is no mechanical method of retaining each voter's choices.

The lack of an audit trail prevents identification and correction of machine failures. If, for example, 220 voters were recorded as voting on a particular machine in a two-candidate contest, where one candidate is recorded on a three-digit counter as receiving 099 votes and the other 106, it cannot be easily determined what happened to the missing 15 votes. Either these 15 voters failed to vote for either candidate, or they voted and the machine failed to record their choices, or some of each occurred. There are no documents in the system that will bring light to the problem, or determine if there is any problem at all. Only a technical review of the innards of each machine could determine what actually happened. No such general technical review has ever been required or carried out. Furthermore, there can be no "recount" as there are no ballots. There can only be a re-canvass, that is, a review of the values on each of the counters to assure that their values were copied down correctly.

What is astonishing is that there was so little questioning of the operations of these machines for so long. One can suppose that their positive attributes so outweighed their downside that they were widely accepted until technological change made them obsolete. Their value was their elimination of writing instruments and paper ballots, elimination of questions of intent of the voter in contentious recounts, the reduction in the number and cost of citizens needed to count the results, and the reduction in the time required to report the results.

When DREs began to be used, electronic storage was possible. If DREs were logically identical to lever machines, then they would have the same limitation: there could be no audit trail whatsoever. However, as proposed in 1988:

> Each voter-choice set (i.e., the machine's record of all choices of a voter) should be retained in the machine . . . (Saltman, 1988, p. 113)

The FEC standards, when finally issued, adopted the requirement that DRE systems retain each voter's voter-choice sets (now called electronic ballot images, EBIs). In Section 3.2.4.2.5 Vote Recording, the standards state:

> [DRE systems] shall also maintain an electronic or physical image of each ballot, in an independent data path. (Federal Election Commission, 1990, p. 30)

This requirement has been generally adhered to by manufacturers.

The essential vulnerability of DREs is that there is no independent audit trail. Assurance of correct software is an absolute necessity. As noted:

> The machine cannot be used to independently verify its own correctness . . . For some, this lack of an audit trail for individual transactions is unacceptable. (Saltman, 1988, pp. 42, 121)

If the software has been maliciously manipulated, there is a question as to whether the voter's choices have, in fact, been entered for summation precisely as the voter desired. The retention of EBIs is highly useful, but their presence does not guarantee correct operation. If the EBIs are to generate the final results, then a very clever programmer could, theoretically, manipulate the process. This manipulation would provide the voter with a screen showing what the voter believed he or she selected, but the EBIs would actually record what the manipulator desired. With knowledge that this manipulation is a possibility, it can be guarded against in the testing and protection of the DRE software and hardware. This issue would not go away (see section 7.6).

A relevant interview by Dan Rather, anchorman for CBS television news, occurred a few days before the November 8, 1988 presidential election. Rather showed a PPC to the viewers with one hole punched. The issue was whether the punched hole could be misinterpreted by a computer. Howard Jay Strauss, previously cited in *The New York Times* article of 1985, was asked about the possibility of altering computer software to change the outcome of a national election:

> *Rather:* For the right kind of money, could you put the fix in, in a national election; realistically could it be done?
>
> *Strauss:* Yes, get me employed by the company that writes this program. In that case, you need bribe one person; one person writing the software for this company. You would have access to a third of the votes in the country. Is that enough to throw the election?

Rather allowed Penelope Bonsall, director of the NCEA, to reply:

> *Bonsall:* If you are talking about the ability or capability to compromise the presidential election coming up on a wide-scale basis, I would say that that theoretical potential is close to nil. (Saltman, 1991, p. 257)

The complex issue of employing technology to assist in the national administration of the democratic process had been reduced to just a few words: a sensationalistic charge and a pro forma denial. It was as if the many hours work put in by many earnest professionals in identifying problems, writing papers, proposing improvements, and planning standards had not occurred.

6.12 THE STANDARDS INSTITUTIONALIZED ON A SHOESTRING

The development of a certification and escrow system for software was necessary to assure institutionalization of the standards process. Voting System Testing Laboratories (VSTLs), initially called Independent Testing Authorities (ITAs), would be needed that would test voting equipment against the standards. The concept was that a single national set of laboratory certifications would be used by any state, eliminating duplicate testing.

In 1989, a highly useful organization had been formed. It was called the National Association of State Election Directors (NASED). It was a voluntary professional association of senior election officials in each state, the District of Columbia and American territories. Some of the officials involved in its formation were Tom Harrison of Texas, Constance Slaughter Harvey of Mississippi, Hoyt Clifton of New Mexico, Dot Joyce of Florida, Donnetta Davidson of Colorado, Anita Tatum of Alabama, Tom Wilkey of New York, and Chris Thomas of Michigan. All of these election directors had served as presidents of the organization between 1990 and 1997. Their respective states most likely paid their travel and meeting costs.

In 1989 and 1990, as the FEC standards were nearing completion, NASED agreed to serve as the certifying agency for the VSTLs. It established an Accreditation Board for this purpose. The Election Center agreed to serve as the secretariat for that function. That organization had been established in 1984 by Gary Greenhalgh after he left the FEC. The center trains election administrators with courses and conferences. It appears to be unique in that regard. Beginning in 1987, the center was led by Carol Garner and then from 1994 to the present by R. Doug Lewis. While the center received foundation money for its initial start, it now runs primarily on tuition and fees from administrators being trained. The center has an arrangement with the public administration program of Auburn University to provide in-service courses. Election officials may earn the status of Certified Elections/Registration Administrator (CERA) through this process.

Robert J. Naegele served as NASED's technical advisor and produced the handbook for accreditation (NASED, 2001 (1992)). The laboratories that were accredited had carried out similar work for federal agencies or their contractors. The first lab to be accredited for hardware testing was Wyle Laboratories of Huntsville, Alabama, in 1994. Soon after, Nichols Research of Huntsville was accepted to certify voting equipment software. Nichols, through mergers, became Ciber in 1997. More recently, SysTest Labs of Denver has been accredited to certify both hardware and software. The certification process is financed through fees assessed against equipment vendors.

The issue of escrow of software arose and continues to be a problem, since the equipment vendors treat their software as proprietary under trade secret protection. However, there is a need for the software to be available in case a question of its correctness arises. The VSTL that has tested the software will have signed a nondisclosure agreement with the vendor. A state may require that the software be deposited with it, with no public disclosure permitted except in the case of an official inquiry. If a state does not wish to serve as a repository, it may ask the vendor to deposit the software with an organization specifically established to serve for escrow purposes.

6.13   THE FEC STANDARDS FAIL IN FLORIDA

In January 1990, the first edition of the FEC's Voting System Standards were issued. The standards applied to "punchcard, marksense, and direct recording electronic voting systems." There were no performance standards for human factors in use of the machine, despite that recommendation by NCEA's Advisory Committee in 1977. Within a few years, some two-thirds of the states had incorporated the standards into their laws and/or regulations. In these states, only election equipment that had been tested and certified could be used in any of the state's jurisdictions. In 1996, the name of the NCEA was changed to the Office of Election Administration (OEA).

With regard to PPC ballots, the standards made clear that their use was acceptable. Section 3.2.4.1.2 Punching Devices stated:

> Punching devices shall be suitable for the type of ballot card used. When pre-scored ballot cards are used, the punching device shall consist of a suitable frame for holding the ballot card, and a stylus which the voter uses to remove a scored area of the card to cast a vote. The stylus shall be designed and constructed so as to facilitate its use by the voter, and to minimize damage to other parts with which it comes in contact. It shall incorporate features to ameliorate the effect of skewed insertion, and to ensure that the chad (debris) is completely removed. (Federal Election Commission, 1990, p. 27)

To the best of this author's knowledge, no stylus without spring loading has been able at any time "to ensure that the chad (debris) is completely removed." Furthermore, no Votomatic or equivalent system was ever tested prior to use and rejected for its inability to completely remove chad. The tendency of the Votomatic system to produce "hanging" or "bulging" chad or to have human factor difficulties did not result in attempts to end its use before the 2000 election in California, Florida, Georgia, Illinois, Ohio, or other states that were users of PPC ballots. While many administrators knew of the problems of the Votomatic system, they did nothing except express the pious hope that elections in their jurisdictions would not be close. In close elections, all of the sloppy procedures and equipment malfunctions that were bound to happen with poorly functioning systems run on a minimal budget would be brought to light.

The availability of a spring-loaded stylus, which would remove chad without the necessity for prescoring the ballot card, was discussed by Saltman (Saltman, 1988, p. 5). It was believed at that time that such a stylus would be widely adopted, but that was not the case. The product did not appear to catch on, and there is no record of its use in 2000. The standards, adopted in Florida in the 1990s, were totally useless in preventing the debacle of 2000 in that state due to the use of PPC ballots.

6.14   OMENS FORETELLING A DISASTER ARE IGNORED

Three situations that occurred in the 1990s are reported here. One was a simulation but two were the outcomes of real elections. There is no evidence that the obvious lesson was taken into account by anyone with any responsibility for election administration.

A simulation of a multi-candidate city council election was undertaken by three political scientists in the Cincinnati area in 1990. Their intent was to evaluate voter ability to use a PPC system compared with a hand-marked, hand-counted paper ballot system and a DRE pushbutton system. A demographic mixture of citizens were recruited involving variations in race, age, income, gender, and other characteristics. The problem given the subjects was to select up to 9 candidates out of a field of 18. Random assignments to one of the three voting methods were made. Each voting unit carried the instruction "VOTE FOR NO MORE THAN NINE."

Hypotheses for the experiment were that:

1. The percentage of subjects using the punchcard ballot who vote for the nine candidates will be less than the percentage of subjects using the other two forms of voting technology who exercise their full franchise by voting for nine candidates.
2. The percentage of subjects using the punchcard ballot who overvote will be greater than the percentage of subjects who overvote using the paper ballot. (Overvotes on DREs were not possible.)
3. The mean number of valid votes cast by the punchcard voter group will be less than the mean number of valid votes cast by the other two groups.

The experiment validated all three hypotheses. Furthermore, the authors point out, "many subjects were generally familiar with paper ballots from everyday life experiences and with computerized punch cards since they have long been used in Cincinnati municipal elections." The authors concluded that their

> empirical findings clearly indicate that voters using the punchcard method do not cast as many valid votes as voters using the alternative systems.

They also stated that

> punchcard systems may present greater obstacles to voting than alternative ballot technologies and may result in more undervoting, overvoting and misvoting. . . . The disenfranchising impact of voting technology should not be ignored. (Shocket, Heighberger, and Brown, 1993, pp. 521–537)

In 2000 and 2004, Cincinnati voters were still using PPCs.

An election in Wisconsin in 1993 provided some additional understanding of the human factors problem in the use of PPC ballots. A special election for the U.S. Representative from the First Congressional District was held on May 4, 1993, because of the resignation of the incumbent, Les Aspin. There was just one contest on the ballot, and five candidates for the office. Peter Barca defeated his strongest competitor Mark Neumann by 675 votes out of more than 110,000 cast. Difficulties in the election were significant in three counties: Racine, Walworth, and Green. In Racine, 3 percent of the punch-card ballots were invalidated, many because of votes cast for more than one candidate and others for votes cast on a line on the ballot showing no candidate. In Walworth, 5 percent of the ballots were invalidated for the same reasons (Hunter, 1993, p. 6A). In these counties, there were many more voters who signed in than votes that were counted. A reasonable surmise was that voters did not come to vote for a one-contest election and then not vote for any candidate.

This election occurred in a stable area where PPC ballots had been used for many years. The single contest on the ballot had forced observers to focus on the inability of voters to convert their choices accurately into the corresponding ballot holes. Following this election, the Wisconsin State Elections Board ordered local jurisdictions not to procure any more PPC systems. The use of these systems declined in Wisconsin towns from 400 in 1993 to 51 in 2000.

In Massachusetts, a primary election for nomination for the office of U.S. Representative for the 10th District was held on September 17, 1996. The main contenders were William D. Delahunt and Philip W. Johnston. A PPC voting system was used. Johnston was initially declared the winner, first by 266 votes and later by 175 votes. Delahunt took the situation to the courts, where it eventually reached the highest in the state, the Supreme Judicial Court. Excerpts from the final decision of the highest court are as follows:

> The trial judge counted as votes for either Delahunt or Johnston many ballots that had previously been recorded as blank. Reflecting the newly identified votes, the judge concluded that Delahunt was the winner . . . The critical question in this case is whether a discernible indentation made on or near a chad should be recorded as a vote for the person to whom the chad is assigned. The trial judge concluded that a vote should be recorded for a candidate if the chad was not removed but an impression was made on or near it. We agree with this conclusion . . . We find unpersuasive Johnston's contention that many voters started to express a preference in the congressional contest, made an impression on a punch card, but pulled the stylus back because they really did not want to express a choice on that contest. The large number of ballots with discernible impressions makes such an inference unwarranted, especially in a hotly contested election . . . Once one accepts, as we have, the presence of a discernible impression made by a stylus as a clear indication of a voter's intent, our task is to assess each of the 956 ballots [previously recorded as blank]. We have done so and agreed with the trial judge's conclusion on all but twenty-eight ballots . . . (Supreme Judicial Court of MA, 1996, 423 Mass. 731)

The situation described here is a microcosm of what occurred in Florida just four years later. On October 8, 1997, William Francis Galvin, the secretary of the Commonwealth of Massachusetts, revoked approval for use of the PPC system. The report announcing the revocation included the following:

> Municipalities using punch cards have consistently reported a significantly higher percentage of blank ballots than has been reported in municipalities

using optical scanners, lever machines, and paper ballots. Additionally, in recounts of election results where punch cards have been used, review of such ballots has shown that often the paper tab, which must be cleanly severed to indicate a vote, has not been so severed and remains partially attached to the ballot. Such recounts have also demonstrated that often a ballot than does not appear to be marked will actually show an indentation on the tab, which is stall fully attached to the ballot. These systemic flaws have changed the outcome of a number of elections, as ballots read by the computer as blank have actually found to contain voters' identifiable choices. (Galvin, 1997, p. 1)

6.15   LACK OF RESOURCES APPLIED

The failure of the federal government to commit resources devoted to election technology and administration is an important factor that facilitated the Florida fiasco. The states complained about the "unfunded mandates" of federal requirements such as the NVRA, but they failed to pick up the slack. The states failed to adequately fund the function about which they are so protective. The result was poor implementation of voting systems in many states.

The problems in preparing new voting technologies for public use were not understood to be significant. There were failures to appreciate the technical complexities of implementation, lack of technical expertise, and funding in local administrations, as well as lack of recognition by the states and federal government that it was a field worthy of important investment. After Representatives Keating and Frenzel were instrumental in the early 1970s in pointing out problems and assuring the establishment and continuation of the Clearinghouse, no priority whatsoever was given to that organization's function.

Comparisons may be made with federal involvement in other areas of civic endeavor, such as agriculture, education, health, and ground transportation. In these other areas, the federal government does not carry out the operational activities (similar to its mission in elections), but recognizes that effective functioning in these fields is essential to public well being. Often, the argument for federal involvement involves concern for "public health" or "public safety" (as was noted in sections 2.11 and 2.12). A strong indication of the federal government's commitment is demonstrated by the establishment of Cabinet posts and fully staffed agencies. Each of these federal departments includes an office that collects data and develops statistics about the status of its assigned field of concern. Other agencies in the department undertake significant research, issue grants, set standards (some mandatory), and sometimes set funding incentives. Data from research and analyses are published that enable state and local governments, and individual citizens, for example, farmers, educators, physicians, and truck manufacturers, to make decisions that are better informed. The mutually supporting arrangements of these departments with their constituencies demonstrate how successful federalism is carried out.

For voting technology and systems, even if limited to federal elections, there was neither a Cabinet position nor an independent office; that is, there was no Democracy Protection Agency. The five-person Clearinghouse/ Office of Election Administration did not constitute a meaningful federal program, stuck as it was in a commission regulating campaign financing. Its minuscule funding prevented any quantitative research, for example, on the effectiveness of different types of voting equipment or on the human factors connected with their use. Obviously, no data on these subjects could be disseminated. When the Clinton administration wanted a study undertaken on voting over the Internet (begun with a workshop in October 2000), it had to turn to the National Science Foundation for the funding (Internet Policy Institute, 2001, pp. 1–52). The result of the lack of data and direction was the disaster in Florida four weeks later. In effect, *failed federalism fueled the Florida fiasco.*

7

THE GREAT AWAKENING AFTER
FLORIDA, THROUGH JULY 2005

Following the ruling of the U.S. Supreme Court in *Bush v. Gore* on December 12, 2000, there was no longer any bar to the appointment of Electors for George W. Bush by the elected Republican leadership in Florida. The Electors were appointed on the day established under federal law, which was December 18. When the Congress met in joint session to count the Electoral votes on January 6, 2001, Vice President Al Gore, as the president of the Senate, was in the chair. Several African American members of the House attempted to object to the counting of the votes of Florida. However, no senator had joined the effort, a requirement of the Electoral Count Act (see section 3.9) for the protest to move forward. The loser of the election ruled the objection out-of-order. During the similar Congressional action in January 2005, it was reported that Senator Barbara Boxer, Democrat of California, "regretted granting Gore's request not to object to the 2000 electoral-vote process" (*The Washington Post*, January 7, 2005, p. A4).

After the legal resolution, there was an outpouring of views on the election by thoughtful individuals in the professions of journalism, law, political science, and industrial design. A number of relevant articles and books have been cited in chapter 1 and listed in the references section, but these citations do not begin to identify the entire body of works on the subject. The failure to examine and understand the voting technology issue beforehand was dismaying to some, for example:

> In . . . 2000 . . . the election of the President of the United States came down to an aspect of the election system that received scant attention from political scientists over the preceding century—the functioning of voting equipment. (Ansolabehere and Stewart, 2002, p. 1)

Following the 2000 election, social scientists began to examine voters' capability to record their choices on the several machine types according to their race, education, income, and other factors of socioeconomic status (SES). The media began to report events about the voting process more often and in greater detail. In 2001, several universities and professional and government-related organizations established studies and produced reports with policy and legislative recommendations. Two were by the (privately funded) National Commission on Federal Election Reform and by the California Institute of Technology (Caltech) and MIT (see the references section). Many bills mandating reforms were submitted in the Congress and significant legislation was adopted. The date of November 7, 2000 was to election administration as September 11, 2001 would become to homeland security.

7.1   Comparison of Residual Rates with Use of Different Technologies

The "residual rate" has begun to be widely used as a measure of human performance in using voting systems (Caltech/MIT, March 2001, p. 6). The term means the percentage of ballots cast for the first contest in a consolidated election for which no legitimate choice has been made. The first contest is believed to be the one least likely to be deliberately undervoted by a voter, implying that it gives the best available measure of human error in failing to vote. A study has estimated that about 0.25 to 0.75 percent of voters deliberately omit voting for the top contest (Knack and Kropf, 2001, p. 4), but the residual rate is typically larger than that. Rates may vary strongly by circumstance. "Fall-off" is a term used to describe reductions in total votes cast for contests down the ballot, and the residual rate could be called "top-contest fall-off." Fall-off generally rises consistently for lower level contests, but there are cases where that does not happen.

While the criterion of residual rate has gained considerable credence since the 2000 election, there is a much earlier example of its use. During research in 1934, Joseph P. Harris compared votes failed to be cast in 1925 on paper ballots in New York City with the votes cast on lever machines in 1929 for the same offices. The term that he used was "wasted votes" rather than residual rate. In 1925, the first contest on the ballot, for the office of mayor, had 1.9 percent wasted votes, whereas the 1929 figure was 2.3 percent (Harris, 1934, p. 275).

Results from the following studies support the conclusion that the PPC system was the worst of all commonly used systems in the ability of voters to successfully use it.

The Caltech/MIT Voting Technology Project reported:

> Punch cards . . . lose at least 50 percent more votes than optically scanned paper ballots. Punch cards have averaged a residual vote rate of 2.5 percent in presidential elections and 4.7 percent down the ballot. Over thirty million voters used punch cards in the 2000 election . . . (Caltech/MIT, July 2001, p. 21)

Researchers at the University of California at Berkeley, led by Henry E. Brady, director of the Survey Research Center, have provided a comparison of residual rate by technology employed for the 2000 election. According to their report, "we invested heavily in collecting and cleaning these data" (for

Table 7.1   Residual rates for 2,219 counties—averages over all ballots

System type	Average residual rate (%)
Punchcard	2.64
Paper ballots	1.99
Lever machines	1.72
DREs	1.68
Marksense	1.37
National average	1.94

Note: Adapted from Brady et al., 2001, p. 29.

2,219 U.S. counties, about 70 percent of all of them). Their data over all ballots is shown in table 7.1 (results for PPC and Datavote systems are combined).

Voters in the City of Detroit used a PPC system in 1996 to cast their ballots. In 1998, the city replaced all its PPC systems with a precinct-counted marksense system, which provided ballot return for overvotes. A report of their results stated:

> The percentage of uncounted ballots in Detroit decreased significantly in the 2000 election . . . In the 1996 election, 3.1% of ballots cast in Detroit were not counted in the Presidential race. In 2000, only 1.1% of ballots were not counted . . .
>
> The decrease was across-the-board . . . The reduction in the undercount was especially large in precincts with high rates of uncounted votes in 1996. Precincts that had over 7% uncounted votes for President in 1996 had less than 1% uncounted votes in 2000. (Minority Staff, April 2001, p. 1)

The State of Georgia used four voting technologies in 1998: punch card, marksense, lever machines, and paper ballots. Georgia adopted a statewide uniform DRE system soon after the 2000 election. In 1998 and 2002, the contest for U.S. Senate was at the top of the ticket. In 1998, the undervote for the Senate contest was 4.8 percent of ballots cast, but in 2002, with the new system, the undervote was 0.88 percent. (Only undervotes were compared since the new system does not allow overvotes.) In 2002, of 29 of Georgia's 159 counties that each had an undervote of at least 15 percent, 26 had undervotes of less than 3 percent. In DeKalb county, the first county in the country to adopt a PPC system in 1964, the undervote dropped from 3.7 percent in 2000 to 0.52 percent in 2002, and in adjacent Fulton County, the 2000 undervote was 6.3 percent while in 2002, it was 0.67 percent (Office of Secretary of State Cathy Cox, 2003, pp. 1, 2).

In Maryland, John T. Willis, secretary of state in 2001, compared residual votes longitudinally in three counties. His data showed that when marksense systems were used in 1996 and 2000, residual rates were considerably lower in each of these counties than when PPC systems were used in 1984, 1988, and 1992. Inspection of the numbers easily shows the differences (table 7.2).

Table 7.2   Residual vote percentages for three Maryland counties: 1984–2000

County/Year	PPC system used			Marksense system used	
	1984	1988	1992	1996	2000
Carroll	1.65	2.54	1.79	0.45	0.12
Frederick	2.94	2.62	1.05	0.47	0.25
Harford	2.78	7.64	1.47	0.62	0.27

Note that the residual rates when marksense systems were used were at the low end of the Knack and Kropf estimated average of deliberate undervotes.

The State of Ohio prepared a plan in 2003 in order to receive federal financial assistance under the Help America Vote Act (HAVA). The plan included replacement of punch-card voting systems, used by more than 70 percent of voters in Ohio's 88 counties. The plan's report, prepared by a committee led by Secretary of State J. Kenneth Blackwell, noted:

> The data shows 29 counties with the highest over/under vote percentage in the 2000 election were all counties that used the punchcard method of voting. The seven counties with the lowest over/under vote percentage in the 2000 election were all counties that did not use punch cards as their primary voting system. (State Plan Committee, 2003, p. 16)

7.2   SOCIOECONOMIC STATUS AND DIFFERENCES IN RESIDUAL RATES

A summary of research that analyzed the percentage of residual votes by African Americans in the 2000 presidential election using different voting equipment has been undertaken by Tova Andrea Wang (Century Foundation, 2004, pp. 1–15).

The report of the University Of California at Berkeley, discussed earlier, also provided two graphs detailing the relationship of SES variables with the size of the residual vote (Brady et al., 2001, p. 27). Without taking into account the type of voting system as a variable, this report determined that the percentage of residual of vote correlated in 2000 with lack of education and with a higher percentage of minorities, larger than 30 percent.

In a comparative study of 40 Congressional Districts (CDs), undertaken by the minority party members (Democrats) of a Congressional committee, each of 20 CDs had a low average income and a high percentage minority population, while each of the other 20 had a high average income and a low percentage minority population. The report determined the residual rates in each of the 40 districts and compared those rates between the two types. The effect of different voting technologies on the residual rates was also reported.

The twenty low-income, high-minority districts each had less than 50 percent of their population consisting of non-Hispanic whites. The twenty

Table 7.3 Percentage of residual vote for two disparate groupings of Congressional Districts, by type of technology used

Type of technology	Residual vote (%)	
	Low income, high minority CDs	High income, low minority CDs
Punch card	7.7	2.0
Marksense—Central Count	4.7	0.7
Lever	4.5	0.9
DRE	2.4	0.8
Marksense—Precinct Count	1.1	0.5
All ballots	4.0	1.2

districts selected had the lowest average income except that no more than two were selected from one state. The twenty high-income, low-percentage minority districts were selected from those having more than 70 percent non-Hispanic whites in their population. The selected CDs had the highest median income consistent with the requirement that not more than two were taken from the same state. Some states had one or two CDs from each group.

The results of the study are summarized in table 7.3 (Minority Staff, July 2001, figure 1 and table 3). It can be seen in the table that, with each type of technology, the percentage residual vote of the low-income, high-minority CDs is considerably higher than the percentage residual vote of the high-income, low-minority CDs. Clearly, the use of punch cards resulted in the highest residual rates for both groupings whereas the use of precinct-counted marksense ballots with overvote return had the lowest residual rates. The residual rates are given for the sum of all ballots, regardless of technology. The latter includes ballots from the few areas where paper ballots were used, as well as areas in which more than one technology was used.

Associates of Henry E. Brady at University of California at Berkeley separately studied the correlation between use of PPC voting systems and the residual rate by minority voters. They report:

> The vote invalidation gap between minorities and non-minorities is higher when a county uses punchcard voting systems . . . The important point is that punch cards are significantly worse than all other systems . . . Punchcard counties tend to have higher residual vote rates than we would expect even after controlling for education.

This study evaluated changes in minority residual rates among two groups of counties in California. One group consisted of nine counties that used PPC systems in both 1996 and 2000. The second group consisted of three counties that had used PPC systems in 1996 but switched to precinct-count marksense systems in 2000. The researchers used data from each census tract in the twelve counties to plot residual rate as a function of percentage of minorities in the tracts. The nine counties retaining the PPC voting system had similar plots of their residual rates in both 1996 and 2000, clearly showing an upturn associated with higher percentages of minorities in the census tracts. In 2000, these nine counties had about a 1.8 percent residual rate with 0 percent minorities per tract, increasing to about 4 percent for tracts with 100 percent minorities.

The three counties that eliminated PPC systems in 2000 showed a much lower average rise with increasing percentage of minorities in the tracts. For 1996 data, the line of average residual rates begins at 1 percent with 0 percent minorities and ends at 5 percent with 100 percent minorities per tract. For 2000, the line of average residual rates begins at 0.3 percent with 0 percent minorities per tract and ends at about 1.5 percent for 100 percent minorities per tract. Thus, the change from PPC systems to precinct-count marksense systems was significant in reducing minority residual vote (Buchler et al., 2004, table 1 and figures 2, 3a, and 3b).

7.3   CAUSES OF HIGHER RESIDUAL RATES AMONG BLACKS

Judge Richard Posner reported the results of regression analyses that he undertook on the Florida vote in 2000. He experimented with a number of regression equations and candidly discussed their separate determinations of significant variables (Posner, 2001, pp. 67–82). His overall conclusion was:

> The equations . . . taken as a whole, indicate that the punchcard ballot and county counting [instead of precinct counting], together with the correlated factors of low literacy, low income, and being black, had a significant effect in increasing the frequency of spoiled votes . . . (pp. 81, 82)

The U.S. Commission on Civil Rights (USCCR) undertook hearings in 2001 and released an extensive report. It appears that the intent of the commission, with Mary Frances Berry as chair, was to provide evidence of violations of the 1982 amendments to the Voting Rights Act. The commission used the term "disenfranchisement" to refer to the high residual rate:

> This disenfranchisement of Florida voters fell most harshly on the shoulders of African Americans. Statewide, based on county-level statistical estimates, African American voters were nearly 10 times more likely than white voters to have their ballots rejected in the November 2000 election. (USCCR, 2001, p. 100)

The use of the term disenfranchisement in this context was vigorously contested by two of the eight commissioners in their dissent included in the separate Appendix to the main report. Calling the majority's report "prejudicial, divisive, and injurious to the cause of true democracy and justice in our society," they wrote that "disenfranchisement is not the same thing as voter error" (Thernstrom and Redenbaugh, 2001, Appendix IX, pp. 1, 3).

Allan J. Lichtman, professor of history at American University, Washington, DC, was the statistical expert hired by the USCCR. His work for the commission appears in the Appendix volume of the USCCR report (Lichtman, 2001, Appendix VII). The first point made by Professor Lichtman in his report was that:

> When we look at the variation in the ballot rejection rates for each county in Florida, one-quarter of that variation can be explained solely by knowing the percentage of blacks who were registered to vote in that county.

Prof. Lichtman does not state what variables contributed to the other three-quarters of the variation in residual rates. He does state, however, that:

> A multiple regression analysis that controlled for the percentage of high school graduates and the percentage of adults in the lowest literacy category failed to diminish the relationship between race and ballot rejection or to reduce the statistical significance of the relationship. (p. 4)

The U.S. Department of Justice investigated the situation in Florida and did not file any suits based on the 1982 amendments. The department, in a letter to Congress signed by Assistant Attorney General Ralph F. Boyd, Jr., noted that it had investigated voting irregularities in three Florida counties: Miami-Dade, Orange, and Osceola. Boyd wrote:

> While the Civil Rights Division discovered evidence of significant confusion and delay in the three counties, there were relatively few voters who actually did not vote because of these problems . . . [This small number of voters] doesn't reasonably cast any doubt on President Bush's several hundred vote margin of victory in Florida . . . The Civil Rights Division found no credible evidence in our investigations that Floridians were intentionally denied their right to vote . . . (*The Washington Post*, May 30, 2001, p. 2)

It seems clear from the letter's wording that the Department of Justice, under its new Republican leadership, would not find a violation of the Voting Rights Act unless it could be shown that a significant number of persons were actually denied the right to vote. Apparently, the department did not view the high residual rates among blacks as a violation.

7.4   REEVALUATIONS IN THE STATES, AND LAWSUITS AGAINST PUNCH-CARD VOTING

At the start of 2001, a number of states, for example, Florida (Governor's Select, 2001, pp. 1–78) and Maryland (Special Committee, 2001, pp. 1–124), established studies to evaluate the voting equipment being employed and to review the relationships between the state and local governments in election administration. In Georgia and Maryland, selection of voting equipment by individual counties was ended. Both states adopted the Diebold

AccuVote-TS DRE system statewide (in Maryland, Baltimore city was exempted). In Wisconsin, PPC systems were decertified. Florida eliminated use of punch-card systems, central-count optical scan systems, hand-counted paper ballots, and lever machines, as recommended by its study. Then, the state certified some DRE systems to make them available for county adoption.

In California, this state's leaders decided to eliminate punch-card voting systems before the 2006 general election, but a lawsuit by civil rights organizations (*Common Cause v. Jones*) contested that date. In their view, the continued use of PPC systems was a civil rights violation. According to Daniel P. Tokaji of the ACLU, one of the plaintiff's lawyers, "judgment was granted plaintiffs as a matter of law." An agreement was reached in which the state moved up the date for removal of punch-card voting systems to March 2, 2004.

In 2003, a petition drive to recall the governor of California succeeded, and a statewide vote was scheduled for October 7 of that year. After the scheduling, civil rights organizations asked the federal district court (*Southwest Voter Registration Education Project v. Shelley*) to delay the recall until after the date that punch-card systems would have to be eliminated. One legal argument put forth by the plaintiffs, with counsel from the ACLU, was that the poor performance of PPC systems, compared to other systems, violated the "equal protection" requirement of the 14th Amendment. A second argument was that:

> people of color in California are more likely to live in counties that continue to use PPC systems and because, within those counties, PPC systems lead to high rates of undervotes and overvotes for people of color and those with lower levels of education. (reported by Brady, 2004, p. 27)

Two expert reports were submitted by the plaintiffs in this case. One, by Henry E. Brady, cited statistics showing that the residual rate in California in 2000 was about 2.2 percent for PPC systems, and about 0.8 percent for each of the other systems in use, that is, DRE, Datavote, central-count marksense, and precinct-count marksense. Brady presented additional data produced by his associates and discussed earlier. He stated that the residual rate for census tracts that retained PPC systems was greater by at least one percentage point than the others that changed systems, using statistical procedures that guarded against spurious results due to correlated SES characteristics. It was estimated by Brady that 40,000 votes would be lost through continued use of the PPC voting system (Brady, 2004, pp. 28–30).

The second expert report, by Roy G. Saltman, cited unacceptable characteristics of PPC systems:

1. *The ballot is inherently fragile:* all of the voting locations in an unvoted ballot are pre-scored and the voter must further violate the ballot's integrity by punching holes in it. This characteristic promotes unplanned changes in the results after the ballot is voted.

2. *Pre-scoring and vote-recorder design produce hanging chad and prevent reproducible results:* a changed result due to manual handling or machine recounting reduces public confidence in the voting process.
3. *Voter ease-of-use is unacceptably poor:* a significant proportion of voters cannot translate their intentions into punchings corresponding to their choices.
4. *Training is no solution:* some PPC systems have been in place for twenty or thirty years with no improvement in voters' capability to use them successfully.
5. *Voters do not see their errors:* the lack of candidate names on the ballot card makes it unacceptably difficult for voters to verify that that their punchings match their intentions.

The plaintiffs were unsuccessful in the federal district court, but achieved success at a three-judge panel of the Ninth Circuit Court of Appeals (see *The New York Times*, September 16, 2003, pp. A1, A18). That decision was reversed by an eleven-judge Ninth Circuit Court sitting "en banc." The latter indicated that its ruling was a balancing of equities, with the state's interest in a timely election having the greater weight. It did not rule on the merits of the plaintiffs' claims.

In Ohio, the ACLU again employed Daniel P. Tokaji as counsel. The organization hoped to accelerate elimination of PPC voting systems. It sued the state on that basis (*Stewart v. Blackwell*), concentrating on three counties that used PPC systems: Hamilton (Cincinnati), Montgomery (Dayton), and Summit (Akron). Although Secretary of State Blackwell stated that white Appalachians in southeast Ohio also had higher residual rates, it must be noted that the Voting Rights Act protects against discrimination due to race or color, not due to lower levels of education, income, or literacy.

The decision on December 14, 2004, by Judge David Dowd, Jr., of the U.S. District Court for the Northern District of Ohio, favored the defendants. Judge Dowd stated that, in Ohio, the size of the residual vote "bears a direct relationship to economic and educational factors." He denied the plaintiffs' Voting Rights Act claim on the basis that the plaintiffs did not show that they were denied access to the polls or that punch-card ballots are employed disproportionately in African American areas of the state. The judge denied also the plaintiffs' Equal Protection claim, saying that

> Local variety in voting technology . . . does not violate the Equal Protection Clause, even if the different technologies have different levels of effectiveness in recording voters' intentions, so long as there is some rational basis for the technology choice.

In the case of PPC voting systems, the rational basis cited by the defendants was that those systems were inexpensive and easy to transport; furthermore, central counting eliminated the necessity for poll workers to learn to operate a local computerized counting system.

In January 2005, Secretary of State Blackwell ordered counties to adopt precinct-count marksense voting systems. Daniel P. Tokaji, speaking for the ACLU, has stated that the organization will appeal: "The state's been promising for years that it would get rid of its machines and has failed to deliver. The state's saying it will do something and it happening are two different things," he has said.

7.5   THE HELP AMERICA VOTE ACT

This groundbreaking Act of Congress (Public Law 107–252, October 29, 2002) was adopted almost two years after the 2000 general election. The Act has been called "an anemic piece of legislation" in an editorial (*The New York Times*, October 24, 2004) but, considering the situation beforehand, it was a giant step forward. Many would not consider a $3 billion appropriation for a function never previously funded to be anemic. There was a strong desire in Congress to adopt some relevant legislation before the next general election, which would occur just a week later. The intervention of the September 11, 2001 attack and the necessity of responding to it was a partial reason for the delay. While there was much negotiation during crafting of the legislation about respective roles of the states and the federal government, a most contentious subject concerned requirements for voter registration by mail. A failure of agreement on that single point would have derailed passage; that nearly happened.

Establishment of the Election Assistance Commission (EAC) was a core decision of the act. The EAC enables the function of election administration to have visibility and provides a forum for interest groups. The four members of the commission are appointed by the president with the advice and consent of the Senate. Commissioners, two from each major party, serve a term of four years with the possibility of reappointment for one additional term; they are to have experience with or expertise in election administration.

The first four commissioners were not confirmed until December 2003, effectively delaying the start of the commission's work until the beginning of 2004. Two were given two-year terms and two others four-year terms. After that, two commissioners are to be appointed every two years. With each set of appointments, not more than one commissioner is to be from the same political party. The chair and vice chair are selected by the members themselves and they serve for a term of one year; they may not be from the same political party.

The commission has no federal regulatory authority. Any action by the commission can only be carried out with the approval of at least three members. The first revision of the 1990 voting system standards, adopted in 2002 by the FEC (Federal Election Commission, 2002, Vols. I and II), were specified to serve as the initial "Voluntary Voting System Guidelines" (VVSG).

The functions of the commission include:

- holding hearings;
- serving as a clearinghouse;

- adopting new and updated VVSG;
- implementing a national testing and certification program for hardware and software of voting systems;
- funding studies on many issues related to elections;
- taking over from the FEC responsibilities related to the NVRA (see section 5.11).

Directly reporting to the commission is an executive director. In May 2005, Tom Wilkey, former New York state director of elections, was competitively selected. All the functions of the OEA and its four professional staff members were transferred to the EAC.

The Standards Board and Board of Advisors were created to include many stakeholders in the official process. The boards may hold hearings, take testimony, and receive evidence to carry out their responsibilities, but they have no power of subpoena. They receive no compensation for their work, except that they receive expenses for travel. They must meet at least once a year in order to vote on the VVSG.

The Standards Board is to be made up of 110 officials, 55 state and 55 local election officials (for this purpose, American Samoa, District of Columbia, Guam, Puerto Rico, and U.S. Virgin Islands are defined as states). The members of the Standards Board must meet at least once every two years to select an Executive Board of nine members.

The Board of Advisors is composed of 37 members, 25 from state and local government organizations and from federal agencies concerned with civil rights, access for disabled persons, and military and overseas voters. Election-focused organizations that are members include NASED, Election Center, National Association of Recorders, Election Administrators, and Clerks (NACRC), and International Association of County Recorders, Election Officials and Treasures (IACREOT). Four other members are to be professionals in the field of science and technology appointed by the majority and minority leaders of the two Houses of Congress. Eight members are to "represent voter interests," appointed by the chair and ranking minority members of the appropriate committees of the House and Senate.

The Technical Guidelines Development Committee (TGDC) was created under the act to develop the VVSG and recommend VSTLs. The chair of the TGDC is the director of NIST and the committee includes 14 additional individuals. Members of the TGDC receive no compensation, but are reimbursed for travel expenses. NIST is to provide technical support to the TGDC. The support is to include research and development in several identified areas.

Certification and testing of voting systems is given official status in the act, replacing NASED's function. Now, the director of NIST is to submit to the commission a recommended list of laboratories to be accredited to carry out the testing, certification, decertification, and recertification of voting systems. The director of NIST is to continually monitor and review the performance of accredited laboratories. Only the commission can accredit or revoke accreditation. The laboratories accredited previous to enactment of HAVA will remain accredited until the new procedures are in place.

NIST needs to determine the practices laboratories must use in order to recommend those that agree to use those practices and can do so effectively.

Several studies of election administration issues are required to be carried out periodically by the EAC. These studies include the following subjects:

1. *best practices for facilitating military and overseas voting*, in consultation with the secretary of defense; the commission has posted its report on this subject on its website;
2. *human factors research*, in consultation with the director of NIST, including usability engineering and human-machine interaction, which feasibly could be applied to voting products and systems designed to reduce voter error and the number of spoiled ballots;
3. *voters who register by mail*—topics to be included are the impact on voter registration, the accuracy of voter rolls, the use of signature verification procedures, and an analysis of other changes that may be made to improve the voter registration process;
4. *the feasibility and advisability of using social security identification numbers* in the voter registration process, in consultation with the U.S. commissioner of social security; issues to be included are the impact on national security concerns and voter privacy;
5. *electronic voting and the electoral process*, concerning the potential for election fraud presented by incorporating communications and Internet technologies; issues covered are to include the application of these technologies in both voter registration and voting.

Voting system requirements are included in HAVA. For precinct-count systems,

1. the voter shall be able to verify, in a private and independent manner, the votes selected on the ballot before the ballot is cast;
2. the voter shall be able to change the ballot or correct any error before the ballot is cast;
3. the voter shall be notified of an overvote, informed of the effect of that overvote, and provided with the opportunity to correct the ballot with the issuance of a new ballot, if necessary.

States are not required to adopt precinct-count systems at polling stations. A jurisdiction that uses a paper ballot voting system, a punch-card voting system, or a central-count voting system (including mail-in ballots or absentee ballots) does not have to meet the requirements mentioned earlier if it establishes a voter education program that informs voters of the effect of overvotes and provides the voter with instructions on how to correct the ballot or obtain a replacement ballot before the ballot is cast.

Audit trails are required, but a hard-copy ballot is not needed as votes are cast. In DRE equipment, the record of each voter's choices, that is, the EBI, is retained in the machine until the polls are closed. Then, if needed, the set of EBIs may be copied out on paper for review. As noted in section 6.11, some technical experts do not agree that the retention of EBIs constitutes an audit trail, as it is produced by the computer itself and not created or verified by an independent process.

Accessibility for individuals with disabilities is necessary, including accessibility for the blind and visually impaired. Accessibility must be provided in a manner that grants the same opportunity for access and participation (including privacy and independence) as for other voters. This requirement may be satisfied through the use of at least one DRE voting system equipped for individuals with disabilities at each polling place. Note that if paper audit trails that are unreadable by the visually impaired are required for verification by voters using DRE equipment, this arrangement may not be consistent with equal access and participation.

This provision on accessibility has strongly affected decision-making in the states and local governments in the selection of new voting equipment. The interest groups for persons with disabilities have been eminently successful in obtaining the assistance of Congress in responding to their needs.

Provisional ballots must be available on election day. If the name of an individual believing that he or she is entitled to vote at a particular polling place does not appear on the official list of eligible voters for that polling place, the individual is to be permitted to cast a provisional ballot. The ballot will be counted if the assertion of the provisional voter is found to be correct.

A single, statewide computerized list of registrants is to be implemented by each state for federal elections. A unique identifier is be assigned to each such voter. Any state or local government election official is to be able to obtain immediate electronic access to the information in the list. All voter registration information obtained by any local election official from a registering voter is to be entered into the list on an expedited basis. Removal of names from the list is to be done in accordance with the NVRA (see section 5.11). Coordination with state records on deaths and felony status is to be undertaken.

New requirements for assured identification of new voters are specified. Applicants who have a current and valid driver's license must provide the identification number. Applicants without a driver's license must submit the last four digits of their social security number, if they have such a number. Applicants without either will be assigned a unique number by the state. The chief state election official will enter into agreements with the state motor vehicle authority and the U.S. commissioner of social security to verify the information provided. (New registrants may show a driver's license from a different state, requiring interstate communication for verification. This possibility is not specifically recognized in HAVA.)

Strict requirements are imposed for new voters who register by mail, if the voter has not previously voted for federal office in the state. If the voter then votes in person, he or she must present a current and valid photo identification or a copy of a current utility bill, bank statement, government check, paycheck, or other government document that shows his or her name and address. If the voter votes by mail after having registered by mail, he or she must submit with the ballot the same identification that would have been required if he or she had voted in person. None of the provisions mentioned earlier apply to voters entitled to vote an absentee ballot under VAEHA or UOCAVA (see sections 5.9 and 5.10).

This requirement was strongly opposed by Senators Hillary Clinton (D-NY) and Charles Schumer (D-NY). They said that it would disadvantage the poor. They attempted to eliminate this provision and, failing that, voted against final passage of HAVA. They were the only senators recorded as opposed.

Payments and grants to the states for different purposes are provided for in several sections of the new law. In FY 2004, the commission was able to disburse a total of approximately $1.3 billion of appropriated funds to 42 states, American Samoa and District of Columbia (U.S. Election Assistance Commission, 2005). There are specified payments for efforts to improve election administration and for replacement of punch-card and lever voting machines.

In addition, the commission must make "requirements payments" each year for several years to each state that meets the funding conditions. The money can be used to meet the federal standards for voting systems and for voter registration. It may also be used as reimbursement for new voting equipment that meets all federal requirements. States do not have to implement the VVSG as a condition for receiving payment.

Grants are specified to be made for accessibility for disabled persons. These grants are to be administered by the secretary of the U.S. Department of Health and Human Services.

To improve military and overseas voting, additional resources are to be given to voting assistance officers of the Armed Forces. Measures are to implemented by the secretary of defense that ensure that a postmark or official proof or mailing date is provided on each absentee ballot collected at any overseas location or vessel at sea for which the U.S. Department of Defense is responsible. Each state is to designate a single office to be responsible for providing information regarding voter registration and absentee ballot procedures to be used by military and overseas voters.

7.6   FEAR OF SOFTWARE FRAUD—ROUND III (2001–2004)

Concern over the correctness of results produced by touchscreen DREs increased significantly following the 2000 general election, but active opposition started to become highly vocal in 2003. DREs had been used in rising quantities since mid-1980s. In 2000, they were used by 13 percent of the voting population, apparently without much opposition. Adding the use of lever machines by 18 percent to that total, nearly one-third of the public voted on a non-ballot system in 2000. In 2004, more than 31 percent voted on DREs and about 15 percent voted on lever machines.

The problem in determining the final result in Florida was translated into a loss of confidence in touchscreen DREs by some portion of voters, even though there were no charges of software fraud in that election and DREs were not used there. Those who backed Gore in 2000 appear to be far more concerned about touchscreen DREs than those who backed Bush. It may be a sense of loss—that something precious was wrongly taken away—that continues to drive the demand by Gore partisans for more assurance of voting system correctness. For example, Representative Robert Wexler (D-FL) filed a lawsuit in his state challenging the use of DREs, but was unsuccessful in court. Serious failures of Internet-connected systems due to hackers has contributed to the unease, even though touchscreen DREs are not connected to it.

By comparison with touchscreen DREs, concern over the results produced by lever machines and full-face DREs has been negligible. Lever machines have produced results without paper ballots since their first use in 1892 and continue to be required throughout the State of New York as of mid-2005. A series of editorials in *The New York Times* has championed paper records, for example, "Voting Machines for New York," May 18, 2004:

> the Legislature should require that all electronic voting machines in the state produce a voter-verifiable paper trail.

These editorials were written in a city that used lever machines in every precinct in the 2004 election and has used them for over 75 years. Not one of the *Times* 40-or-so editorials and op-ed columns on current issues in voting in 2004 compared the likelihood of incorrect results between the two types of machines. As indicated in section 6.11, lever machines cannot have an audit trail, whereas DREs have their EBIs. Apparently, a significant percentage of the public is unaware of the retained ballot images. This retention should make the public less apprehensive about DREs than about lever machines, but that has not been the case.

The lack of concern about lever machines seems to carry over to the public's perception of full-face DREs. This type of device was introduced into Baltimore city, replacing lever machines, in the 1990s without any articulation of concern for software fraud from any quarter in Maryland. The question of possible software fraud would not become a serious issue for Maryland's elected officials until 2003, after some computer scientists at Johns Hopkins University in Baltimore released a report, discussed later. The Hopkins researchers had paid no attention to the full-face DREs used for voting in the very city where their ivory tower was located. It was the use of touchscreen DREs that piqued their interest in discovering security flaws.

Johns Hopkins computer scientists released a report in July 2003, made possible by a download from an unsecured website of Diebold Election Systems (Keiger, 2004, pp. 50–56). Included in the data downloaded was a computer

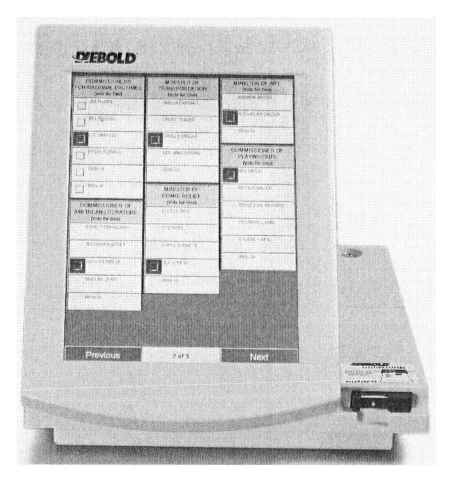

Figure 7.1 AccuVote-TS direct recording touchscreen voting machine, in use ca. 2002. Manufactured by Diebold, Incorporated, North Canton, OH. The touchscreen shows three columns of contests. Each contest is headed by a dark rectangle stating the name of the office. Candidates are listed in series in the whiter rectangles under the offfice title. The smaller darker squares indicate selections by a voter. The original photograph shows colors. The slot to the lower right of the screen is for entry of the voter's smartcard.

program for Diebold's AccuVote-TS touchscreen voting system (see figure 7.1). Eventually, the download was put in the hands of Aviel D. Rubin, technical director of the Information Security Institute at Johns Hopkins. Rubin and associates mounted the Diebold voting machine software on a personal computer and analyzed it for security flaws. They did not assume the existence of a real polling situation in their considerations, and they assumed that the Internet might be used in some data transmissions. Their report described their analysis (Kohno et al., 2003, pp. 1–23).

A major accusation of poor security concerned the smartcard given to a voter whose identity has been verified at the polling station. (A smartcard is similar in size to a credit card, but it contains electronic storage and logic for data interchange.) The voter is to insert the smartcard in a slot in the

AccuVote-TS terminal in order to begin voting. It was claimed that it would be easy to disable the voting machine's deactivation of the smartcard after voting and use the same smartcard to vote repeatedly, or to duplicate a smartcard and vote many times with a succession of counterfeits. Other claims concerned passwords and cryptography: either they were not used when they should have been, or if used, they were used improperly. There were "vulnerabilities to network threats," the report stated, and a voter-verified paper audit trail should be used with DREs.

After Rubin read that Maryland was planning to buy 11,000 more Diebold AccuVote-TS machines beyond the 5,000 already used in four counties in 2002, he decided that he needed to have his report publicized. Rubin contacted Cable News Network (CNN) and technology reporter John Schwartz of *The New York Times*.

The response by Diebold was swift. The company published a rejoinder in about a week, which replied one-by-one to a list of 87 allegations in the Johns Hopkins report (Diebold, 2003, pp. 1–27). In summary, the Diebold reply stated:

> the authors of the report focused solely on the part the AccuVote-TS software plays in the voting process, while ignoring the other critical checks and balances present in our electoral system . . .
>
> In addition to expressing an incomplete understanding of the full scope of the electoral process, the report is explicitly based in large part on false assumptions. One such assumption the authors made is that the system is somehow connected to the Internet during the voting process. This is absolutely not the case . . .

Maryland's top officials were worried about the effect of the Johns Hopkins report on public confidence. It was embarrassing that a senior scientist at the state's leading private university had independently found flaws in the manner in which the state was running its elections. It should be embarrassing to the researcher himself that instead of approaching the State Board of Elections (SBE) to report what he found and to offer the assistance of his part of the university's resources to correct the defects, he preferred to publicize the problems through major national news outlets. When asked if Rubin had made any attempt to discuss the issue before releasing his report, a top official of the SBE replied that he had not. In addition to discomforting the state's leadership, the report also energized segments of the population already predisposed to oppose an *electronic* non-ballot voting system.

The state asked Science Applications International Corporation (SAIC), with which it already had a contract, to undertake an additional task. The work would be to perform a risk analysis of the Diebold AccuVote-TS voting system and the process of employing it in Maryland elections. SAIC produced its review on September 2, 2003, just about six weeks after the release of the Hopkins report.

The conclusions of SAIC (Maryland Department of Budget . . . 2003, pp. iii–v) included the following:

> The State of Maryland procedural controls and general voting environment . . . do not, in many cases meet the standard of best practice or the State

of Maryland Security Policy . . . This assessment of the current security controls . . . is dependent upon the system being isolated from any network connections. . . .

The valuable result of a risk assessment is that the failings uncovered are often easily rectified. The SAIC technical recommendations were of that type, but the Democrat-controlled legislature was not satisfied. The SAIC report was sponsored by the state's Executive Branch headed by Governor Robert L. Ehrlich Jr., a Republican, and some conflict-of-interest by SAIC was claimed by the Democrats. A new effort was instituted by the Department of Legislative Services on order of the Maryland General Assembly. A contract was issued to RABA Technologies LLC of Columbia, MD. The company reviewed system arrangements again and conducted a "red team" exercise. This procedure permits "teams . . . to experiment with attack scenarios without penalty."

The RABA report, released in January 2004 (Maryland Department of Legislative . . . , 2004, pp. 1–25), identified risks that could cause disruptions if the flaws were exploited. The report said,

> each of these vulnerabilities has a mitigating recommendation that can be implemented in time for the March 2004 primary. *With all these near-term recommendations in place*, we feel, for this primary, that the system will accurately render an election that is worthy of voter trust.

In addition, the report provided an unusually even-handed discussion of the pros and cons of implementing voter-verifiable paper audit trails (VVPATs). It noted the resources required to assure a secure system, but stated that systems using paper ballots have serious accuracy problems. In conclusion, the RABA report stated that if the computer software is digitally signed, "reconciling the results of a single, randomly selected terminal with its paper receipts is sufficient . . ."

During 2004, a lawsuit filed by TrueVoteMD.org to force the state to use VVPATs was rebuffed by a Circuit Court judge.

In Ohio, Secretary of State Blackwell contracted with Compuware Corporation to undertake a study similar to the SAIC review carried out in Maryland. Compuware investigated the DREs from four vendors whose equipment was certified for use in Ohio. The equipment analyzed was:

- AccuVote-TS from Diebold Election systems,
- iVotronic from ES&S,
- eSlate 3000 from Hart InterCivic, and
- AVC Edge from Sequoia Voting Systems.

The Compuware report, issued in November 2003, identified risks for each system and provided risk mitigation strategies for each. The administrative recommendations made were very similar to the SAIC recommendations presented earlier (Ohio Secretary of State, 2003, pp. 17–20).

As a result of the Compuware study and the concerns elsewhere about voter-verifiable paper audit trails, the secretary of state reversed course from a requirement he imposed on counties to adopt either DREs or marksense systems. As of January 2005, only marksense systems could be used. It was reported in February 2005 that Ohio attorney general Jim Petro stated that "the secretary does not have the authority to dictate how independent boards conduct their elections" (*Cleveland Plain Dealer*, February 9, 2005). In this confusing situation, it may be that the ACLU will have to appeal, after all, to get Ohio to eliminate PPC voting systems.

In Nevada, Secretary of State Dean Heller decreed in 2003 that DREs, used throughout the state, must have printouts that each voter would have to approve before leaving the voting booth. It is interesting to compare the Nevada solution with the proposal by computer scientist Rebecca Mercuri, a well-known and long-time advocate for VVPATs. In Mercuri's view, each DRE should be required to print out the set of each voter's final choices as well as display them on its screen. The process, as she had described it recently, is as follows:

> The voter confirms that the printout concurs with their [*sic*] choices (if not, an election worker is notified in order to initiate a corrective process) and then deposits the printout into a sealed ballot box. At the end of the election session, electronic tallies produced by the machine provide unofficial results and are subsequently confirmed by the paper counts. If these totals differ, the printouts are used to produce the final result. Since the printed versions were prepared by a computer, in a human-readable format, they can be optically scanned or hand-tabulated. (Mercuri and Neumann, 2003, p. 40)

By the primary election of September 7, 2004, the capability to generate printouts had been implemented in Nevada. The procedure used was that the printout was provided to the voter under transparent plastic. Before the voter was able to complete the voting process, he or she had to press a button that indicated the printout had been accepted. Then the printout would be filed. However, as noted by Richard Smolka, the editor and publisher of the newsletter *Election Administration Reports*, who observed the election:

> Some voters checked the printed 'receipt' against their marked sample ballots but most seemed to ignore this verification feature (*Election Administration Reports*, September 13, 2004, p. 2).

Here is seen the essential problem with the Nevada solution. If the hard copy is to serve as a genuine audit trail, every voter must review and approve it. If only a few voters examine them, the printouts *not* examined are just pieces of paper produced by a computer program that was suspect at the start. It might be an incorrect record of the choices of any voter failing to examine it to assure correctness.

Consider the difference between Rebecca Mercuri's description of the process and the Nevada solution. Mercuri requires that the voter confirm the printout's agreement with his or her choices *before* depositing the printout in a sealed ballot box. The Nevada solution, requiring that the voter not handle the printout in order to prevent him or her from walking out of the polling station with it, nevertheless, provides the voter with the opportunity not to examine the printout at all. Most voters will not review their printouts because they have finished voting and simply want to leave immediately. They will just press the button and depart. Thus, the paper record is voter verifiable *but not necessarily voter verified.*

Those voters who examine their printouts provide a "sampling" solution to a complete audit, but no records are kept on the percentage of voters undertaking the effort. Whether or not the percentage of voters performing the audit is enough to provide a sufficiently high confidence level in software correctness is not known. Furthermore, the necessary percentage of voters performing the audit for a high confidence level depends on the closeness of the vote: the closer the vote, the higher the sampling percentage that is required (Saltman, 1975, pp. 113–122). The loss by U.S. Penator John Ensign (R-NV) in a very close race in 1998, two years before his subsequent victory, was one reason for support of VVPATs by Nevada Republicans. Nevada's form of implementation, resulting in a small sampling of ballots, would not have assured a more confident outcome than was officially reported.

A different solution is the use of a new type of equipment in which a touchscreen device used by a voter prints a human-readable and computer-readable ballot when voting is complete. After examination by the voter, the ballot is entered into a marksense balloting computer. The examination provides the audit trails.

In California, David L. Dill, professor of computer science at Stanford University, has been one of the leaders in the demand for the use of VVPATs for DREs. In early 2003, Dill made a presentation to his local county board of elections, proposing that the board not procure DREs as it had planned. Also, he mounted a website at www.verifiedvoting.org and founded the Verified Voting Foundation. Additionally, he wrote a Resolution on Electronic Voting, posted it on his website, and requested endorsement with signatures from others. Several thousand individuals have signed on. The resolution includes the following:

> Computerized voting equipment is inherently subject to programming error, equipment malfunction, and malicious tampering. It is therefore crucial that voting equipment provide a voter-verifiable audit trail, by which we mean a permanent record of each vote that can be checked for accuracy by the voter before the vote is submitted, and is difficult or impossible to alter after it has been checked . . .

Dill has willingly admitted that correct software is possible. As a speaker at a NIST symposium on voting standards, December 10, 2003, he said:

> In life-critical software, such as flight control, or something like that, we try a lot harder to get the software correct, but we also have accountability. If our

planes are crashing, or our medical equipment is killing patients, hard questions are asked and the problem gets looked into and it gets fixed. If we didn't know that something bad was happening, because the wrong candidate was winning the election and we couldn't tell, it's not clear that the problem is going to get fixed or that we ever knew about it.

In February 2003, California secretary of state Kevin Shelley created the Ad Hoc Touch Screen Task Force in response to concerns expressed over the security of this type of voting equipment. The task force's report was issued in July 2003 (California Secretary of State, 2003, pp. 1–54). On the subject of the voter-verified paper audit trail, the report stated:

> There was no consensus on the issue of whether a voter-verified paper audit trail (VVPAT) should be required on all voting systems . . . the Task Force did agree that systems with a VVPAT should be an option for local jurisdictions to choose, if such systems can meet the disabled and language accessibility requirements of State and Federal law.

Despite the failure of the Task Force to endorse a mandatory VVPAT, the secretary of state adopted and issued a standard for paper audit trails in DRE voting systems on June 15, 2004 (California Secretary of State, 2004, unpaged). The standard was adopted into law by the California legislature. The requirement applies to DRE systems for which the electronic record has been considered the official record. The system described in the standards is essentially the same as that used in Nevada. As a result of the standard, the paper copy is to be considered the official record. Voters must be able to verify their votes in the same language in which they voted, implying that Asian language type-fonts and Spanish diacritical marks would be needed in some counties. (Shelley was forced to resign in early 2005 over alleged misuse of HAVA funds.)

In Georgia, the state is highly pleased with its statewide AccuVote-TS system and the public appears to be satisfied as well. Dr. Brit Williams, professor emeritus of computer sciences at Georgia's Kennesaw State University (KSU) was one of the speakers at the NIST Symposium on December 10, 2003. He has served as Chair of the NASED Voting Systems Board Technical Committee. Along with Kathy Rogers, director of the Georgia Elections Division, he testified to the U.S. House of Representatives Committee on Administration on July 7, 2004. Their testimony is part of the public record.

In his presentation at NIST, Williams specifically noted that Maryland's SAIC study had proposed four technical changes as a result of the review of the Johns Hopkins report and the AccuVote-TS voting system. Williams said that Georgia has implemented three of the four. The fourth concerned Internet or other network connections and did not have to be implemented since Georgia's system has no network connections.

Williams noted the distinction between the software provided by the vendor and software as specialized for an election by the state. The vendor's software is provided in an unspecialized manner so that it may be reused in many elections. As it is not specialized, an included Trojan Horse (unauthorized malicious code set to be activated at a future time) cannot be designed to know in advance which storage register will be used to accumulate votes for a particular candidate. The most a Trojan Horse could be designed to do would be to look for a particular political party. To foil this type of attack, Williams said, the political party names are embedded in data fields. Then, the Trojan Horse program would have to parse the data fields (examine them in detail) to identify the party by its name or abbreviation, and that this type of programming would be easily noticed.

Williams said, also, that voting machine results and precinct results are posted on the wall of the precinct after the polls are closed. Any manipulation of the memory cards on the way to the central summarizing station would be at variance with the posted results.

The thrust of Williams and Rogers's presentation to the House committee was that Georgia's system of certification of election equipment and implementations of security techniques are sufficient to the extent that paper audit trails are unnecessary and possibly counterproductive. They testified that

> the conjecture, that using current technology, we are unable to make such a simple system [as a voting machine] secure and accurate is contradicted by the facts of our daily existence.

They noted that modern life involves the use of computer programs that must be correct, for example, in chips that fly airplanes and in controls for an artificial heart and lung machine during open heart surgery. Their statement responded to Dill's claim, made at the NIST symposium, that a failure resulting in serious injury or death would have to occur before software would be reviewed to correct the errors.

Georgia created the Center for Election Systems at KSU in 2002 to provide support and independent testing for all of its 159 counties. The Center tested every touchscreen unit, encoder, optical scan ballot reader, and server used in the 2002 general election. Tens of thousands of voting terminals and related components were tested, and its staff continues to travel to each of Georgia's counties to independently test and validate all new equipment purchases. The Center now offers support to counties and their staff in areas of poll worker training and courses for new election officials on election management. State legislation enacted in 2003 requires that all chief local election officials successfully complete 64 hours of training. The training program includes election law, ethics, and election procedures.

The process used by Georgia to assure system integrity starts when the VSTL complete the qualification tests on the product that the state is planning to use. The system to be tested for the state is not obtained from the vendor but is transported to the KSU Center for Election Systems directly from a VSTL. The software is digitally signed, which means that any subsequent alteration would be identified by a changed value of the checking polynomial associated with it. The Center then conducts tests to certify the system for use in the state. One test is designed to detect fraudulent or malicious code that might be hidden in the system. In all tests, a known pattern of votes is cast and compared with the output of the system.

7.7   REMOTE INTERNET VOTING: AND NOW FOR SOMETHING COMPLETELY DIFFERENT

The increasing popularity of the Internet in the late 1990s suggested its extension to public voting. The idea was promoted by several software companies that had developed Internet voting programs for use by private corporations for proxy voting. Certain individuals were interested, also, because they believed that Internet voting had the potential for increasing turnout.

Remote Internet Voting (RIV) is similar to a central-count voting system or a vote-by-mail voting system. The latter, including voting absentee, allows voters to fill out ballots at home and cast them through the postal system ("snail mail," in the vernacular of Internet buffs). There seems to be little concern about a loss or alteration of ballots because of use of the public mail system. That system is familiar to everyone and has a very long history of success, but occasionally mail does not get delivered. A few miscreants could destroy mail or delay it beyond the required date for final receipt.

Opposite requirements, compared with precinct-count voting systems, are a hallmark of RIV. Network technology must be used for the votes to reach their intended destinations. The possibility of software manipulation is a significantly larger problem with RIV than with precinct-count voting. There are many methods that a malicious "hacker" could use to hijack a set of votes and get them lost in cyberspace.

Privacy is a serious concern with RIV. A non-ballot voting machine may be considered to be designed in two parts: a vote-entry section and a vote-summarizing section (Saltman, 2003, pp. 132–136). In a precinct-count voting machine, the two sections of the machine are in the same physical location, often in the same box. In voting over the Internet, the vote-entry section and the vote-summarizing section are not co-located. When the voter indicates to the vote-entry section, probably a downloaded program in a personal computer, that voting is complete, the choices are communicated, hopefully, to a vote-summarizing section. The latter may be located in another continent. It may not be possible to prevent the voter from printing or transmitting his or her selections and distributing them to a briber, a supervisor, or an employer. If the machine is not owned by the voter, the owner may have the right to review any activities that have taken place on the machine.

Voting by mail has a similar privacy problem. The casting of absentee ballots in nursing homes or other locations where voters may be subject to the pressures of aggressive activists has been a source of concern. Oregon has abolished polling stations and has used all-mail ballots since December 1995. The process was made permanent under a statewide referendum in 1998. A benefit to the state and its local governments is that polling stations do not need to be commandeered or rented and then outfitted with election equipment. Poll workers do not have to be hired and trained, and no concern need be evidenced that disabled voters have access to nonexistent polling stations. In a survey of Oregon voters taken after an all-mail-ballot in 1996, 1.4 per cent stated that because another person was present when they filled out their ballots, they felt "under pressure to vote a certain way." Furthermore,

0.5 percent said that if they had been alone instead of having another person with them, they "would have voted differently" (Alvarez and Hall, 2004, p. 114). These responses, minimal but existing nevertheless, demonstrate the downside of voting outside of a private booth at a polling station.

In a discussion of turnout, it was pointed out that "vote-by-mail does not tend to pull in new voters—registered voters who traditionally have not voted" (Alvarez and Hall, 2004, p. 117).

The March 2000 Arizona Democratic primary was one of the first uses of RIV. The same authors note that:

> the turnout . . . was extremely low. Only 10.6% of Arizona Democrats partici-pated in this election, despite the novelty of the Internet voting option, despite the campaign . . . to get voters involved, and despite the great deal of media attention . . . By contrast, about 24% of Arizona's Democratic electorate participated in statewide primaries held in the 1990s. (pp. 130–131)

The Digital Divide is an economic disparity that results from the require-ment for a certain personal investment as well as user education for participa-tion in Internet voting. If the income and educational differential among groups results in a racial imbalance among the voters using the method, that condition might be a violation of the 1982 Amendments to the Voting Rights Act. Concerning the Arizona primary, it was stated that:

> counties with small nonwhite populations had the highest turnout rates, and counties with large nonwhite populations had the lowest turnout rates. . . . [There is] strong evidence that race played an important role in deter-mining the relative turnout rates across Arizona counties . . . (pp. 132–133)

Two significant studies on RIV were undertaken around the year 2000. The California Internet Voting Task Force was convened in late 1999 and reported in January 2000 (California Secretary of State, 2000, pp. 1–32). The National Workshop on Internet Voting met in October 2000 and reported in March 2001 (Internet Policy Institute, 2001, pp. 1–52). Neither report was optimistic about Internet use for voting until better methods of system security could be developed and implemented.

The project called Secure Electronic Registration and Voting Experiment (SERVE) was a follow-on to an earlier project of the Department of Defense's FVAP (see section 5.10) called Voting Over the Internet (VOI). The VOI, a "pilot project," handled a total of 84 votes in four states in the 2000 general election. The states were Florida, South Carolina, Texas, and Utah. All votes were real, not test ballots. About 50 votes were cast in Florida.

When SERVE was begun, in July 2003, it was intended to allow approxi-mately 100,000 Americans overseas to cast ballots over the Internet in the 2004 primaries and general election. Its purpose was to enable military per-sonnel, along with some civilians, to vote on any computer equipped with a few basic components, such as Microsoft Windows software. SERVE would apply to overseas voters whose U.S. residence was in one of 50 counties in the 7 states that agreed to participate.

In connection with its ongoing project, the FVAP paid for several computer security experts to examine the system's proposed architecture and provide a report. The report, issued on January 31, 2004 (Jefferson et al., 2004, pp. 1–34), was highly critical of the planned security and called for the project's end. Surprisingly, the FVAP took the experts' advice and cancelled SERVE within a week. The experts had stated in their report that the issues of "malicious software, denial of service, and other threats have not been resolved."

In the long term, overseas voters would appear to be the prime target for promoters of RIV because of the uncertainty of delivery time of international mail. The time frame of solutions to security problems cannot be predicted, but there are researchers throughout the developed world working on the issues. It must be noted that those states in which VVPATs are now required may not be able to adopt RIV under current regulations. The voter is not at the point of vote summarization to examine a receipt.

7.8   THE 2004 GENERAL ELECTION

In view of the difficulties experienced in the 2000 presidential election, there was much trepidation nationwide as to what might happen the next time. Democrats, anticipating the possibility of legal challenges, made sure to arrange for the assignment of lawyers supporting their cause in all the most likely locations. However, no drawn-out situations occurred in the presidential contest in which a final decision could not be made in a few days. Nevertheless, some occurrences are worthy of comment.

North Carolina's Carteret County, containing about 60,000 people, is positioned along the Atlantic Ocean at the southern end of the Outer Banks. The statewide contest for commissioner of agriculture foundered in Carteret County because some touchscreen machines in that county had failed to include the votes of 4,438 voters. The votes for two major candidates for that office had differed by only 2,287 when results were tallied. No other statewide race was affected because none had a margin of less than 4,438 votes.

The problem occurred with the machines set up for early voting. They were initialized to accept the votes of just 3,005 voters, but 7,443 voters had voted on them. Apparently, a message window available to poll workers reported "Voter Log Full," but the officials did not understand the implication and permitted voting to continue. The machines did not stop, but continued to record the number of additional voters voting. Additional votes were not recorded. The names of the voters who lost their votes were known, due to the availability of the sequential sign-in log (*Election Administration Reports*, January 10, 2005, pp. 4, 5).

Of course, the impasse was seized upon by opponents of DRE voting as an example of why a hard-copy ballot or receipt should be required. The situation was similar to a case in which the same number of punch-card ballots intended for central counting had been stolen or destroyed in a car crash while being transported. A number of different methods were proposed by officials in North Carolina to resolve the problem, all of them rejected by the courts. The issue was ultimately concluded when one of the statewide candidates voluntarily conceded.

The State of Ohio was a major battleground in the 2004 presidential election. Both the state's executive and legislative branches were in the hands of Republicans, as well as both seats in the U.S. Senate and 12 of the 18 seats in the House of Representatives. Democrats would have an uphill battle.

Immediately after the election, a statewide recount was undertaken on the request of the two minor parties that also had participated in the election. The final popular vote of over 5.6 million votes resulted in a slight majority for Bush. The advantage of about 119,000 votes was, on a percentage basis, 51–49 percent, a credible but losing effort by Kerry.

There were charges of vote manipulation and fraud in certain places such as Hocking County, but these allegations evaporated under scrutiny. This view was confirmed by the Election Science Institute (formerly called VoteWatch), a nonpartisan, nonprofit organization. The group had undertaken an extensive review of results.

At the Congressional meeting on January 6, 2005, to review and certify the Electoral votes of each state, Representative Stephanie Tubbs Jones (D-OH), with the agreement of Senator Barbara Boxer (D-CA), raised an objection to the count of the Ohio Electoral votes. Under the Electoral Count Act, this resulted in separate but simultaneous debates by each House to discuss and resolve the question of the state's Electoral votes. Two hours were allotted for this process to proceed to its obvious conclusion.

Democrats knew that they would be outvoted; their purpose was to raise the issue of certain administrative failures by Ohio's Republican secretary of state. Not shamed by Florida in 2000, J. Kenneth Blackwell served in 2004 as the cochair of the Republican state campaign to reelect President Bush. In addition, Democrats wanted to raise issues of poor election administration in Ohio's counties, which included improper denial of provisional ballots and other actions that they implied were tinged with racial discrimination. They used these to suggest revisions and strengthening of HAVA. Two of the Democrats speaking in the House debate, besides Tubbs Jones, were Representatives Sherrod Brown (D-OH) and Marcy Kaptur (D-OH). Brown had served previously as Ohio secretary of state. With regard to Blackwell, the most substantive comment was by Kaptur. She stated:

> Our secretary of state repeatedly took actions to make it more difficult for as many Ohioans as possible to have their votes fairly cast and accurately recorded. . . . Just prior to the election, the secretary of state continued to frustrate the enfranchisement of Ohioans with actions ranging from specifying paper weight standards for voter registration forms that even his own office couldn't meet, and then fighting the availability of provisional ballots right up to 3 p.m. on election day. In fact, people who had requested absentee ballots and had not received them were denied provisional ballots until a Federal Court ruling issued at 3 p.m. on Election Day.

Democrats' other issues were that voters had to wait in line to vote for as long as six hours, and they said that this was particularly the case in urban areas and not so in suburban areas. Franklin County (Columbus) and Cuyahoga County (Cleveland) were noted in particular.

Republican speakers included Majority Whip Roy Blunt of Missouri and Bob Ney of Ohio, chairman of the House Administration Committee, responsible for HAVA. Blunt's point was that people have to have confidence that the process works in the proper way but they don't need to believe that it is absolutely perfect. (That is a comfortable view if your candidate wins. See later for Washington State where the Republican candidate lost.) Ney quoted from an article in a Columbus, Ohio, newspaper:

> Franklin County Board of Elections Chairman William A. Anthony, Jr. said that long lines were not caused by the allocations of machines, a process controlled by a Democratic supervisor, but by the high voter turnout, the overall lack of machines and the one hundred choices that voters had to make . . . Anthony is also chairman of the Franklin County Democratic Party . . . Anthony was quoted, saying that "I am a black man. Why would I sit here and disenfranchise voters in my own community? I feel like they're accusing me of suppressing the black vote. I fought all of my life for people's right to vote."

At the end of the debates, the certificates from Ohio were accepted and the Congress finished the process of electing George W. Bush to serve as president for the next four years.

In the contest for governor of Washington State, about 60 percent of Washington voters had mailed in their ballots in this election, a percentage that has steadily increased over the past decade. After all counties reported their totals and an automatic recount was triggered, Republican Dino Rossi led Democrat Christine Gregoire by 42 votes on November 30. On December 2, Democrats requested a hand recount of the 2.9 million ballots cast in the governor's race. They solicited funds from Democrats nationwide to pay for it. Included in the hand recount were several hundred ballots that had been mistakenly thrown out in King County (Seattle). As a result of the final recount, Gregoire was certified as the winner by 129 votes on December 30 by Secretary of State Sam Reed. The Democrats' recount money was returned to them, since the previous outcome was reversed in their favor.

In this state, ballots may be "enhanced" or "duplicated" by officials to assure correct machine counting. Washington State has an "intent of the voter" standard and, unlike Florida in 2000, no one attempted to subvert its meaning. Signature-matching software is used with some mailed-in and absentee ballots.

The state Republican Party did not give up the fight easily. They argued for a new election. Among other charges, they claimed that, statewide, some felons voted without having their rights restored, some persons voted for their dead relatives, and there were other invalid votes. "We think it's sufficient to show there are more illegal votes than the margin of votes," said a Republican lawyer. On June 6, 2005, a Republican lawsuit, filed in a supposedly favorable county, was dismissed. The judge said that state law did not allow the election to be set aside merely because the number of illegal or invalid votes, 1,678 according to the court, exceeded the margin of victory. There were 1,401 votes by felons, 19 votes by dead persons, six double votes, 177 erroneous provisional votes, and 77 extra votes from Pierce County (Tacoma) beyond the number of voters casting ballots (*Election Administration Reports*, June 13, 2005, pp. 3, 4). The Republican Party did not appeal the decision to a higher court.

Charges of registration fraud were made in Nevada, Oregon, and other states during July through October 2004, based on observed multistate activities of a particular organization. In Nevada, an investigation was conducted at the request of Secretary of State Dean Heller. The alleged fraud involved the acceptance of voter registration applications by the organization and destruction of the ones that did not specify registration in the Republican party. In a news release on October 28, 2004, Heller stated that he "initially asked the Investigations Division [of the Nevada Department of Public Safety] to review the charges against Voter Outreach of America, due to the fact that similar allegations of tearing up voter registration forms have surfaced in other states . . ." The news release noted that "the FBI has taken the lead on the investigation into claims of possible voter fraud allegedly engaged in by [this] private voter registration company . . ." As of July 25, 2005, nothing more has been officially released.

7.9   SOME RELEVANT EVENTS FOLLOWING THE 2004 GENERAL ELECTION

Maryland adopted legislation in March 2005 requiring a study to review and evaluate independent verification systems, including VVPATs.

On March 17, 2005, 23 Democratic members of the House of Representatives sent a threatening letter to nine of the nation's voting machine vendors. The letter stated that the representatives "would do everything in their power to encourage federal election officials to only allow the purchase of equipment from vendors who endorse and implement" certain enumerated principles. Reminiscent of demands for "loyalty oaths" during the anti-Communist hysteria soon after World War II, the letter stated that vendors "have a moral and patriotic duty to help . . . voters trust our electoral process." The letter said further that "only firms that abide by these principles should be entitled to federal funding." The signers included John Conyers, Jr. (MI), Maxine Waters (CA), Stephanie Tubbs Jones (OH), Marcy Kaptur (OH) and Robert Wexler (FL). Among the principles listed was the inclusion of a "verifiable paper ballot" for voters to verify their votes and "open and accessible software code." What the signers hoped to achieve with this hostile missive is not clear. With Republicans in control of the White House and Congress, these Democrats have no say over implementation of current federal law.

In April 2005, a response was issued by the Election Technology Council (ETC) representing seven of the nine vendors receiving the letter. The ETC is a committee of a trade association called Information Technology Association of America (ITAA). The response, signed by the ITAA president, stated that "open software code is unnecessary, impractical, and detrimental to the security of U.S. elections," and that voting devices with paper receipts were being manufactured and offered for sale to jurisdictions who desire them (*Election Administration Reports*, May 2, 2005, pp. 3, 4).

The TGDC, created under HAVA, is now at work. The draft of Version I of new VVSGs was presented to the EAC by May 9, 2005. Areas addressed by Version I included accessibility, usability, and computer security. Version II, to be completed by the end of 2005, will rewrite the 2002 voting system standards to make them more precise and testable, and will address human factors (*Election Administration Reports*, May 2, 2005, pp. 1, 2).

A new concept of security presented by the TGDC in Version I is called "Independent Dual Verification (IDV) Voting Systems." IDV systems "have as their primary objective the production of ballot records that are capable of being used in audits in which their correctness can be audited to very high levels of precision." Version I also presents security requirements for VVPATs. The use of VVPATs is not mandatory; the requirements for them are to be implemented "if a State chooses to require them" (Technical Guidelines Development Committee, 2005, pp. 6–1, 6–2).

The Election Center, in May 2005, released a report by its National Task Force on Election Reform. This group of 39 election officials from state and local governments undertook a study of the 2004 general election and made "recommendations about what should—and should not—be done" (Election Center, 2005, pp. 1–59). The report's publication demonstrated that election officials have now come together as an important interest group attempting to influence public policy in its area of expertise. Three topics were considered in the report: voter registration, election technology, and election redesign.

For voter registration, the task force indicated concern about collection of registrations by private groups. The report called for establishment of specific laws and penalties relating to violations of voter registration laws. It proposed, also, an automatic or expedited process for the restoration of voting rights for convicted felons who have satisfied their sentences. Other topics addressed were updating procedures related to provisional voting and maintenance of statewide voter registration lists under requirements of the NVRA.

For election technology, the report recommended that guidelines be developed by NIST, through the EAC, for an independently verifiable audit trail for DRE voting systems. Guidelines should provide for a redundant record of votes on a secure medium. The subject of the guidelines should not be restricted to paper, but could include other media such as electronic, audio, or video.

For election redesign, the report recommended the consideration of combinations of polling stations into multi-precinct "universal vote centers." The new arrangement "enables election officials to reduce the number of polling places . . . to a smaller, more manageable number." The task force also addressed the problem of poll worker recruitment and retention, proposing actions to promote the participation of students and working citizens.

In an appendix, the report provided information from the Maryland State Board of Elections about its use of digital signatures for its statewide voting system software. (The process is the same as that used in Georgia and recommended by Maryland's RABA report.) The state computes a "digital fingerprint" from the software received from the VSTL, using the same mathematical function computed by NIST when its National Software Reference Library received the same software from its vendor. The computed value is unique to the particular software. Values from the NIST copy and the VSTL copy should be identical to each other if the software has not been modified.

A hearing held on June 21, 2005 by the U.S. Senate Committee on Rules and Administration delineated opposing views of VVPATs. Senator John Ensign (R-NV) said that a separate paper record would giver voters "confidence that their votes have been cast and recorded accurately." Also predictably favoring VVPATs was Professor David L. Dill of Stanford University. He said that a poll of members of the Association for Computing Machinery, the largest professional association of computer technologists, heavily favored a paper trail. Of course, computer technologists don't run elections.

Speakers on the other side included Conny B. McCormack, who officially manages elections for Los Angeles (LA) County, now the nation's largest local jurisdiction. She stated that:

> The fact is that existing DRE systems without VVPAT have the proven track record of doing the best job of all available voting systems. . . . The suppositions and theories espoused by critics contending that DRE systems are more susceptible to tampering are completely false. . . . By contrast, there is ample documented evidence that fraud has been perpetrated with paper-based voting systems. . . . A video [of Nevada voters] confirms that . . . very few voters even glanced at the paper printout. . . . Printing the paper record adds more time to the voting experience. Everyone is in agreement that it is anathema to voters to add waiting time. . . . The principal authors of HAVA . . . espressed their concerns that pending federal legislative proposals mandating VVPAT would "undermine essential HAVA provisions, such as the disability and language minority access requirements, and could result in more, rather than less, voter disenfranchisement and error." (U.S. Senate Committee on Rules and Administration, Hearing on Voter Verification in the Federal Electoral Process, June 21, 2005)

It may be reasonably inferred that Ms. McCormack would have wanted DREs without receipts for LA County, but that cannot be allowed because of California's legislated requirement. Instead, LA County is using the "InkaVote" system at polling stations. This equipment is similar in design to a pre-scored punch card (PPC) system, but employs a pen to darken voting locations instead of a stylus to remove chad. The newer system has some of the same human factor problems as PPCs, in that the names of the candidates are not on the ballot card.

Jim Dickson of the American Association of People with Disabilities told the committee that "the disability and civil rights communities oppose opening up HAVA for any amendments." Senator Chris Dodd (D-CT), ranking member of the committee, stated "strong opposition to any requirement (such as the use of paper) that would make it more difficult for blind and disabled voters to vote in the same manner as others" (*Election Administration Reports,* June 27, 2005, pp. 2, 3).

In July 2005, it was reported that Georgia had adopted legislation that would require voters to show a photo ID in order to vote. Considerable opposition has been expressed, on the basis that many older and poorer citizens do not have photo IDs because they do not drive and do not travel out of the country. Apparently, in Georgia, a photo ID in lieu of a driver's license may be obtained at a cost of $20 and the new law does not change this situation. A requirement to purchase a photo ID in order to vote in a federal election may be a violation of the Voting Rights Act. If the cost of a photo ID is seen equivalent to a poll tax, then the requirement would be unconstitutional under the 24th Amendment and the U.S. Supreme Court's decision in *Harper vs. Virginia State Board of Elections* (see sections 5.3–5.5).

7.10 RECOMMENDATIONS FOR ADMINISTRATIVE ACTIONS

The software testing process should be open to review. An editorial in *The New York Times,* May 30, 2004, entitled "Who Tests Voting Machines?," reported that one of the currently accredited VSTLs "refused to tell us anything about how it tests, or about its testers' credentials." Certainly, the VSTL had no obligation to do so under the procedures in place before HAVA. Now that federal government agencies, that is, NIST and the EAC, are handling the accreditation, a greater openness based on "freedom of information" regulations should result. Independent experts serving in an auditing capacity should be able to determine the criteria used to accredit VSTLs as well as the procedures used by the VSTLs to determine software correctness and presence and absence of malicious code. An accredited VSTL has an obligation to the voting public that it does not have to its private clients. "Trade secret" should not be able to prevent the citizenry from assuring that the software that counts their votes has been tested with the most thorough means available by competent laboratories that have no conflicts of interest.

Testing of all software used in precinct-count voting equipment should be required. Under current standards in place, so-called Commercial Off-The-Shelf (COTS) software need not be tested. Such software may include complex operating systems. These are unnecessary because of the simplicity of what the voting equipment is doing. Nevertheless, some manufacturers base their software on them. This arrangement raises that possibility that, first, all software claimed to be COTS is sometimes not really so (there is reason to believe that this is the case) and, second, that malicious code may be located in such untested software.

A reduction in complexity of software is essential to make it possible for full testing of correctness to be achieved. Individuals asserting that correctness is impossible to attain base their opinion on their experience with complex operating systems using multitasking and network connections. Precinct-based vote-counting software must appear as little like that as possible and as much as possible like the single-function process-control programs that stabilize airplanes and manage combustion in newer automobile engines.

For states in which no requirement for VVPATs is in place, there is a trade-off. A state using DREs may follow the lead of Nevada and require paper trails, or follow the lead of Georgia and insist that they are unnecessary and costly. The trade-off for a state is the establishment of a strong, highly competent technical capability at the state level versus the easy-out of not having to face embarrassments like Maryland after the Johns Hopkins report or North Carolina after the unrecoverable loss of votes in Carteret County. If NIST and the EAC adopt strong procedures for accrediting VSTLs and for the tests that the VSTLs perform, then together with highly capable voting equipment administration and effective controls to assure integrity and security, states on the fence can feel comfortable in rejecting paper trails for DREs. States using DREs without paper trails might find it useful to print out the lists of EBIs in 5 percent of the precincts and add the results manually. This action would be expected to demonstrate that the manually summed results match the computer-generated results.

Future actions of the TGDC and the EAC in the adoption of IDV may make the argument moot, in that security procedures may be defined that assure correctness at a level equivalent to or exceeding that which is achieved by VVPATs.

Undervote and overvote data should be collected automatically at precincts with the generation of results. These data for the top contest will be used to calculate residual rates. The latter are needed to determine the ability of voters to effectively use the machines. Additionally, these data provide the ability to reconcile the votes cast with the number of voters voting. Each voter at a particular precinct may cast the same maximum number of votes. The number of votes actually cast plus the number of votes not cast (due to overvotes and undervotes) should be the same number for each voter.

In the use of DREs, each EBI should show the number of undervotes as well as votes actually cast. Then, the reconciliation available should supply additional confidence to voters that their votes were counted.

Manual collection of auditing data at precincts needs to be improved. The data required for assurance of correctness of results are often not collected or not collected correctly. In earlier times, there was considerably more concern about ballot reconciliation, due to the possibility of ballot stuffing and similar precinct-based crimes. The lack of public concern would seem to validate the view that, in recent times and in areas where computer-processing is used, such crimes are no longer an important issue. Other concerns have superceded them, but the issue must not be forgotten.

The lack of correct collection of the needed data has been documented. Authors of a study of residual rates in Louisiana observed that "invalidation [of ballots] may be abnormally low . . . precisely because official data understate turnout" (Tomz and Van Houweling, 2003, p. 54). In the Washington State court review discussed in section 7.8, the 77 extra votes in Pierce County demonstrated the problem. In the 2004 presidential election in Ohio, the group now called the Election Science Institute found that they could not audit many precinct results because the reports filed by precinct officials were blank, even though they were signed as required. In Milwaukee, the *Journal Sentinel* newspaper reported on February 1, 2005 that data from the 2004 general election showed that, in 17 wards, there were at least 100 more votes recorded than people listed as voting.

7.11   RECOMMENDATIONS FOR LEGISLATIVE ACTIONS

The future of the EAC is uncertain because funding has been assured only through fiscal year 2006, and its existence is opposed by certain "states' rights" advocates. The attitude demonstrated by the attempt by Anti-Federalists to reject the Congressional oversight written into the Election Clause in 1787 continues to this day. In the late nineteenth century, the assurance of a nonpartisan ballot and true voter privacy in federal elections could have been achieved by a single federal law. Instead, individual states had to accomplish this—a process begun in 1888 and not completed by all states until well into the twentieth century (see sections 3.11 and 4.11). In the late twentieth century, a strong federal response to the problems caused by the introduction of computer technology was not possible because of the continuation of the same views. The result was several serious failures in local government election administration and minimal federal funding, capped by the Florida fiasco.

In February 2005, the National Association of Secretaries of State (NASS), most of whose members are the chief elections officials of their respective states, adopted a statement demonstrating that opposition to a meaningful Election Clause is alive and well after more than 200 years. This appalling resolution, in its entirety, is as follows:

> Recognizing the role of the Election Assistance Commission as a limited one, Congress, in the Help America Vote Act of 2002, (HAVA), wisely authorized the EAC for only three years. Any duties assigned to the EAC can be completed by the National Institute of Standards and Technology or by the state and local election officials who make up the HAVA Standards Board and its Executive Committee. The National Association of Secretaries of State encourages Congress not to reauthorize or fund the Election Assistance Commission after the conclusion of the 2006 federal election, and not to give the EAC rulemaking authority.

The elimination of funding of the EAC means the end of federal involvement in VSTL certification, issuance of grants for useful studies, and guidance for improvements in administration. NIST is part of the U.S. Department of Commerce, headed by a partisan official appointed by the president. Without the direction of the EAC, and the unavailability of the EAC to certify VSTLs and approve the VVSG, NIST would be unlikely to be allowed to carry out its HAVA responsibilities. NASS's concern may be driven by attempts by liberals, such as the signers of the letter of March 17, 2005 to turn the EAC into a regulatory agency.

The work of the EAC is essential and all its current responsibilities should be funded for the foreseeable future.

Restoration of felons' voting rights was a recommendation made by one of the national studies of 2001 and the Election Center's report discussed in section 7.9. It seems reasonable that persons under restraint should not be permitted to vote, but it seems reasonable also that ex-felons' rights should be restored. This may be accomplished by each state, but it also could be accomplished uniformly for federal elections by a single federal law. Federal requirements are typically extended by the states to registrations for all elections, as maintenance of separate systems is too costly.

Revision of the NVRA has been important for Senator Christopher "Kit" Bond (R-MO) and certain other Republicans. The senator made his views clear in an op-ed column in a major newspaper (Bond, 2001, p. A25). In that column, he discussed the situation in the city of St. Louis. He wrote:

> The number of registered voters threatens to outnumber of voting age population. A total of 247,135 persons are registered to vote compared with the city's voting age population of 258,532 . . . Almost 70,000 St. Louis city residents . . . cannot be located by the US Postal Service . . . More than 23,000 people on St. Louis' voting rolls are also registered elsewhere in Missouri . . . Though dead for 10 years, St. Louis Alderman Albert "Red" Villa actually registered to vote this spring in the city's mayoralty primary. Ritzy Mekler, a mixed breed dog, was also registered to vote . . . hundreds of city voters apparently are mailing in absentee ballots from abandoned buildings and vacant lots . . . The legacy of the motor voter bill [NVRA] is that it boosted voter participation while reducing the integrity of and confidence in our elections . . .

The concerns about the inaccuracies of voter registration rolls need to be addressed by Congress. In 2001, the OEA (see section 6.12) released a report stating that in 18 states, departments of motor vehicles (DMVs) had trouble getting registration information to election officials expeditiously for the 2000 general election. The OEA received hundreds of calls from voters who submitted applications through a DMV but found on election day that they were not on the rolls (*Los Angeles Times*, June 23, 2001). In 2004, voter roll inaccuracies may have been responsible for the large volume of provisional ballots that have been experienced; more accurate voter registration lists could reduce the need for such ballots. Secretary of State Rebecca Vigil-Giron of New Mexico recently pointed out this connection. A national analysis of voter rolls in six states found more than 181,000 registered dead people. Thousands more voters were registered to vote in two places (*Chicago Tribune*, December 4, 2004).

The assurance of accurate and up-to-date statewide voter registration lists is a very large data systems problem. Data must enter the system from many different sources. The failure of the promoters of the NVRA to include in the act a specific systems design project along with funding to carry it out was a serious error. The legislated elimination of purging, even after five years of nonvoting, prevented the use of the major tool to clean the rolls. Its replacement, using the mails to identify movers, has not been totally satisfactory, as the studies mentioned earlier demonstrate.

Now is an appropriate time to provide funding to undertake projects to improve the accuracy and integrity of voter registration rolls. The current concern about terrorists who may be hiding among us with false identification has increased the number and variety of decision-makers interested in an accurate list of persons in this country. Voters entitled to register are a subset of that list. Very recently adopted is "The Real ID Act" (Public Law 109–13, Division B, May 11, 2005). This law, in its Title II, concerns "Improved Security for Drivers' Licenses and Personal Indentification Cards."

Legislation aimed more specifically at voter registration was introduced in early 2005 by Senators Bond and Mitch McConnell (R-KY). The proposed act, S.414, would allow use of Social Security Numbers in voter registration files, require the use of photo ID at the polls, and require each HAVA-mandated statewide registration file to include a common format to facilitate data communication with the files of other states. As previously mentioned, there is considerable opposition to the requirement for photo IDs at the polls, but if there were no cost to voters to obtain such identification, opposition might be considerably reduced.

Activities of partisan registration drives, in which registration applications not consistent with the sponsor's partisanship are torn up (as alleged in Nevada), should be a federal felony, if they are not already.

A Constitutional amendment should provide the District of Columbia with voting rights in Congress. The District, as presently constituted, is entitled to a voting seat in the House of Representatives. It should be able to obtain that, provided that it maintains a reasonably sized population, for example, in excess of one-half the population of the least populated state.

Representation in the U.S. Senate is more problematical. A proposed Constitutional amendment to provide DC with two seats in the Senate failed (see section 5.3). A more likely possibility is one seat in the U.S. Senate, as long as the District maintains a reasonably sized population. Another possibility is the division of DC into districts in which voters are assigned to vote in Senate contests in (say) the five most populous states.

The process of Congressional redistricting has been significantly altered by the availability of computer software. The use of computer programs with census data on very small areas has made possible the most cynical designs of Congressional districts as well as districts for state legislatures. The tortured designs of districts now possible make a mockery of the idea that districts represent citizens living in a limited area. Gerrymandering is too mild a word to describe the forms looking like multiheaded worms. In Maryland, as a result of the 2000 census, the state's eight districts, which had resulted in the election of four Republicans and four Democrats, were altered to elect two

Republicans and six Democrats. In Texas, a second redesign of districts in 2003 following the 2000 census resulted in the loss of five Congressional districts for the Democrats. These bald power grabs reduce the value of elections as the essential expression of public choice.

A problem of the current arrangement is that it is self-perpetuating. If legislative districts are designed to retain power for a particular party, then that party will be able to continue its control over district design, barring a massive change in public sentiment.

One proposal now achieving some backing is for each state to turn over redistricting responsibility from the state legislature to a bipartisan commission. One "good government" interest group, *Common Cause*, is promoting such an arrangement. Iowa is a state that already uses a redistricting commission, but it is also a state that is more demographically homogeneous than many others. If Congress should require "compact" districts, as it did temporarily many years ago, it might have to call on mathematicians to define the meaning of compact for the benefit of district designers and the federal courts. Such a definition might fail for districts bounded by winding rivers or non-compact state boundaries, such as the oddly shaped panhandles of western Maryland and northern and eastern West Virginia. Furthermore, the requirement for majority–minority districts might be difficult to factor into the definition.

As a partial solution, Congress could adopt a requirement that redistricting be allowed only once with every 10-year national census. An entirely different possibility is the elimination of Congressional districts and the assignment of a number of representatives to each political party according to its statewide percentage of votes. The actual persons elected would be determined by the position of each in a priority list put forth by each party.

Partisanship by election officials and by executives of voting equipment vendors may significantly reduce public confidence. In most places, local boards of election are officially bipartisan although in areas where one party is heavily dominant, genuine representation by the other party may be difficult to achieve. In Florida, the three-person county Canvassing Board guarantees one-party dominance. Accusations of very hurtful partisanship have named Secretaries of State Katherine Harris in Florida in 2000 and J. Kenneth Blackwell in Ohio in 2004 as culprits. Both individuals served as co-chairs of their state Republican party's efforts for George W. Bush. The service of the chief state election official in the most partisan of positions seems to this author to be a deliberate flouting of fairness. Legislation at the federal or state levels should prevent this hangover from the spoils system of the nineteenth century. Additionally, review and revision of election laws and regulations should be able to minimize situations where partisan judgments may be made to upset the balance of fair competition.

Vendors of voting equipment have an obligation, similarly, to prevent involvement of their senior employees in partisan politics. Voters of all points of view must vote on the machines provided and they should be able to have confidence that they are not voting on a machine that has been "fixed" for one party or the other. An egregious example of partisanship surfaced in 2004 when a particular incident was reported by many sources. According to one source, the magazine *Science*, there was "an actual pre-election statement by Diebold's chief executive officer, a prominent Bush fundraiser, that he would 'deliver' the state of Ohio to the president." Diebold, Inc. of North Canton, Ohio, the CEO's company, manufactures and sells DRE equipment that some voters distrust because of its lack of a paper audit trail. As noted by the magazine (*Science*, vol. 306, October 29, 2004, p. 770), "a savagely partisan U.S. election turns into a field day for conspiracy theorists, and trust in government takes another hit."

The Diebold company, following this incident, revised its "business ethics" requirements for its employees to prevent such situations from happening again, but only its Board of Directors could call the CEO on the carpet. In addition, state governments should review their campaign contribution laws that permit voting equipment manufacturers to contribute in large amounts to political parties or candidates. One may never know whether such a contribution is a payoff for equipment selection. Larger contributions are in the public record and voting machines have the manufacturer's name on them.

Squelching rumors and reporting facts are additional ways to improve public confidence. When elections are poorly administered or equipment fails, a certain percentage of the public will assume that a conspiracy is afoot. Rumors will fly and they will infect normally rational citizens. The National Transportation Safety Board (NTSB) has been created to determine the causes of accidents and to make recommendations for improvements. Our democratic voting process has no equivalent organization to investigate questions of major failures. Such an organization, a Voting Incident Investigations Board, could concentrate on the few incidents that have risen to the point of serious concern about conspiracies. The board's job would be to investigate and report exactly what really happened and to recommend changes in procedures or equipment design, just like the NTSB. Each state should have such a group, and a federal group should report to the EAC.

PPC voting systems may have to be abolished by a law of Congress. Despite the offers of buyouts, some states and/or counties may not get around to replacing them. Their use is so detrimental to the concept of a fair election that they are an embarrassment to this nation. A particular year should be named, for example, 2008, by which time they should no longer be in use anywhere.

7.12   SUBJECTS NEEDING FURTHER EXAMINATION

The earlier sections have noted some problems needing a solution. Additionally, in Section 241 (b) of HAVA, 19 subjects of study are listed. Three of them, not previously considered here, are:

• The feasibility and advisability of conducting elections for federal office on different days, at different places, and during different hours, including the advisability of establishing a uniform poll closing after time.

- Methods of recruiting, training, and improving the performance of poll workers (also mentioned in the Election Center's report). Note that if election day were a holiday, or if financial incentives were given to employers for employees' time off, a much greater number of potential poll workers might be available.
- Additional uniformity among the states for federal elections in treatment of intent of the voter, casting of provisional ballots, and recount procedures. (Intent of the voter is not specifically included, but it deserves to be added.)

Another possible subject is:

- A change in the current method of electing the president through the Election College system. A thorough in-depth analysis of alternatives needs to be undertaken, specifying the likelihood of adoption of each. The possibility of incremental change as opposed to a complete change to a plurality of the popular vote needs to be considered. An example of an incremental change would be the elimination of the persons called Electors and their replacement with the numerical values that they represent. At least, this would eliminate the problem of the "faithless Elector."

REFERENCES

Albright, Spencer D., 1942, *The American Ballot*, American Council on Public Affairs, Washington, DC.

Allen, Howard W. and Kay Warren Allen, 1981, "Vote Fraud and Data Validity," in Clubb, Jerome M., William H. Flanigan, and Nancy H. Zingale (eds.), *Analyzing Electoral History: A Guide to the Study of American Voter Behavior*, Sage Publications, Beverly Hills, CA, pp. 153–193.

Almond, Gabriel A., 2004, "Who Lost the Chicago School of Political Science?," in *Perspectives on Politics*, Vol. 2, No. 1 (March), pp. 91–93.

Alvarez, R. Michael and Thad E. Hall, 2004, *Point, Click and Vote: The Future of Internet Voting*, Brookings Institution Press, Washington, DC.

American University Institute of Election Administration and National Scientific Corporation, 1973, *A Study of Election Difficulties in Representative American Jurisdictions*, Office of Federal Elections, General Accounting Office, Washington, DC.

Ansolabehere, Stephen and Charles Stewart III, 2002, *Voting Technology and Uncounted Votes in the United States*, MIT, Cambridge, MA.

Argersinger, Peter H., 1984, "Electoral Processes," in Greene, Jack P. (ed.), *Encyclopedia of American Political History*, Scribner, NY, pp. 489–512.

———, 1986, "New Perspectives on Election Fraud in the Gilded Age," in *Political Science Quarterly*, Vol. 100, No. 4 (Winter 1985–1986), pp. 669–687.

Asbury, Herbert, 1928, *The Gangs of New York*, Thunder's Mouth Press, NY.

Austrian, Geoffrey D., 1982, *Herman Hollerith, Forgotten Giant of Information Processing*, Columbia U. Press, NY.

Automatic Voting Machine Corporation, 1958, *The Voting Machine and American Democracy* (2nd ed.), Published by the Corporation, Jamestown, NY.

Aylsworth, Leon E., 1930, "The Presidential Short Ballot," in *The American Political Science Review*, Vol. 24, Issue 4 (November), pp. 966–970.

Barrows, Robert G., 1996, "Urbanizing America," in Calhoun, Charles W. (ed.), *The Gilded Age: Essays on the Origins of Modern America*, SR Books, Wilmington, DE, pp. 91–110.

Barstow, David and Don Van Natta, Jr., 2001, "How Bush Took Florida: Mining the Overseas Absentee Vote," *The New York Times*, July 15, pp. 1, 17, 18.

Bass, Herbert J., 1961, *"I am a Democrat;" The Political Career of David Bennett Hill*, Syracuse U. Press, Syracuse, NY.

Becker, Carl L., 1958 (1922), *The Declaration of Independence*, Vintage Books, NY.

Bensel, Richard F., 2004, *The American Ballot Box in the Mid-Nineteenth Century*, Cambridge U. Press, NY.

Bergholz, Richard, 1969, "Experts' Game: How Elections Can Be Rigged Via Computers," *The Los Angeles Times*, July 8, p. 1.

Blodgett, Geoffrey, 1966, *The Gentle Reformers: Massachusetts Democrats in the Cleveland Era*, Harvard U. Press, Cambridge, MA.

Board of Aldermen of New York City, 1878, *Report of the Special Committee of the Board of Aldermen Appointed to Investigate the "Ring" Frauds Together with the Testimony Elicited During the Investigation*, New York.

Bond, Christopher S. "Kit," 2001, " 'Motor Voter' Out of Control," *The Washington Post*, June 27, p. A25.

Boorstin, Daniel J., 1965, *The Americans: The National Experience*, Vintage Books, NY.

———, 1973, *The Americans: The Democratic Experience*, Random House, NY.

Borden, Morton, 1984, *Jews, Turks and Infidels*, U. Of North Carolina Press, Chapel Hill, NC.

Brace, Kimball W., 2004, *Overview of Voting Equipment Usage in United States*, Presentation to U.S. Election Assistance Commission, May 5, Washington, DC.

Brady, Henry E., 2004, "Postponing the California Recall to Protect Voting Rights," in *Political Science and Politics*, Vol. XXXVII, No. 1 (January), pp. 27–32.

Brady, Henry E., Justin Buchler, Matthew Jarvis, and John McNulty, 2001, *Counting All the Votes: The Performance of Voting Technology in the United States*, Survey Research Center and Institute of Government Studies, U. of California, Berkeley, CA.

Buchler, Justin, Matthew Jarvis, and John McNulty, 2004, "Punch Card Technology and the Racial Gap in Residual Votes," in *Perspectives on Politics*, Vol. 2, No. 3 (September), pp. 517–524.

Burke, Albie, 1970, "Federal Regulation of Congressional Elections in Northern Cities," in *The American Journal of Legal History*, Vol. XIV, No. 1 (January 1970), pp. 17–34.

Burke, John G., 1997, "Bursting Boilers and Federal Power," in Cutliffe, Stephen H. and Terry S. Reynolds (eds.), *Technology & American History*, U. of Chicago Press, Chicago, pp. 105–127.

Burnham, David, 1985, "Computerized Systems for Voting Seen as Vulnerable to Tampering," *The New York Times*, July 29, p. 1.

California Institute of Technology and Massachusetts Institute of Technology Voting Technology Project, March 2001, *Residual Votes Attributable to Technology*, Pasadena, CA and Cambridge, MA.

———, July 2001, *Voting: What Is, What Could Be*, Pasadena, CA and Cambridge, MA.

California Secretary of State, 2004, *State of California Standards for Accessible Voter Verified Paper Audit Trail Systems In Direct Recording Electronic (DRE) Voting Systems*, Sacramento, CA.

California Secretary of State Bill Jones, 2000, *A Report on the Feasibility of Internet Voting*, Sacramento, CA.

California Secretary of State Kevin Shelley, 2003, *Ad Hoc Touch Screen Task Force Report*, Sacramento, CA.

Callow, Jr., Alexander B., 1966, *The Tweed Ring*, Oxford U. Press, NY.

Campbell-Kelly, Martin and William Aspray, 1996, *Computer: A History of the Information Machine*, Basic Books, NY.

Century Foundation, 2004, *Issue Brief: African Americans, Voting Machines, and Spoiled Ballots: A Challenge to Election Reform*, New York and Washington, DC (www.tcf.org).

Chiles, James R., 1990, "Civic Pride, Old West-Style; County Seats were a Burning Issue in the Wild West," in *Smithsonian*, Vol. 20, No. 12 (March) pp. 100–110, 154.

Chudacoff, Howard P. and Judith E. Smith, 1994, *The Evolution of American Urban Society* (3rd ed.), Prentice Hall, Englewood Cliffs, NJ.

Cohen, I. Bernard, 2000, "Howard Aiken and the Dawn of the Computer Age," in Rojas, Raul and Ulf Hashagan (eds.), *The First Computers—History and Architecture*, MIT Press, Cambridge, MA, pp. 107–120.

Cordata, James W., 1987, *Historical Dictionary of Data Processing Organizations*, Greenwood Press, NY.

Correspondents of *The New York Times*, 2001, *36 Days*, Times Books, NY.

Council of State Governments, 1973, *Modernizing Election Systems*, Lexington, KY.

Cunliffe, Marcus, 1971, "Elections of 1789 and 1792," in Schlesinger, Jr., Arthur M. (ed.), *History of American Presidential Elections, Volume I, 1789–1844*, Chelsea House, NY, pp. 3–55.

Cunningham, Jr., Noble E., 1971, "Election of 1800," in Schlesinger, Jr., Arthur M. (ed.), *History of American Presidential Elections, Volume I, 1789–1844*, Chelsea House, NY, pp. 101–156.

Dauer, Manning, 1971, "Election of 1804," in Schlesinger, Jr., Arthur M. (ed.), *History of American Presidential Elections, Volume I, 1789–1844*, pp. 159–182, Chelsea House, NY.

Davenport, John I., 1894, *The Election and Naturalization Frauds in New York City, 1860–1870* (2nd ed.), published by the author, NY.

Diebold Election Systems, 2003, *Checks and Balances in Elections Equipment and Procedures Prevent Alleged Fraud Scenarios*, North Canton, OH.

Dinkin, Robert J., 1982, *Voting in Revolutionary America*, Greenwood Press, Westport, CT.

Dionne, E. J. and William Kristol (eds.), 2001, *Bush V. Gore*, Brookings Institution, Washington, DC.

Dudley, Robert L. and Alan R. Gitelson, 2002, *American Elections: The Rules Matter*, Longman, NY.

Dugger, Ronnie, 1982, *The Politician*, Norton, NY.

———, 1988, "Annals of Democracy: Counting Votes," *The New Yorker*, November 7, pp. 40–108.

Duval County Election Reform Task Force, 2001, *Final Report*, Jacksonville, FL.

ECRI, 1988, *An Election Administrator's Guide to Computerized Voting Systems*, Plymouth Meeting, PA.

Election Center, 2005, *Election 2004: Review and Recommendations by the Nation's Election Administrators*, Houston, TX.

Election Administration Reports, a newsletter published bi-weekly at 5620 33rd Street, N.W., Washington, DC 20015.

Elkins, Terry and Eva Waskell, 1987, "Bugs in the Ballot Box," in *Campaigns & Elections*, Volume 8 (March/April), pp. 20–24.

Elliot, Jonathan (ed.), 1836, *The Debates in the Several State Conventions on the Adoption of the Federal Constitution, Vol. III*, Library of Congress, Washington, DC (http://memory.loc.gov/ammem/amlaw/lawhome.html).

Evans, Eldon Cobb, 1917, *A History of the Australian Ballot System in the United States*, U. of Chicago Press, Chicago.

Federal Election Commission, 1990, *Performance and Test Standards for Punchcard, Marksense, and Direct Recording Electronic Voting Systems*, Washington, DC.

———, 2002, *Performance and Test Standards for Punchcard, Marksense, and Direct Recording Electronic Voting Systems*, Vols. I and II, Washington, DC.

Ferrand, Max (ed.), 1911, *The Records of the Federal Convention of 1787*, Yale U. Press, New Haven, CT (http://memory.loc.gov/ammem/amlaw/lawhome.html).

Fischer, Claude S., 1997, " 'Touch Someone': The Telephone Industry Discovers Sociability," in Cutliffe, Stephen H. and Terry S. Reynolds (eds.), *Technology & American History*, U. of Chicago Press, Chicago, pp. 271–300.

Fredman, L. E., 1968, *The Australian Ballot; The Story of an American Reform*, Michigan State U. Press, East Lansing, MI.

Galvin, W., 1997, *Report Concerning Revocation of Approval for Votomatic 235 Punch Card Devices*, October 8, Office of the Secretary of Commonwealth, Boston, MA.

Goldberg, Robert, 1987, "Election Fraud: An American Vice," in Reichley, A. James (ed.), *Elections American Style*, Brookings Institution, Washington, DC, pp. 180–192.

Goldman, Robert M., 2001, *A Free Ballot and a Fair Count*, Fordham U. Press, NY.

Governor's Select Task Force on Election Procedures, Standards and Technology, 2001, *Revitalizing Democracy in Florida*, Tallahassee, FL.

Gustafson, John, 2000, "Reconstruction of the Atanasoff-Berry Computer," in Rojas, Raul and Ulf Hashagen (eds.), *The First Computers—History and Architecture*, MIT Press, Cambridge, MA, pp. 91–106.

Hanson, Dirk, 1982, *The New Alchemists*, Little, Brown & Co., Boston.

Harris, Joseph P., 1929, *Registration of Voters in the United States*, Brookings Institution, Washington, DC.

———, 1934, *Election Administration in the United States*, Brookings Institution, Washington, DC.

Heffner, Richard D., 1999 (1952), *A Documentary History of the United States* (6th ed.), Mentor, NY.

Hoffman, Lance J., 1988, *Making Every Vote Count: Security and Reliability of Computerized Vote-Counting Systems*, George Washington University, Washington, DC.

Hunter, J. P., 1993, "Barca Victory Built on Solid Reputation," *Capital Times*, May 11, Madison, WI.

Imai, Kosuke and Gary King, 2004, "Did Illegal Overseas Absentee Ballots Decide the 2000 U.S. Presidential Election?," in *Perspectives on Politics*, Vol. 2, No. 3 (September), pp. 537–549.

Internet Policy Institute, 2001, *Report of the National Workshop on Internet Voting: Issues and Research Agenda*, March, Washington, DC.

Ifrah, Georges, 2001, *The Universal History of Computing*, John Wiley & Sons, NY.

Ivins, William Mills, 1970 (1887), *Machine Politics and Money in Elections in New York City*, Arno Press, NY.

Jefferson, David, Aviel D. Rubin, Barbara Simons, and David Wagner, 2004, *A Security Analysis of the Secure Electronic Registration and Voting Experiment (SERVE)*, Federal Voting Assistance Program, Washington, DC.

Johnson, Paul, 1999, *A History of the American People*, Harper Perennial, NY.

Josephson, Matthew, 1938, *The Politicos*, Harcourt, Brace & World, NY.

Kaplan, David A., 2001, *The Accidental President*, William Morrow, NY.

Karlan, Pamela S., 2001, "Equal Protection: *Bush v. Gore* and the Making of a Precedent," in Rakove, Jack N. (ed.), *The Unfinished Election of 2000*, Basic Books, NY, pp. 159–199.

Keating, Dan, 2002, "Democracy Counts: The Media Consortium Florida Ballot Project," presentation to the annual meeting of the American Political Science Association, Boston.

Keiger, Dale, 2004, "e-lective Alarm," *Johns Hopkins Magazine*, February, pp. 50–56.

Ketchum, Ralph (ed.), 1986, *The Anti-Federalist Papers and the Constitutional Convention Debates*, Mentor Books, NY.

Keyssar, Alexander, 2000, *The Right to Vote*, Basic Books, NY.

Knack, Stephen and Martha Kropf, 2001, *Roll Off at the Top of the Ballot: Intentional Undervoting in American Presidential Elections*, U. of Maryland and U. of Missouri, Kansas City.

Kohno, Tadayoshi, Adam Stubblefield, Aviel D. Rubin, and Dan S. Wallach, 2003, *Analysis of an Electronic Voting System*, Technical Report TR-2003-19, Johns Hopkins University Information Security Institute, Baltimore, MD.

Kramer, Larry, 2001, "The Supreme Court in Politics," in Rakove, Jack N. (ed.), *The Unfinished Election of 2000*, Basic Books, NY, pp. 105–157.

Kramnick, Isaac (ed.), 1987, *James Madison, Alexander Hamilton and John Jay: The Federalist Papers*, Penguin Books, NY.

Lichtman, Allan J., 2001, "Report . . . on the Racial Impact of the Rejection of Ballots Cast in the 2000 Presidential Election in the State of Florida," in *Appendix to Voting Irregularities in Florida During the 2000 Presidential Election*, U.S. Commission on Civil Rights, Washington, DC.

Ludington, Arthur C., 1911, *American Ballot Laws, 1888–1910*, U. of the State of New York, Albany, NY.

Macpherson, C. B. (ed.), 1980, *John Locke: Second Treatise of Government*, Hackett Publishing, Indianapolis, IN.

Maier, Pauline, 1998, *American Scripture: Making the Declaration of Independence*, Vintage Books, NY.

Main, Jackson Turner, 1973, *Political Parties Before the Constitution*, U. of North Carolina Press, Chapel Hill, NC.

———, 1974 (1961), *The Anti-Federalists: Critics of the Constitution, 1781–1788*, Norton, NY.

Mandelbaum, Seymour J., 1965, *Boss Tweed's New York*, John Wiley & Sons, NY.

Maryland Department of Budget and Management, 2003, *Risk Assessment Report: Diebold AccuVote-TS Voting Systems and Processes*, Annapolis, MD.

Maryland Department of Legislative Services, 2004, *Trusted Agent Report: Diebold AccuVote-TS Voting System*, Annapolis, MD.

McCormick, Richard P., 1953, *The History of Voting in New Jersey, 1661–1911*, Rutgers U. Press, New Brunswick, NJ.

Mercuri, Rebecca T. and Peter G. Neumann, 2003, "Verification for Electronic Balloting Systems," in Gritzalis, Dimitris A. (ed.), *Secure Electronic Voting*, Kluwer Academic Publishers, Norwell, MA, pp. 31–42.

Merzer, Martin et al., 2001, *The Miami Herald Report: Democracy Held Hostage*, St. Martin's Press, NY.

Miller, Worth Robert, 1995, "Harrison County Methods: Election Fraud in Late Nineteenth Century Texas," in *Locus: Regional and Local History*, Vol. 7, No. 2 (spring), pp. 111–128.

Minority Staff, Committee on Government Reform, April 2001, *Election Reform in Detroit: New Voting Technology and Increased Voter Education Significantly Reduced Uncounted Ballots*, U.S. House of Representatives, Washington, DC.

———, July 2001, *Income and Racial Disparities in the Undercount in the 2000 Presidential Election*, House of Representatives, Washington, DC.

Monroe, Kristen Renwick, 2004, "The Chicago School: Forgotten but Not Gone," in *Perspectives on Politics*, Vol. 2, No. 1 (March), pp. 95–98.

Morris, Jr., Roy, 2003, *Fraud of the Century: Rutherford B. Hayes, Samuel Tilden, and the Stolen Election of 1876*, Simon & Schuster, NY.

Nathan, Harriet, 1983, *Joseph P. Harris, Professor and Practitioner: Government, Election Reform, and the Votomatic*, The Bancroft Library, U. Of California, Berkeley, CA.

National Association of State Election Directors (NASED), 2001 (1992), *Accreditation of Independent Testing Authorities For Voting System Qualification Testing*, Council of State Governments, Washington, DC.

National Clearinghouse on Election Administration, 1983, *A Report to the Congress on the Development of Voluntary Engineering and Procedural Performance Standards for Voting Systems*, Federal Election Commission, Washington, DC.

National Commission on Federal Election Reform, organized by the Miller Center of Public Affairs at the University of Virginia and the Century Foundation, August 2001, *To Assure Pride and Confidence in the Electoral Process*, Charlottesville, VA.

Neumann, Peter G., 1995, *Computer-Related Risks*, ACM Press, NY.

Office of Secretary of State Cathy Cox, 2003, *Analysis of Undervote Performance of Georgia's Uniform Electronic Voting System*, Atlanta, GA.

Ohio Secretary of State, 2003, *Direct Recording Electronic (DRE) Technical Security Assessment Report*, Columbus, OH.

Overacker, Louise, 1932, *Money in Elections*, Macmillan, NY.

Piven, Frances Fox and Richard Cloward, 1989, *Why Americans Don't Vote*, Pantheon Books, NY.

Posner, Richard A., 2001, *Breaking Deadlock*, Princeton U. Press, Princeton, NJ.

Pugh, Darrell, 1988, *Looking Back—Moving Forward*, American Society for Public Administration, Washington, DC.

Pursell, Carroll, 1995, *The Machine in America*, Johns Hopkins U. Press, Baltimore.

Reynolds, John F. and Richard L. McCormick, 1986, " 'Outlawing 'Treachery': Split Tickets and Ballot Laws in New York and New Jersey, 1880–1910," in *The Journal of American History*, Vol. 72, Issue 4 (March), pp. 835–858.

Riordan, William, 1963 (1905), *Plunkitt of Tammany Hall*, E. P. Dutton, NY.

Robinson, Lloyd, 2001 (1968), *The Stolen Election: Hayes versus Tilden—1876*, Forge, NY.

Roth, Susan King, 1998, "Disenfranchised by Design: Voting Systems and the Election Process," in *Information Design Journal*, Vol. 9, No. 1, pp. 29–38.

Saltman, Roy G., 1975, *Effective Use of Computing Technology in Vote-Tallying*, NBSIR 75-687 (reprinted as NBS SP 500-30, 1978), National Institute of Standards and Technology, Gaithersburg, MD.

———, 1988, *Accuracy, Integrity and Security in Computerized Vote-Tallying*, NBS SP 500-158, National Institute of Standards and Technology, Gaithersburg, MD.

———, 1991, "Computerized Voting," in Yovits, Marshall C. (ed.), *Advances in Computers, Volume 32*, Academic Press, NY.

———, 2003, "Public Confidence and Auditability in Voting Systems," in Gritzalis, Dimitris A. (ed.), *Secure Electronic Voting*, Kluwer Academic Publishers, Norwell, MA, pp. 125–137.

Schlesinger, Jr., Arthur M., 1993 (1983), *The Almanac of American History* (revised and updated ed.), Barnes & Noble Books, NY.

Shocket, Peter A., Neil R. Heighberger, and Clyde Brown 1993, "The Effect of Voting Technology on Voting Behavior in a Simulated Multi-Candidate City Council Election: A Political Experiment of Ballot Transparency," in *The Western Political Quarterly*, Vol. 45, pp. 521–537.

Shurkin, Joel, 1996, *Engines of the Mind*, W. W. Norton, NY.

Sims, Peggy, 2001, *List Maintenance Provisions of the National Voter Registration Act (NVRA)*, Federal Election Commission, Washington, DC.

Special Committee on Voting Systems and Election Procedures in Maryland, 2001, *Report and Recommendations*, State of Maryland, Annapolis, MD.

State Plan Committee of Ohio Secretary of State J. Kenneth Blackwell, 2003, *Changing the Election Landscape in the State of Ohio*, Columbus, OH.

Taylor, Frederick W., 1978 (1912), "Scientific Management," in Shafritz, Jay M. and Albert C. Hyde (eds.), *Classics of Public Administration*, Moore Publishing, Oak Park, IL, pp. 17–20.

Technical Guidelines Development Committee, Draft Version I Voluntary Voting System Guidelines, May 9, 2005, National Institute of Standards and Technology, Gaithersburg, MD.

Thernstrom, Abigail and Russell G. Redenbaugh, 2001, "Dissenting Statement," in *Appendix to Voting Irregularities in Florida During the 2000 Presidential Election*, U.S. Commission on Civil Rights, Washington, DC, Appendix IX.

Tomz, Michael and Robert P. Van Houweling, 2003, "How Does Voting Equipment Affect the Racial Gap in Voided Ballots?," in *American Journal of Political Science*, Vol. 47, No. 1, pp. 46–60.

Toobin, Jeffrey, 2001, *Too Close to Call*, Random House, NY.

Trattner, Walter I., 1989 (1974), *From Poor Law to Welfare State* (4th ed.), The Free Press, NY.

U.S. Commission on Civil Rights, 2001, *Voting Irregularities in Florida During the 2000 Presidential Election*, Washington, DC.

U.S. Election Assistance Commission, 2005, *Fiscal Year 2004 Annual Report*, Washington, DC.

Wand, Jonathan N. et al., 2001, "The Butterfly Did It: The Aberrant Vote for Buchanan in Palm Beach County, Florida," in *American Political Science Review*, Vol. 95, No. 4 (December), pp. 793–810.

Wesser, Robert F., 1971, "Election of 1888," in Schlesinger, Jr., Arthur M. (ed.), *History of American Presidential Elections, 1789–1968*, Volume II, Chelsea House, NY.

Whoriskey, Peter, 2000, "Report in '88 Recommended Punch Cards Be Abandoned," *Miami Herald*, November 16.

Wiebe, Robert H., 1967, *The Search for Order, 1877–1920*, Hill and Wang, NY.

Wigmore, John H., 1889, *The Australian Ballot System as Embodied in the Legislation of Various Countries* (2nd ed.), Boston Book Company, Boston, MA.

Williamson, Chilton, 1960, *American Suffrage from Property to Democracy, 1760–1860*, Princeton U. Press, Princeton, NJ.

Wills, Garry, 2002 (1978), *Inventing America: Jefferson's Declaration of Independence*, Mariner Books, NY.

Wilson, Woodrow, 1978 (1887), "The Study of Administration," in Shafritz, Jay M. and Albert C. Hyde (eds.), *Classics of Public Administration*, Moore Publishing, Oak Park, IL, pp. 3–17.

Yarbrough, Tinsley E., 2002, *Race and Redistricting: The Shaw-Cromartie Cases*, The U. Press of Kansas, Lawrence, KS.

Young, H. Peyton, 2001, *Dividing the House: Why Congress Should Reinstate an Old Reapportionment Formula*, Policy Brief #88, Brookings Institution, Washington, DC.

Zukerman, T. David, 1925, *The Voting Machine*, Political Research Bureau of the Republican County Committee of New York, New York.

INDEX